The Archaeology of Villages in Eastern North America

Florida Museum of Natural History: Ripley P. Bullen Series

FLORIDA MUSEUM
OF NATURAL HISTORY

The Archaeology of Villages

IN EASTERN NORTH AMERICA

Edited by Jennifer Birch and Victor D. Thompson

UNIVERSITY OF FLORIDA PRESS

Gainesville

This book may be available in an electronic edition.

23 22 21 20 19 18   6 5 4 3 2 1

Library of Congress Cataloging-in-Publication Data
Names: Birch, Jennifer, 1980– editor. | Thompson, Victor D., editor.
Title: The archaeology of villages in eastern North America / edited by
      Jennifer Birch and Victor D. Thompson.
Other titles: Ripley P. Bullen series.
Description: Gainesville : University of Florida Press, 2018. | Series:
      Florida Museum of Natural History: Ripley P. Bullen series | Includes
      bibliographical references and index.
Identifiers: LCCN 2018000535 | ISBN 9781683400462 (cloth : alk. paper)
Subjects: LCSH: Indians of North America—East (U.S.)—Antiquities. |
      Woodland Indians—East (U.S.)—Antiquities. | East (U.S.)—Antiquities.
      Classification: LCC E78.E2 B57 2018 | DDC 977/.01—dc23
LC record available at https://lccn.loc.gov_2018000535

University of Florida Press
15 Northwest 15th Street
Gainesville, FL 32611-2079
http://upress.ufl.edu

UF PRESS

UNIVERSITY
OF FLORIDA

Contents

Illustrations

TABLES

Foreword

Crafting Community and Identity in the Eastern Woodlands

The emergence and socially generative qualities of coalescent, nucleated, and in some cases fortified settlements occupied much or all of the year is a topic of interest to archaeologists and historians in every area of the world where such communities appeared. The chapters in this volume document this epochal transformation in the human condition in eastern North America, using a diverse series of case studies spanning many times and places, from remote antiquity to the recent past (Figure i). Thompson and Birch's introductory chapter provides a broadly based and globally informed theoretical overview encompassing definitions, approaches, and guiding questions associated with the exploration of the origins, maintenance, and in some cases failures of settled life. How communities served as loci and indeed crucibles of social change and identity formation in the East and beyond is examined, beginning with the definition of fundamental concepts like "village" (i.e., "a restricted geographic place where some portion of the population lived year-round" with "semiregular face-to-face interactions among the majority of a population that included a wide variety of coresidential groups") and "power" (i.e., the ability "to create new societal forms developed through processes of emplacement, negotiation, cooperation, and competition at multiple social and spatial scales"). The importance of community, and settled life in general, in shaping complex human societies, and how these developments played out at various times and places in the Eastern Woodlands, forms the central organizing theme of the volume. The specific case studies and historical trajectories that follow show, furthermore, that examining community formation and function is an important means by which local or regional archaeology may be described and interpreted. With its extensive and diverse historic and archaeological record of village life, the chapters in this volume demonstrate that eastern North America is an excellent region to explore these subjects.

Examining some of the oldest evidence in the region for the emergence of village life, Thompson examines Late Archaic shell ring settlements on the southeast-

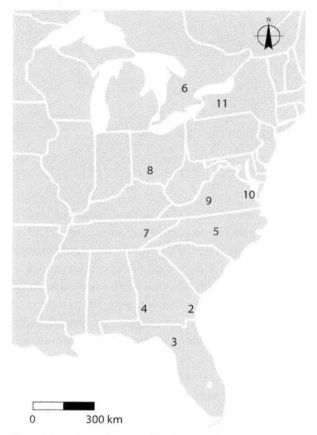

Figure i. Locations of case studies discussed in text.
Numbers correspond to chapters in this volume.

ern Atlantic seaboard between ca. 5,000 and 3,000 years ago. These rings were the center or organizational hub of activities for local hunter-gatherer communities over much or all of the year, persistent places shaped by relations of production and practice in a host of realms sacred and secular. Instead of focusing on specific sites, Thompson explores how community life played out over the broader coastal and marine landscape, describing the complex web of relationships, ceremonial and quotidian, that had to have been present and that were essential to this lifeway continuing for millennia. Community life and identity creation were entangled with ceremony and monumentality in these societies, involving mechanisms facilitating interaction, resource use, and dispute resolution within and beyond specific communities, in an ongoing process that continued for centuries. The fact that village communities occurred among hunter-gatherers, preceding and independent of the adoption of agricultural food production, is another reason why eastern North America is an important region for examining the emergence and consequences of settled life.

Moving forward in time, Neill Wallis explores how Middle Woodland community location and growth in the Deep South were shaped by landscape characteristics and planned accordingly from the start at some centers, with a final layout in mind, following what the author describes as something of a "Calvinist quality" of predestination. A pattern of large mounds opposite a U-shaped opening appears to be about as close to a standardized form as may have been present. Incorporation of astronomical alignments, dualities in aspects of the site setting, and natural features such as rises and open areas shaped and delimited the built environment. Traditional explanations for the emergence of the largest circular and U-shaped villages present at the time, like population growth, the adoption of intensive agriculture, or an increase in warfare, are not readily apparent in the north Florida/south Georgia area under examination. Instead, these communities were created to bring large numbers of people together in ritual practice, accompanied by feasting, monumentality, and other social activities, which were instrumental to the creation and maintenance of larger social collectives and organizational spheres. Identity formation occurred at a scale far beyond that at dispersed households and hamlets. Locations were selected because they fit into consciously selected or unconsciously accepted human visual dominance relations and information-processing capabilities, and the need to integrate peoples at a specific setting on the landscape. These community plans were simultaneously sociograms and cosmograms, structurally reinforcing social relations and statuses, and tying the community into larger worlds both social and sacred using ancient architectural grammars and cosmological themes. Community was thus constituted in many arenas, and can be examined in many ways archaeologically.

The Middle/Late Woodland Kolomoki site in southwest Georgia, for example, is discussed by West, Pluckhahn, and Menz, who examine the concept of the hypertrophic community, a form of cultural practice with a long history in the Eastern Woodlands. Oversize artifacts like Benton and Sloan points, or bannerstones, grooved axes, and flint swords occur back to Paleoindian times in the region, and have been interpreted as symbols of personal status and cultural identity, and for use in collective ceremony and ritual. The authors argue that the later Woodland was a time when large and dispersed centers like Kolomoki began to appear more widely in the Deep South. Although the authors caution against making a generalized hypertrophic community site type, they provide examples from many times and places of seemingly oversized communities in the Eastern Woodlands. Unusually large, indeed hypertrophic sites are, in fact, a common feature in the regional archaeological record, dating back to Bull Brook during the Paleoindian period, Watson Brake during the terminal Middle Archaic, Poverty Point during the Late Archaic, numerous Hopewellian sites a few centuries later in the Woodland, and Cahokia in the Mississippian era, to name a few better-known examples. Size has a compelling logic, an agentive capability of its own, as a powerful symbol of a community and identity. There is an old adage in archaeology that the more we dig, the more we have a better chance of knowing what was going on at a site, and this is certainly true at Kolomoki, where excavation size and extent, the authors demonstrate, have been critically important in interpretative efforts.

Several authors examine communities in the centuries immediately before and after European contact. Eric Jones explores the formation of nucleated circular villages after ca. AD 1300 in the upper Yadkin River basin in the North Carolina Piedmont, and their relationship to more traditional patterns of dispersed house-holds, which in this area continue to occur into late precontact times. Jones evaluates site locational characteristics using a settlement ecology approach linking evidence from archaeological ground truthing with landscape reconstructions based on catchments, water sources, and distance to trails, and site viewshed analyses. Settlement locational characteristics were also evaluated against a control sample of random locations using discriminant function analysis. The data are readily accessible, reflecting an open approach to information management and sharing that is becoming widespread in the region. Defensible locations and proximity to productive soils and biota were important factors promoting large, coalescent community development locally. Less-populated areas appear to have been buffer zones between differing societies, in part because these areas were less productive. Jones argues that the need to maintain exchange networks kept such areas lightly occupied, with dispersed small settlements present, rather than totally uninhabited. Conflict within such areas, if occurring at all, was of sufficiently low intensity as to be archaeologically almost invisible. Regional political geography was also important in shaping these developments, with the coalescence of villages occurring in reaction to Mississippian expansion into the area, which was ultimately checked. The chapter serves as a reminder that nucleated villages can appear amid normally dispersed populations in reaction to larger, regional-scale changes in exchange and warfare.

Birch and Williamson's chapter on initial Northern Iroquoian coalescence examines how gender relations and enculturation processes, and the rate and intensity at which the adoption of agriculture occurred, all shaped the development of village life in their study area. Their chapter also highlights the importance of having complete community plans for the interpretation of settled life. While remote sensing is a critically important first step in modern archaeological fieldwork, their chapter shows that there is no substitute for large-scale excavation and ground truthing to document the distribution and content of features, which may not always be interpreted accurately from remote sensing data alone. The interpretation of even excavated archaeological features, their work further shows, needs to proceed carefully. Fence lines in the Iroquoian area early on appear to have been as much about defining communities as defending them. Ditches, embankments, and fence lines thus do not have to imply martial behavior, although their function and elaboration can change over time, as happened when warfare became common in later centuries. That some village locations were occupied continuously for centuries, and hence were truly persistent places, is a settlement positioning strategy dating well back into the Archaic in various parts of the Eastern Woodlands. At the same time, the nature of the subsistence base, intensive maize agriculture, and the need to regularly move fields resulted in more frequent relocations of some settlements. The change from flexible and varied to more standardized and consistent community structure in the Iroquoian area, the authors argue, indicates community life was becoming more routinized and fixed. Counterintuitively, more formal settlement *structure* did not always result in settlement *permanence*, something also noted in other chapters.

Community development and identity creation during the Mississippian era in eastern Tennessee are examined by Sullivan, who looks at changes in architecture, mortuary behavior, ceramic form and style, and leadership and gender roles over time and space. Most people lived in dispersed smaller settlements well into Mississippian times, but cultural identity was, as in earlier periods throughout the region, at least partially if not substantially shaped and reinforced at the centers. Nucleated villages appear in the fourteenth century in eastern Tennessee, which Sullivan argues was because the region became a refuge for populations relocating from areas farther to the west. These peoples came from what is known as the Vacant Quarter, or at least those parts of it in the Middle Cumberland and Tennessee River valleys. While drought has been implicated in these Mississippian population movements, a host of factors were apparently in play shaping the diaspora and coalescence of late precontact era peoples, some of which Sullivan demonstrates are recognizable archaeologically in their communities. Indeed, both droughts and periods of excessive rainfall, as well as large areal abandonments and periods of coalescence, happened in many times and places in the East, at least well back into the Archaic period, and can be examined from a perspective emphasizing communities. Abandonment of an area, this case further demonstrates, does not necessarily mean the death of the people within it. Instead, we need to be thinking about where people might have gone instead of why they are no longer present, or simply assuming they died out. As Sullivan argues, the creation of new and coalescent communities followed its own logic in each area and even at each site, making broad generalizations difficult, and specific historical situations important to document. The East Tennessee example shows that earlier instruments of community creation, such as council houses, could continue in use even as new architectural and organizational features like platform mounds and more rigidly hierarchical leadership forms were added. Sullivan, like Birch and Williamson, also examines the importance of gender in the everyday practices creating community, from the maintenance of kin groups to distinguishing different leadership spheres via mortuary segregation, highlighting the fact that examining community involves much more than the study of monumentality and architecture.

Cook's chapter on Fort Ancient villages examines late precontact developments in another part of the region, the lower Midwest, which may have also witnessed an influx of people due to processes creating the Vacant Quarter. Becoming Fort Ancient culture, Cook demonstrates, was as much about migration and coalescence as local or in situ development, something we have been recognizing in many areas of the East in recent years, not the least at Cahokia, where significant in-migration preceded the elaborate developments of the eleventh through thirteenth centuries. Cook's use of isotope and biodistance analyses to explore possible source populations for Fort Ancient sites highlights the importance of working with legacy skeletal collections, and what can be learned when this can occur. It is also heartening that legacy assemblages and ideas, such as some of those used and advanced by James B. Griffin on Fort Ancient origins, are still viable, which should give us all hope for the utility and durability of our own investigations, and the importance of curating field and analysis records for posterity. Cook and several other authors herein also show how concepts like migration, coalescence, and hybridity can be explored archaeologically by examining where people, structures, and other architecture occurred within sites and, in the case of fortifications, over the larger region. Finally, as the case studies draw closer to the present, use of historical narratives, ethnohistorical sources, and even oral historical accounts of likely descendant populations are increasingly used, as they should be, to explore aspects of community structure, ceremony, and interaction that might not be readily detectable archaeologically.

Jefferies examines the emergence of circular villages in southwestern Virginia in the Late Woodland period from ca. AD 1000 to AD 1650, documenting a change from dispersed small settlements to large circular nucleated villages after AD 1200, a pattern similar to that observed to the east in the Powhatan area by Gallivan, Shephard, and Jenkins and to the south by Jones in the Yadkin, albeit with enough differences in each area to highlight the importance of thoroughly documenting local historical trajectories and avoiding broad generalizations made on the basis of one or a few attributes. As Jefferies demonstrates, southwestern Virginia was near the headwaters of rivers that could be used to reach late precontact cultures as diverse as Dan River, Dallas, Monongahela, and Fort Ancient, making the area a cultural crossroads of a sort, and also an excellent place for populations to relocate upstream from more heavily trafficked or attacked areas. Changes in community layout and fortification, and in some cases relocation into more defensible spaces, occurred in a number of areas in the post–AD 1200 period in the East. These appear directly related to a marked increase in the intensity of warfare at this time, which is tied to communities characterized by a need to integrate socially distinct groups and an equally strong concern for defense. Fleeing peoples joined resident populations located elsewhere, coalescing for mutual protection while simultaneously creating challenges related to community integration and identity formation. As several scholars herein argue, constructed boundaries, whether fences or ditches, helped create a sense of identity and possibly social distinctions or equivalences, depending on layout and whether multiple precincts were present. Finally, Jefferies's work and that of several other authors herein also highlight how dramatic changes in settlement were often concurrent with the intensive use of maize, and not its initial cultivation. Changes in community organization could be used to explore the consequences of maize intensification and such questions as to whether it was a time-transgressive phenomenon, earlier in the western part of the region than in the eastern portion.

Specific events and rituals in early contact period Powhatan society that helped bind people together into communities are examined by Gallivan, Shephard, and Jenkins, who demonstrate how richly detailed ethnohistoric records and the use of what they describe as "deep historical anthropology" can be used to understand the "power of Powhatan places." How outsiders and foreign objects were socialized or made part of a community is examined, while the community itself was considered a social agent by virtue of its continuing creation and maintenance. As in other areas examined herein, palisades and fence lines were as much about defining community as about defense. The enlargement of Werowocomoco as Powhatan's principal town appears to be another example of hypertrophic community creation and emplacement, symbolizing the unification of the area. The ritual progressions residents followed in and around Powhatan sites during ceremonies documented ethnohistorically likely had parallels at many other centers in the Eastern Woodlands where, unfortunately, such written records are lacking. Gallivan, Shephard, and Jenkins additionally examine the role of canoes and waterways in shaping tribute flow and delimiting political relationships, demonstrating that movement over the landscape took many paths, and not just overland both in this case and no doubt throughout the human occupation of the region.

Indeed, consideration of least-cost movement pathways should always be considered the default option when examining how people traversed the landscape, with exceptions likely indicating something interesting, like the presence of communities structuring or constraining interaction.

In the final case study, Kurt Jordan examines Seneca Iroquois community structure in the early historic era, where a shift from nucleated to dispersed settlements occurred, a reversal of the trend documented in other areas, but for many of the same reasons. Like Gallivan, Shephard, and Jenkins's examination of Powhatan, Jordan makes use of the rich historic literature on Senecas and their neighbors to show that settlement changes were often highly varied, yet were carefully considered and guided by pragmatism. Nucleated communities with substantial fortifications were an early response to threats, as was a switch to dispersed settlements during a subsequent time of peace, followed a generation later by the adoption of nucleated hilltop communities during a period of conflict. These rapid changes in Seneca settlement took place in less than a century and remind us that community change in the precontact era may have been equally rapid and varied, and that settlement systems were rarely if ever static over long periods. Likewise, the way decisions regarding settlement change were made among Senecas, via consensus or alternatively fissioning, were highly varied. An important lesson, Jordan concludes, is that while cultural traditions may shape change, novel responses could also happen.

Cobb closes the volume with a synthesis and commentary that brings a broad anthropological, historical, and geographic perspective to the study of village and community while concurrently masterfully and thoughtfully tying together many of the threads articulated by the various authors. As such, his chapter complements the theoretical overview by Thompson and Birch that began the volume and, if I may be so bold, the commentary in this foreword; all offer different perspectives on the study of settled life, while highlighting the importance of the subject and the individual contributions to the volume. The emergence of village life is viewed as a tipping point by Cobb, with varied causes and consequences, as important a change in human existence as the establishment of hereditary inequality, multi-community political entities, or state-level societies. The community is a new way of experiencing and relating to the world, continually constituted and changing, a process and not just a place. The origins, maintenance, and meanings of settled life is thus one of the big questions facing anthropology, a worthy subject for archaeological investigation.

Indeed, community life underpins much of our cultural identity, albeit manifest in many different ways, and at a larger scale our national and global civilization. The study of how settled village or community life came about, its varied possibilities, and how and why it can change for the better or the worse are thus important and relevant subjects to all of us. In a region as extensively studied as eastern North America, furthermore, where over half a million archaeological sites have been recorded, archaeology offers the chance to examine variability in what is meant by community with samples encompassing great time depth and geographic scale. Indeed, the chapters herein draw heavily upon and illustrate the utility of this record, and for the study of archaeology in general. This volume offers readers an intellectually exciting opportunity to rethink what is meant by community, how it can be examined with archaeological and historic materials, and the lessons life in ancient communities have for the modern world.

David G. Anderson
Department of Anthropology, University of Tennessee

1

The Power of Villages

VICTOR D. THOMPSON AND JENNIFER BIRCH

Throughout eastern North America, pivotal cultural transformations took place when people came together into villages. Such transformations included new traditions and social milieus that had no prior analogues. For the purposes of this volume, we define village-communities along a number of social and spatial dimensions (*sensu* Kolb and Snead 1997; Canuto and Yaeger 2000). As Copeland Reining (1980:8) points out, there are a number of components that define the village, which include aspects such as physical attributes (e.g., population size, composition, house structures, territories, site permanence), what it means to be a villager (e.g., identity, face-to-face interactions, households), and the structural organization of such entities (e.g., continuity of membership, residence rules, marriage). While mainly based on ethnographic observations, archaeologists must consider these aspects when we talk about villages. However, in order to have a consensus on what constitutes a village in archaeological and historical records, we suggest that at its base two aspects are important. Thus, we define the village as a restricted geographic place where some portion of the population lived year-round. This definition also presumes that there were semiregular face-to-face interactions among the majority of a population that included a wide variety of coresidential groups, often including multiple extended families. This definition closely follows the Bandy and Fox (2010:6) notion of a sedentary village as consisting of "relatively permanent, multifamily residential clusters." However, our emphasis on face-to-face interaction provides, as we detail below, another dimension by which to differentiate such formations.

We recognize that there are a certain number of deficiencies in the definition presented above. Framing it this way, however, allows us to focus on those societies that did not engage in such traditions both before and after the emergence of villages. This permits us to focus our narratives on groups as engaging in a different way of life than the highly mobile hunter-fisher-forager groups that preceded such formations (see Anderson and Sassaman 2012), as well as the dispersed farming communities and households characteristic of some parts of the uplands of eastern North America during the later prehistoric and contact eras (e.g., Pauketat 2003; Williams and Shapiro 1990). Such a definition permits comparison of structurally similar social formations irrespective of their means of subsistence. It also gives us an analytical unit to work from, separate from some of the largest aggregate communities (e.g., Cahokia) where the vast majority did not participate in semiregular face-to-face interaction, and where social relations were more closely aligned with interactions typical of urban environments. We note that this would not preclude villages that were a part of such entities. The particular behaviors that transpire during and by virtue of copresence in residential settings are a unique form of human sociality (Goffman 1967). The immediate physical material of face-to-face interactions include facial, gestural, and verbal cues. We would argue that in order to sustain coresidential village-communities, these interactions required the development of qualitatively different social behaviors and postures compared to earlier, more mobile communities. Such patterned interactions may have required the development of formalized mechanisms and institutions that structure relationships, communication systems, and the nature of strategic interactions. The outcomes of such social transformations warrant focused study by archaeologists.

There were a number of factors that led people to come together into these new social formations, including environmental, climatic, cultural, and sociopolitical inputs, though nowhere were these mutually exclusive (Bandy and Fox 2010:2; Birch 2013a). The relative permanence and stability of these village-communities were also variable. They range from the early, sedentary villages of the coastal Southeast, where community and intervillage ties were negotiated and reinforced through ritualized feasting over centuries (e.g., Sanger 2015; Thompson 2007; Thompson and Andrus 2011; Thompson and Moore 2015), to the large, aggregated villages of the Northeast, where generational patterns of village relocation did not preclude significant investment in fortifications and the built environment (Birch 2012).

While the settings for village formation in eastern North America differ widely, the cultural materials that peoples used to craft village-communities and the social processes that played out within them were not so different. The power of villages to create new societal forms developed through processes of emplacement, negotiation, cooperation, and competition at multiple social and spatial scales. As such, the way individuals and groups expressed power operated under different societal constraints than under other kinds of social formations. The focus of this volume is to examine the nature of power dynamics in village societies and how such relationships played out at the local village level, as well as among interacting village-communities.

Global Perspectives on Villages

There is a vast global literature regarding the archaeology of village societies (see Pluckhahn and Thompson 2018 and Birch 2013b for a summary). Much of it focuses on how such formations develop along with the concomitant emergence of related social institutions and traditions (e.g., Bar-Yosef and Belfer-Cohen 1989; Bandy and Fox 2010; Flannery 2002; Parkinson 2002). Other studies tend to focus on village economics, particularly the development of agrarian economies (Hodder 1990; Kuijt and Goring-Morris 2002), demography (Bandy 2008; Bocquet-Appel 2002; Warrick 2008), social structure (e.g., Byrd 1994; Kuijt 2000; Wills and Leonard 1994), and the integration of single villages into larger political units (e.g., Anderson 1994; Gibson 2011). As a part of such discussions, power dynamics among villages and villagers, in general, emerge as key issues in many of the central problems in village studies (e.g., McGuire and Saitta 1996), although they are perhaps less often identified as such. We see no reason to restrict discussions of power and sociopolitics to more complex organizational forms when it is clear that these dynamics are also apparent in small-scale, segmentary societies (Hastorf 1990; Roscoe 2009; Vaughan et al. 2010). To our knowledge, however, few, if any, edited volumes focus solely and explicitly on the dynamics of power in village societies. This includes how power is enacted in village settings at the community level, smaller social groups, and the individual level. We assert that such understandings are important if we are to understand how villages and villagers engage in suprahousehold endeavors (e.g., communal labor projects) and relationships (e.g., ritual societies), as well as the points of articulation between village-level and pan-regional institutions.

Our intention with the title of this chapter, "The Power of Villages," was to invoke many different meanings and questions regarding the nature of village societies. In our minds some of the more important dimensions of such inquiries include the following: What compels people to live in villages (i.e., village emergence)? How do villages deal with the social and economic problems of coresidence (i.e., cooperation)? How do villages and villagers assert power over their respective scalar peers (i.e., competition, sanctioning)? And, finally, how are the bonds of villages broken (i.e., fission) or transformed into something altogether different (i.e., polities, nations)? In what follows, we explore the particulars of these questions in more detail and offer some commentary regarding archaeological inquiry into each broadly, and in the Eastern Woodlands specifically, in order to elucidate some of the important issues in the examination of power dynamics within village societies.

Social Relations in Village Societies

What are the new forms of social relations that develop in villages, and how do they differ from dispersed communities or prior societal conditions? This question is perhaps the most broadly considered in the literature and at its essence is about the formation of early village life (Pluckhahn and Thompson 2018:8). Indeed, from the European and Asian Neolithic (Byrd 1994, 2005; Hole et al. 1969; Kuijt 2000), to Mesoamerica and South America (Bandy 2004, 2006; Flannery 1976; Lesure et al. 2013; Marcus 2008; Marcus and Flannery 1996), the American Southwest (Kohler et al. 2004; Kohler and Varien 2012; Mabry et al. 1997; Rautman 2014, 2016; Wilshusen and Potter 2010), and the Eastern Woodlands (this volume), this has been a central question among the global archaeological community for decades (see discussions in Birch 2013b; Pluckhahn and Thompson 2018:8).

In the Eastern Woodlands, there are a number of different moments in which early villages first formed. Exactly what compelled each of these communities to come together and to organize themselves in particular ways, from our perspective, varied widely. The earliest villages in the region (ca. 4600 to 3200 cal. BP and perhaps earlier) likely occurred along the southern coasts of both the Gulf and Atlantic regions (DePratter 1979; Russo 1998; Sanger 2015; Thompson 2007; Thompson and Andrus 2011; Turck and Thompson 2016). Among these early villages, there is little evidence for conflict, and populations for each individual village were likely quite low, on the order of some 200 persons or less (Thompson 2006). Interestingly, such early villages were a limited phenomenon and collapsed in various coastal regions, not to emerge again until the Middle and Late Woodland, where again we see limited evidence for conflict in coastal regions (Hutchinson 2004; Pluckhahn and Thompson 2018). This is in contrast to many of the inland riverine areas of the Mid-South, Midwest, and Great Lakes Northeast, where the formation of nucleated villages tends to be in the context of agricultural intensification and, possibly, violence (Birch 2015; Hart and Means 2002).

Taking a long-term view of village formation, we believe that the Eastern Woodlands boasts some of the most diverse villages in the world. We have a long-term record of village formation predicated on nondomesticated resources—from the earliest in the region to historic contact (Thompson and Worth 2011). Even after maize makes its entry into some regions it is varyingly adopted, with some groups relying heavily on it as a staple resource, while others simply added it to a mixed economy (e.g., Birch 2015; Hart and Lovis 2013; Gallivan 2016; Thomas 2008). Further, we see households and extended families articulating into diverse forms, including longhouses, courtyard groups, and circular villages (e.g., Cook 2008; Hart and Brumbach 2003; Means 2007). Thus, the Eastern Woodlands is a prime testing ground for some of the postulates offered by Rosenberg and Redding (2000:41), who suggest that many of the features of sedentary village life emerged before agriculture. In addition, such diversity allows for broader considerations of how power developed, was maintained, and evolved in these social formations.

Heterarchy and Cooperation in Villages

How are power relations in villages expressed when they are part of heterarchical or peer-village networks as opposed to rigid hierarchically organized polities? We recognize that there is no such thing as an autonomous village and that social and cultural phenomena were defined both by intravillage relations and interactions among village-communities and their constituent parts (contra Carneiro 2002; Kowalewski 2013). However, the degree of integration among villages is highly variable, especially across eastern North America. Such interactions may range from peer-village networks (e.g., Griffin 1992; Williamson and Robertson 1994) to confederacies (e.g., Knight 1994; Snow 1994), to tightly integrated hierarchical polities (e.g., Marquardt 2014; Thompson et al. 2016).

As one might imagine, the dynamics of villages that fringed greater Cahokia at its apogee might be very different than those around the Great Lakes region, although both events were occurring ca. AD 1200. However, because larger comparisons have not been carried out, we actually do not know where there may have been convergences in such traditions, or, conversely, where such formulations depart historically from other village formations. Similarly, we might expect changes in the basic structures of regional interaction networks and the power of local leaders or collectives to stay the same or to change through the trajectory of the rise and fall of the network or polity. Such questions are not only dependent upon the degree of integration that villages are articulated with the larger polity but also the temporality of polity development itself. Other factors such as patterns of trade and exchange, climatic instability, or the onset or intensification of conflict have also functioned to alter the nature of intravillage relations and organization (Birch et al. 2017; Blanton et al. 1996).

Power Dynamics in Villages

What is the nature of intravillage power dynamics? Village societies have commonly been thought of as being synonymous with "tribal" social formations and lacking complex forms of political and economic organization. More recent perspectives on sociopolitical organization in middle-range societies recognize the multidimensional nature of power and authority that develop in small-scale social settings (Cobb 2003; Feinman and Neitzel 1984). In many cases, the accumulation of power and the structure of authority was not a goal in and of itself, "but was a means to solve the objectively existing important problems encountered by the society" (Grinin and Korotayev 2011:282). This includes the complex sets of relations that develop in village societies where modular or segmentary forms of social organization are among the most common mechanisms for structuring social and power relations (Roscoe 2009; Sahlins 1968).

In other cases, studies regarding the nature of intravillage dynamics have largely focused on so-called big man problems. What we mean by this is that archaeologists have been primarily concerned in such studies on how "big men" become indebted to by certain sections of the village and/or community (e.g., Clark and Blake 1996; Hayden 1995, 2001). This pursuit of prestige is largely accomplished through competitive generosity, usually in the context of feasting.

The wider literature on feasting and the development of inequality is well represented among scholars investigating villages in the Eastern Woodlands. And the concept of feasting regarding power and authority in such settings has been especially attractive (e.g., Blitz 1993; Russo 2004). However, there is an essential tension between approaches that view group-oriented events as venues for the aggrandizement of leaders and those that argue that feasting, ritual, and associated group events within village settings also functioned to promote group integration (Hayden 2014; Spence 1999; Wilshusen and Potter 2010). These frameworks need not be mutually exclusive (Dye 2009; Gumerman and Dean 1989; Renfrew and Cherry 1986). Facilities associated with group-oriented events, including monumental architecture, plazas, and courtyards, appear concomitantly with early villages in many areas of the northeastern Woodlands. As venues for events including feasts, ceremonies, and funerals, they would have been key settings for positioning groups and individuals vis-à-vis one another in intravillage power structures.

Deeply seated principles of social organization, such as matrilineages and clans, "together with the limited forms of marriage, descent, and residence patterns that are logically possible" (Trigger 1991:557) within overarching social structures, should be viewed as malleable cultural materials that can be mobilized or de-emphasized in the context of distinct organizational strategies (Blanton et al. 1996). While becoming more common in the broader literature (Blanton and Fargher 2007; Carballo 2013), the study of how collectives and collective action work under such conditions has not been fully explored in the Eastern Woodlands (see Pluckhahn 2013 for an exception). As people begin to live together and have daily face-to-face interactions, mechanisms must be in place to mediate potential conflicts that may arise. These mechanisms may be cooperative and based on consensual decision-making, or they may involve the appointment of arbitrators or leaders. How such mechanisms of mediation transform or translate into power relations among intravillage members is a subject that deserves further consideration.

Transformations in Village Societies

How are power relations and organizational strategies transformed during times of reorganization and/or population movement? Critical hinge-points or sequences of events have the ability to drastically remake societies (Beck et al. 2007; Blitz 2010; Sewell 1992). Processes such as migration, settlement aggregation, and warfare have the potential to transform social landscapes and prompt the transformation of power structures and daily practices (Birch 2012; Hill et al. 2004; Cabana and Clark 2011; Haas 2001).

Migration occurred at a variety of scales in eastern North America and included long-distance relocation as well as the ebb and flow of population in response to political, economic, and ecological events (Blitz 1999; Meeks and Anderson 2014). This included patterns identified elsewhere as serial migration (Bernardini 2005) or population circulation (Schachner 2012). Warfare is also a significant factor in the development and transformation of village societies, necessitating reorganization in every aspect of a society and its leadership (Birch 2010; Dye 2009; Kowalewski 1996; Roscoe 2013; Wilson 2012). Heightened conflict is one factor that may cause people to come together into larger, more defensible settlements.

Aggregation and migration involve negotiation between social units undergoing processes of recombination. Mechanisms develop that allow people to manage the challenges of living in larger, more complex social formations (see chapters in Birch 2013b). In larger villages or towns, new problems may arise that relate to community infrastructure, land tenure, communal defense, and scheduling and hosting of important events such as ceremonies and feasts.

In the Northeast, power relations among subcommunity groups in aggregated settlements may have been balanced by the stability of large corporate groups (Hayden 1977; Hayden and Cannon 1982). Here, settlement aggregation led to the increased importance of clan-based, heterarchical political structures such as councils; the internal ordering and integration of subcommunity groups; and the management of cooperative sociopolitical and economic functions (Birch and Williamson 2013; Birch 2015).

The development of organizational complexity also involved significantly more focused processes of place-making (Birch and Williamson 2015; Cobb 2005; Gallivan 2007; Pluckhahn and Thompson 2013; Thompson and Pluckhahn 2012). Serial migration was the most common settlement pattern in Iroquoia, where the periodic relocation of villages was one facet of a cultural system that precluded the development of entrenched social and political inequality. There would have been the constant need to "produce place" (Cobb 2005:570) at new settlements, in part through the reconstruction and manipulation of the built environment that materialized the reconfiguration of social and political relations. In the interior and coastal Southeast, there were persistent places that provided the context for the development of particular kinds of organizational structures.

Large and Powerful Villages

How do some villages become extraordinarily large and powerful? Tuzin's 2001 book, *Social Complexity in the Making*, has in the past fifteen years or so become the go-to ethnographic work for archaeologists who not only want to understand the power of large villages but also how such entities emerge in the first place (see Duffy 2015; Birch 2013a; Pluckhahn 2003; Pluckhahn and Thompson 2018; Thompson 2006; Thompson and Kidder 2007). There are several reasons why this work captured the attention that it did. Chief among these is his explanation of how one particular village became so large that it in effect became a political capital, functioning in a neoevolutionary sense as a chiefdom, but with no single chief (Tuzin 2001). The model that Tuzin presents here is historically contingent and does not follow all the commonly cited dimensions of established archaeological models (or other ethnographic ones heavily relied upon by archaeologists) for polity formation (e.g., Carneiro 1981; Earle 1993). Like those models, Tuzin stresses the role of ideology and warfare in how Ilahita came to be a large and powerful village, but focuses on growth through incorporation rather than suppression or coercion. By stressing how dual organization and ideology fostered both the integration of kin groups and the spiritual unity of the entire village, Tuzin (2001) demonstrates how villages might become large and powerful without developing power and wealth-based inequalities.

There are several examples in the Eastern Woodlands where it appears that certain villages emerge to the level of prominence that Tuzin describes. Most notable among these are some of the Middle and Late Woodland villages of the Deep South, such as Kolomoki and Crystal River (see Pluckhahn and Thompson 2013, 2018; Pluckhahn 2003; Thompson et al. 2017). These emergences were largely predicated on the control of trade in nonlocal items and on ritual gatherings that integrated large numbers of villages at these sites. What is most interesting is that many of these villages not only emerged to prominence but also persisted for long periods (i.e., more than hundreds of years) of time (Pluckhahn and Thompson 2018; Wallis et al. 2015). Large contact-era villages in the Northeast such as the primary towns of Iroquoian (Jordan, this volume; Garrad 2014; Trigger 1976) and Algonquian (Gallivan 2007) Nations served similar functions as centers of trade and diplomacy and were hubs of authority for chiefs and polities.

In the Mississippian Southeast, the landscape and built environment of mound centers created "spatial crucible[s] for the reproduction of social inequality" (Cobb 2003:69). Archaeological (e.g., Pauketat 1994) and ethnohistoric (Knight 1990) analyses of southeastern sociopolitical organization suggest how the hierarchical dual organization of clans was transformed into a division of elites and commoners, disarticulating reciprocal bonds between corporate kin-groups and articulating households with nascent elites during multigenerational processes of "emplacement" (Cobb and Butler 2006; Gallivan 2007; Pauketat 1994). These processes may also play out in reverse, with the migration, disarticulation, or fission of villages causing organizational changes in structures of power and governance.

The Significance of Village Studies in Eastern North America

As we note above, the emergence of villages occurred under different ecological and economic conditions across the globe. Such formations coalesced in the context of the marine and riverine based economies of the coast and interior river valleys, as well as among the horticultural and agricultural groups of interior floodplains. These social groups persisted in varying forms and with diverse relationships and spatial layouts over extended time frames. The fundamental question that we address here is how the institutions that facilitated and maintained village-communities at both local and regional scales operated. That is, what is the power of villages?

There are several reasons why an examination of the power of villages in eastern North America informs global discussions of similarly organized groups in the ancient world. One of the more important reasons for this has to do with, to a large extent, the nature of theoretical perspectives in vogue in eastern North America. Specifically, more historically contingent (e.g., historical processualism [Pauketat 2001]) approaches have been more prevalent as of late, eschewing cultural historical studies and typologies (Birch 2015; Pluckhahn 2010). The advantage to this approach is that it has produced a number of case-specific historical understandings of village formation and social dynamics in the region (e.g., Creese 2013; Barrier and Horsley 2014; Pluckhahn 2013; Pauketat 2003). This, however, is not to say that scholars have ignored cross-comparison and regional data. Rather, researchers have also remained committed to the discussion of the process of village formation and functioning as well (Cobb and Nassaney 2002; Cobb and Garrow 1996; Pluckhahn and Thompson 2018). Our purpose in this volume is to bring together case studies that highlight the similarities and differences in the historical trajectories of village formation and development in eastern North America. In doing that we hope to shed light on the larger processes by which villages have the power to effect large-scale social transformations.

References Cited

Anderson, David G.

1994   *The Savannah River Chiefdoms.* University of Alabama Press, Tuscaloosa.

Anderson, D., and K. Sassaman

2012   *Recent Developments in Southeastern Archaeology.* SAA Press, Washington, DC.

Bandy, Matthew S.

2004   Fissioning, Scalar Stress, and Social Evolution in Early Village Societies. *American Anthropologist* 106:322–333.

2006   Early Village Society in the Formative Period in the Southern Lake Titicaca Basin. In *Andean Archaeology III,* 210–236. Springer, Boston.

2008   Global Patterns of Early Village Development. In *The Neolithic Demographic Transition and Its Consequences,* edited by Jean-Pierre Bocquet-Appel and Ofer Bar-Yosef, 333–357. Springer, Dordrecht.

Bandy, Matthew S., and Jake R. Fox

2010   Becoming Villagers: The Evolution of Early Village Societies. In *Becoming Villagers: Comparing Early Village Societies,* edited by Matthew S. Bandy and Jake R. Fox, 1–18. University of Arizona Press, Tucson.

Barrier, Casey R., and Timothy J. Horsley

2014   Shifting Communities: Demographic Profiles of Early Village Population Growth and Decline in the Central American Bottom. *American Antiquity* 79(2):295–313.

Bar-Yosef, Ofer, and Anna Belfer-Cohen

1989   The Origins of Sedentism and Farming Communities in the Levant. *Journal of World Prehistory* 3:447–498.

Beck, Robin A., Jr., Douglas J. Bolender, James A. Brown, and Timothy K. Earle

2007   Eventful Archaeology: The Place of Space in Structural Transformation. *Current Anthropology* 48(6): 833–860.

Bernardini, Wesley

2005   Reconsidering Spatial and Temporal Aspects of Prehistoric Cultural Identity: A Case Study from the American Southwest. *American Antiquity* 70(1): 31–54.

Birch, Jennifer

2010   Coalescence and Conflict in Iroquoian Ontario. *Archaeological Review from Cambridge* 25(1): 27–46.

2012   Coalescent Communities: Settlement Aggregation and Social Integration in Iroquoian Ontario. *American Antiquity* 77(4): 646–670.

2013a   Between Villages and Cities: Settlement Aggregation in Cross-Cultural Perspective. In *From Prehistoric Villages to Cities: Settlement Aggregation and Community Transformation*, edited by Jennifer Birch, 1–20. Routledge, New York.

2015   Current Research on the Historical Development of Northern Iroquoian Societies. *Journal of Archaeological Research* 23(3): 263–323.

Birch, Jennifer, ed.

2013b   *From Prehistoric Villages to Cities: Settlement Aggregation and Community Transformation.* Routledge, New York.

Birch, Jennifer, and Ronald F. Williamson

2013   Organizational Complexity in Ancestral Wendat Communities. In *From Prehistoric Villages to Cities: Settlement Aggregation and Community Transformation*, edited by Jennifer Birch, 153–178. Routledge, New York.

2015   Navigating Ancestral Landscapes in the Northern Iroquoian World. *Journal of Anthropological Archaeology* 39:139–150.

Birch, Jennifer, Robert B. Wojtowicz, Aleksandra Pradzynski, and Robert H. Pihl

2017   Multi-scalar Perspectives on Iroquoian Ceramics: Aggregation and Interaction in Precontact Ontario. In *Process and Meaning in Spatial Archaeology: Investigations into Pre-Columbian Iroquoian Space and Place*, edited by Eric E. Jones and John L. Creese, 147–190. University Press of Colorado, Boulder.

Blanton, Richard, and Lane Fargher

2007   *Collective Action in the Formation of Pre-Modern States.* Springer Science & Business Media, New York.

Blanton, Richard E., Gary M. Feinman, Stephen A. Kowalewski, and Peter N. Peregrine

1996   A Dual-processual Theory for the Evolution of Mesoamerican Civilization. *Current Anthropology* 37(1): 1–14.

Blitz, John H.

1993   Big Pots for Big Shots: Feasting and Storage in a Mississippian Community. *American Antiquity* 58(1): 80–96.

1999   Mississippian Chiefdoms and the Fission-Fusion Process. *American Antiquity* 64(4): 577–592.

2010   New Perspectives in Mississippian Archaeology. *Journal of Archaeological Research* 18:1–39.

Bocquet-Appel, Jean-Pierre

2002   Paleoanthropological Traces of a Neolithic Demographic Transition. *Current Anthropology* 43(4): 637–650.

Byrd, Brian F.

1994   Public and Private, Domestic and Corporate: The Emergence of the Southwest Asian Village. *American Antiquity* 59(4): 639–666.

2005   Reassessing the Emergence of Village Life in the Near East. *Journal of Archaeological Research* 13(3): 231–290.

Cabana, Graciela S., and Jeffery J. Clark, eds.

2011   *Rethinking Anthropological Perspectives on Migration.* University Press of Florida, Gainesville.

Canuto, Marcello A., and Jason Yaeger

2000   Introducing an Archaeology of Communities. In *The Archaeology of Communities: A New World Perspective*, edited by Marcello A. Canuto and Jason Yaeger, 16–43. Routledge, New York.

Carballo, David M., ed.

2013   *Cooperation and Collective Action: Archaeological Perspectives.* University Press of Colorado, Boulder.

Carneiro, Robert

1981   The Chiefdom: Precursor of the State. In *The Transition to Statehood in the New World*, edited by Grant D. Jones and Robert R. Kautz, 37–79. Cambridge University Press, Cambridge.

2002   The Tribal Village and Its Culture: An Evolutionary Stage in the History of Human Society. In *The Archaeology of Tribal Societies*, edited by William A. Parkinson, 34–52. International Monographs in Prehistory, Ann Arbor, MI.

Clark, John, and Michael Blake

1994   The Power of Prestige: Competitive Generosity and the Emergence of Ranked Societies in Lowland Mesoamerica. In *Contemporary Archaeology in Theory*, edited by R. Preucel and I. Hodder, 258–281. Blackwell Publishers, Oxford.

Cobb, Charles R.

2003   Mississippian Chiefdoms: How Complex? *Annual Review of Anthropology* 32:63–84.

2005   Archaeology and the "Savage Slot": Displacement and Emplacement in the Premodern World. *American Anthropologist* 107(4): 563–574.

Cobb, Charles R., and Brian M. Butler

2006   Mississippian Migration and Emplacement in the Lower Ohio Valley. In *Leadership and Polity in Mississippian Society*, edited by Brian M. Butler and Paul D. Welch, 328–347. Center for Archaeological Investigations, Southern Illinois University, Carbondale.

Cobb, Charles R., and Patrick H. Garrow

1996   Woodstock Culture and the Question of Mississippian Emergence. *American Antiquity* 61(1): 21–37.

Cobb, Charles R., and Michael S. Nassaney

2002   Domesticating Self and Society in the Woodland Southeast. In *The Woodland Southeast*, edited by David G. Anderson and Robert C. Mainfort Jr., 525–539. University of Alabama Press, Tuscaloosa.

Cook, Robert. A.

2008   *SunWatch: Fort Ancient Development in the Mississippian World.* University of Alabama Press, Tuscaloosa.

Copeland Reining, Priscilla

1980   Introduction. In *Village Viability in Contemporary Society*, edited by Priscilla Copeland Reining and Barbara Lenkerd, 9–18. AAAS Symposium 34, Westview Press, Boulder.

Creese, John

2013   Rethinking Early Village Development in Southern Ontario: Toward a History of Place-Making. *Canadian Journal of Archaeology* 37:185–218.

DePratter, Chester

1979   Shellmound Archaic on the Georgia Coast. *South Carolina Antiquities* 11(2): 1–69.

Duffy, Paul R.

2015   Site Size Hierarchy in Middle-Range Societies. *Journal of Anthropological Archaeology* 37:85–99.

Dye, David H.

2009   *War Paths, Peace Paths: An Archaeology of Cooperation and Conflict in Native Eastern North America.* Altamira, Lanham, MD.

Earle, Timothy R.

1993   *Chiefdoms: Power, Economy, and Ideology.* Cambridge University Press, Cambridge.

Feinman, Gary, and Jill Neitzel

1984   Too Many Types: An Overview of Sedentary Prestate Societies in the Americas. *Advances in Archaeological Method and Theory* 7:39–102.

Flannery, Kent V.

1976   *The Early Mesoamerican Village.* Academic Press, New York.

2002   The Origins of the Village Revisited: From Nuclear to Extended Households. *American Antiquity* 67(3): 417–433.

Gallivan, Martin D.

2007   Powhatan's Werowocomoco: Constructing Place, Polity, and Personhood in the Chesapeake, CE 1200–CE 1609. *American Anthropologist* 109(1): 85–100.

2016   *The Powhatan Landscape: An Archaeological History of the Algonquian Chesapeake.* University Press of Florida, Gainesville.

Garrad, Charles

2014   *Petun to Wyandot: The Ontario Petun from the Sixteenth Century.* University of Ottawa Press, Ottawa.

Gibson, D. Blair

2011   Chiefdom Confederacies and State Origins. *Social Evolution and History* 10(1): 215–233.

Goffman, Erving

1967   *Interaction Ritual: Essays in Face-to-Face Behavior.* Aldine, Chicago.

Griffin, James B.

1992   Fort Ancient Has No Class: The Absence of an Elite Group in Mississippian Societies in the Central Ohio Valley. *Archeological Papers of the American Anthropological Association* 3(1): 53–59.

Grinin, Leonid E., and Andrey V. Korotayev

2011   Chiefdoms and Their Analogues: Alternatives of Social Evolution at the Societal Level of Medium Cultural Complexity. *Social Evolution and History* 10(1): 276–335.

Gumerman, G. J., and J. Dean

1989   Prehistoric cooperation and competition in the western Anasazi Area. In *Dynamics of Southwest Prehistory*, edited by Linda Cordell and George Gumerman 99–148. University of Alabama Press, Tuscaloosa.

Haas, Jonathan

2001   Warfare and the Evolution of Culture. In *Archaeology at the Millennium: A Sourcebook*, edited by Gary M. Feinman and T. Douglas Price, 329–350. Kluwer Academic/Plenum Publishers, New York.

Hart, John P., and Hetty Jo Brumbach

2003 The Death of Owasco. *American Antiquity* 68(4): 737–752.

Hart, John P., and William A. Lovis

2013 Reevaluating What We Know About the Histories of Maize in Northeastern North America: A Review of Current Evidence. *Journal of Archaeological Research* 21(2): 175–216.

Hart, John P., and Bernard Means

2002 Maize and Villages: A Summary and Critical Assessment of Current Northeast Early Late Prehistoric Evidence. In *Northeast Settlement Subsistence Change A.D. 700–1300*, edited by John P. Hart and Christina Reith, 345–358. New York State Education Department, Albany.

Hastorf, Christine A.

1990 One Path to the Heights: Negotiating Political Inequality in the Sausa of Peru. In *The Evolution of Political Systems: Sociopolitics in Small-Scale Sedentary Societies*, edited by Steadman Upham, 146–176. School of American Research Advanced Seminar Series. Cambridge University Press, Cambridge.

Hayden, Brian

1977 Corporate Groups and the Late Ontario Iroquoian Longhouse. *Ontario Archaeology* 28:3–16.

1995 Pathways to Power: Principles for Creating Socioeconomic Inequalities. In *Foundations of Social Inequality*, edited by T. Douglas Price and Gary M. Feinman, 15–86. Plenum Press, New York.

2001 Fabulous Feasts: A Prolegomenon to the Importance of Feasting. In *Feasts: Archaeological and Ethnographic Perspectives on Food, Politics, and Power*, edited by M. Dietler and B. Hayden, 23–64. Smithsonian Institution Press, Washington, DC.

2014 *The Power of Feasts: From Prehistory to the Present*. Cambridge University Press, Cambridge.

Hayden, Brian, and Aubrey Cannon

1982 The Corporate Group as an Archaeological Unit. *Journal of Anthropological Archaeology* 1:132–158.

Hill, J. Brett, Jeffery J. Clark, William H. Doelle, and Patrick D. Lyons

2004 Prehistoric Demography in the Southwest: Migration, Coalescence, and Hohokam Population Decline. *American Antiquity* 69(4): 689–716.

Hodder, Ian

1990 *The Domestication of Europe: Structure and Contingency in Neolithic Societies*. Basil Blackwell, Oxford.

Hole, Frank, Kent Flannery, and James Neely

1969 *Prehistory and Human Ecology of the Deh Luran Plain: An Early Village Sequence from Khuzistan, Iran*. Memoirs of the Museum of Anthropology No. 1. University of Michigan, Ann Arbor.

Hutchinson, Dale

2004 *Bioarchaeology of the Florida Gulf Coast: Adaptation, Conflict and Change*. University Press of Florida, Gainesville.

Knight, Vernon James, Jr.

1990 Social Organization and the Evolution of Hierarchy in Southeastern Chiefdoms. *Journal of Anthropological Research* 46(1): 1–23.

1994   The Formation of the Creeks. In *The Forgotten Centuries: Indians and Europeans in the American South, 1521–1704*, edited by C. Hudson and C. Tesser, 373–392. University of Georgia Press, Athens.

Kohler, Timothy A., and Mark D. Varien, eds.

2012   *Emergence and Collapse of Early Villages: Models of Central Mesa Verde Archaeology.* University of California Press, Berkeley.

Kohler, Timothy A., Stephanie VanBuskirk, and Samantha Ruscavage-Barz

2004   Vessels and Villages: Evidence for Conformist Transmission in Early Village Aggregations on the Pajarito Plateau, New Mexico. *Journal of Anthropological Archaeology* 23:100–118.

Kolb, Michael J., and James E. Snead

1997   It's a Small World After All: Comparative Analyses of Community Organization in Archaeology. *American Antiquity* 62(4): 609–628.

Kowalewski, Stephen A.

1996   Clout, Corn, Copper, Core-Periphery, Culture Area. In *Pre-Columbian World Systems*, edited by Peter N. Peregrine, 27–37. Prehistory Press, Madison, WI.

2013   The Work of Making Community. In *From Prehistoric Villages to Cities: Settlement Aggregation and Community Transformation*, edited by Jennifer Birch, 201–218. Routledge, New York.

Kuijt, Ian, ed.

2000   *Life in Early Farming Communities: Social Organization, Identity, and Differentiation.* Kluwer Academic/Plenum Press, New York.

Kuijt, Ian, and Nigel Goring-Morris

2002   Foraging, Farming, and Social Complexity in the Pre-Pottery Neolithic of the Southern Levant: A Review and Synthesis. *Journal of World Prehistory* 16(4): 361–440.

Lesure, Richard G., Thomas A. Wake, Aleksander Borejsza, Jennifer Carballo, David M. Carballo, Isabel Rodríguez López, and Mauro de Ángeles Guzmán

2013   Swidden Agriculture, Village Longevity, and Social Relations in Formative Central Tlaxcala: Towards an Understanding of Macroregional Structure. *Journal of Anthropological Archaeology* 32(2): 224–241.

Mabry, Jonathan, Deborah Swartz, Jeffrey Clark, Helga Wocherl, and Michael Lindeman

1997   Archaeological Investigations of Early Village Sites in the Middle Santa Cruz Valley: Descriptions of the Santa Cruz Bend, Square Hearth, Stone Pipe, and Canal Sites. Anthropological Papers No. 18, Center for Desert Archaeology, Tucson.

Marcus, Joyce

2008   The Archaeological Evidence for Social Evolution. *Annual Review of Anthropology* 37:251–266.

Marcus, Joyce, and Kent V. Flannery

1996   *Zapotec Civilization: How Urban Society Evolved in Mexico's Oaxaca Valley.* Thames and Hudson, London.

Marquardt, William

2014   Tracking the Calusa: A Retrospective. *Southeastern Archaeology* 33:1–24.

McGuire, Randall H., and Dean J. Saitta

1996   Although They Have Petty Captains, They Obey Them Badly: The Dialectics of Prehispanic Western Pueblo Social Organization. *American Antiquity* 61(2): 197–216.

Means, Bernard K.

2007   *Circular Villages of the Monongahela Tradition.* University of Alabama Press, Tuscaloosa.

Meeks, Scott C., and David G. Anderson

2014   Drought, Subsistence Stress, and Population Dynamics. In *Soils, Climate and Society:
Archaeological Investigations in Ancient America,* edited by John D. Wingard and Sue
Eileen Hayes, 61–83. University Press of Colorado, Denver.

Parkinson, William A., ed.

2002   *The Archaeology of Tribal Societies.* International Monographs in Prehistory, Ann Arbor, MI.

Pauketat, Timothy R.

1994   *The Ascent of Chiefs: Cahokia and Mississippian Politics in Native North America.* University of Alabama Press, Tuscaloosa.

2001   Practice and History in Archaeology: An Emerging Paradigm. *Anthropological Theory*
1(1): 73–98.

2003   Resettled Farmers and the Making of a Mississippian Polity. *American Antiquity*
68(1): 39–66.

Pluckhahn, Thomas J.

2003   *Kolomoki: Settlement, Ceremony, and Status in the Deep South, ca. 350 to 750 A.D.* University of Alabama Press, Tuscaloosa.

2010   Household Archaeology in the Southeastern United States: History, Trends, and
Challenges. *Journal of Archaeological Research* 18(4): 331–385.

2013   Cooperation and Competition among Late Woodland Households at Kolomoki,
Georgia. In *Cooperation and Collective Action: Archaeological Perspectives,* edited by
David M. Carballo, 175–196. University Press of Colorado, Boulder.

Pluckhahn, Thomas J., and Victor D. Thompson

2018   *The Archaeology of Village Life at Crystal River.* University Press of Florida, Gainesville.

2013   Constituting Similarity and Difference in the Deep South: The Ritual and Domestic
Landscapes of Kolomoki, Crystal River, and Fort Center. In *The Ritual and Domestic
Landscapes of Early and Middle Woodland Peoples in the Southeast,* edited by Alice
Wright and Edward Henry, 181–195. University Press of Florida, Gainesville.

Rautman, Alison E.

2014   *Constructing Community: The Archaeology of Early Villages in Central New Mexico.* University of Arizona Press, Tucson.

2016   "Circling the Wagons" and Community Formation: Interpreting Circular Villages in
the Archaeological Record. *World Archaeology* 48(1): 125–143.

Renfrew, Colin, and John F. Cherry, eds.

1986   *Peer-Polity Interaction and Socio-Political Change.* Cambridge University Press, Cambridge.

Roscoe, Paul

2009   Social Signaling and the Organization of Small-Scale Society: The Case of Contact-
Era New Guinea. *Journal of Archaeological Method and Theory* 16(2): 69–116.

2013   War, Collective Action, and the "Evolution" of Human Polities. In *Cooperation and
Collective Action: Archaeological Perspectives,* edited by David M. Carballo, 57–82. University Press of Colorado, Boulder.

Rosenberg, Michael, and Richard W. Redding

2000   Hallan Çemi and Early Village Organization in Eastern Anatolia. In *Life in Neolithic Farming Communities: Social Organization, Identity, and Differentiation*, edited by Ian Kuijt, 39–62. Kluwer Academic/Plenum Publishers, New York.

Russo, Michael

1998   Measuring Sedentism with Fauna: Archaic Cultures along the Southwest Florida Coast. In *Seasonality and Sedentism: Archaeological Perspectives from Old and New World Sites*, edited by T. R. Rocek and O. Bar-Yosef, 143–164. Peabody Museum Press, Harvard University, Cambridge, MA.

2004   Measuring Shell Rings for Social Inequality. In *Signs of Power: The Rise of Cultural Complexity in the Southeast*, edited by J. L. Gibson and P. J. Carr, 26–70. University of Alabama Press, Tuscaloosa.

Sahlins, Marshall

1968   *Tribesmen*. Prentice-Hall, Englewood Cliffs, NJ.

Sanger, Matthew Clair

2015   Life in the Round: Shell Rings of the Georgia Bight. Ph.D. diss., Columbia University.

Schachner, Gregson

2012   *Population Circulation and the Transformation of Ancient Zuni Communities*. University of Arizona Press, Tucson.

Sewell, William H., Jr.

1992   A Theory of Structure: Duality, Agency, and Transformation. *American Journal of Sociology* 98:1–29.

Snow, Dean R.

1994   *The Iroquois*. Blackwell, Cambridge.

Spence, Michael

1999   Comments: The Social Foundations of Archaeological Taxonomy. In *Taming the Taxonomy: Toward a New Understanding of Great Lakes Archaeology*, edited by Ronald F. Williamson and Christopher M. Watts, 275–282. Eastendbooks, Toronto.

Thomas, David Hurst

2008   Synthesis: The Aboriginal Landscape of St. Catherines Island. In *Native American Landscapes of St. Catherines Island, Georgia III*, edited by D. H. Thomas, 990–1042. Anthropological Papers No. 88, American Museum of Natural History, New York.

Thompson, Victor D.

2006   Questioning Complexity: The Prehistoric Hunter-Gatherers of Sapelo Island, Georgia. Ph.D. diss., University of Kentucky.

2007   Articulating Activity Areas and Formation Processes at the Sapelo Island Shell Ring Complex. *Southeastern Archaeology* 26(1): 91–107.

Thompson, Victor D., and C. Fred T. Andrus

2011   Evaluating Mobility, Monumentality, and Feasting at the Sapelo Island Shell Ring Complex. *American Antiquity* 76(2): 315–343.

Thompson, Victor D., and T. R. Kidder

2007   Archaeologies of Transformation. Symposium "Complexity and Transformation in World Archaeology" for the 72nd Society for American Archaeology Meeting, Austin, TX.

Thompson, Victor D., and Christopher R. Moore

2015   The Sociality of Surplus among Late Archaic Hunter-Gatherers of Coastal Georgia.

In *Surplus: The Politics of Production and Strategies of Everyday Life*, edited by C. T. Morehart and K. De Lucia, 245–266. University of Colorado Press, Boulder.

Thompson, Victor D., and Thomas J. Pluckhahn

2012   Monumentalization and Ritual Landscapes at Fort Center in the Lake Okeechobee Basin of South Florida. *Journal of Anthropological Archaeology* 31:49–65.

Thompson, Victor D., and John Worth

2011   Dwellers by the Sea: Native American Coastal Adaptations along the Southern Coasts of Eastern North America. *Journal of Archaeological Research* 19(1): 51–101.

Thompson, Victor D., William H. Marquardt, Alexander Cherkinsky, Amanda Roberts Thompson, Karen Walker, and Lee Newsom

2016   From Shell Midden to Shell Mound: The Geoarchaeology of Mound Key an Anthropogenic Island in Southwest Florida, USA. *PlOS ONE* 11(4): e0154611.

Thompson, Victor D., Thomas J. Pluckhahn, Matt Colvin, Justin Cramb, Katharine Napora, J. Jacob Lulewicz, and Brandon Ritchison

2017   Plummets, Public Ritual, and Interaction Networks during the Woodland Period in Florida. *Journal of Anthropological Archaeology* 48:193–206.

Trigger, Bruce G.

1976   *The Children of Aataentsic: A History of the Huron People to 1660*. Mc-Gill-Queens University Press, Montreal and Kingston.

1991   Distinguished Lecture in Archeology: Constraint and Freedom—A New Synthesis for Archeological Explanation. *American Anthropologist* 93(3): 551–69.

Turck, John A., and Victor D. Thompson

2016   Revisiting the Resilience of Late Archaic Hunter-Gatherers along the Georgia Coast. *Journal of Anthropological Archaeology* 43:39–55.

Tuzin, Donald

2001   *Social Complexity in the Making: A Case Study among the Arapesh of New Guinea*. Routledge, New York.

Vaughan, Kevin J., Jelmer W. Eerkens, and John Kantner, eds.

2010   *The Evolution of Leadership: Transitions in Decision-Making from Small-Scale to Middle-Range Societies*. School for Advanced Research Press, Santa Fe, NM.

Wallis, Neill J., Paulette S. McFadden, and Hayley M. Singleton

2015   Radiocarbon Dating the Pace of Monument Construction and Village Aggregation at Garden Patch: A Ceremonial Center on the Florida Gulf Coast. *Journal of Archaeological Science: Reports* 2:507–516.

Warrick, Gary A.

2008   *A Population History of the Huron-Petun, A.D. 500–1650*. Cambridge University Press, Cambridge.

Williams, Mark, and Gary Shapiro

1990   Paired Towns. In *Lamar Archaeology, Mississippian Chiefdoms in the Deep South*, edited by M. Williams and G. Shapiro, 163–174. University of Alabama Press, Tuscaloosa.

Williamson, Ronald F., and David G. Robertson

1994   Peer Polities Beyond the Periphery: Early and Middle Iroquoian Regional Interaction. *Ontario Archaeology* 58:27–40.

Wills, W. H., and Robert D. Leonard, eds.

1994   *The Ancient Southwestern Community: Methods and Models for the Study of Prehistoric Social Organization*. University of New Mexico Press, Albuquerque.

Wilshusen, Richard H., and James M. Potter

2010   The Emergence of Early Villages in the American Southwest: Cultural Issues and Historical Perspectives. In *Becoming Villagers: Comparing Early Village Societies*, edited by Matthew S. Bandy and Jake R. Fox, 1–18. University of Arizona Press, Tucson.

Wilson, Gregory D.

2012   Living with War: The Impact of Chronic Violence in the Mississippian-Period Central Illinois River Valley. In *Handbook of North American Archaeology*, edited by Timothy R. Pauketat, 523–533. Oxford University Press, Oxford.

2

Collective Action and Village Life
during the Late Archaic on the Georgia Coast

VICTOR D. THOMPSON

The emergence of villages has presented a cascade of both theoretical and method-ological issues for archaeologists, from the search for substantive definitions (e.g., Bandy 2010; Birch 2013) to how we measure, for example, year-round settlement (e.g., Rocek and Bar-Yosef 1998). To a great degree, the literature surrounding the nature of the emergence of villages has largely focused on agriculturalists (Bandy and Fox 2010). While researchers certainly have considered hunter-gatherer econ-omies in sophisticated ways in this process of becoming villagers, the larger narra-tive seems to lead back to how various dimensions of domestication and agricul-ture fit into this process. It is not my intent to criticize these studies, as in most of these situations it makes perfect sense to take this approach. Conversely, most of the literature that does focus exclusively on hunter-gatherer economies tends to situate narratives in terms of complexity and the emergence of hierarchy (Arnold 1996; Price and Brown 1985). Certainly, all such studies owe a considerable debt to Price and Brown (1985) and Arnold (1996), whose work made possible research into more varied aspects of hunter-gatherer lifeways than previously considered by researchers. However, as Pluckhahn and Thompson (2018) note, few consider hunter-gatherers exclusively as vectors for the process of village formation without injecting the issue of complexity along with it, despite the latter's rather nebulous formulations (see Sassaman 2004).

This chapter takes as its starting point that at least some shell rings of the Geor-gia Coast represent some of the earliest villages in the region (Figure 2.1). As out-lined in Thompson and Birch (this volume), these represent very different social relationships than other types of settlements engaged by hunter-gatherers (e.g., ag-gregation sites). My aim is to address two fundamental problems that relate to the formation of such entities for the first time in a region. First, there is the question of how emergent villages dealt with economic and social problems of coresidence.

Next, given the creation of a landscape populated with village communities, how then are peer relationships negotiated (see Thompson and Birch, this volume)? I view both of these as collective action questions because at the heart of them resources are involved, and if villagers at any one scale behaved in a selfish way, regardless of whether rooted purely in subsistence economic or ritual economic pursuits, then conflict and tension would arise causing systemic collapse (see Roscoe 2009). As I outline, this is especially challenging for the early villages of the Georgia Coast, as the distribution of resources made it difficult to be insular with regards to the broader landscape.

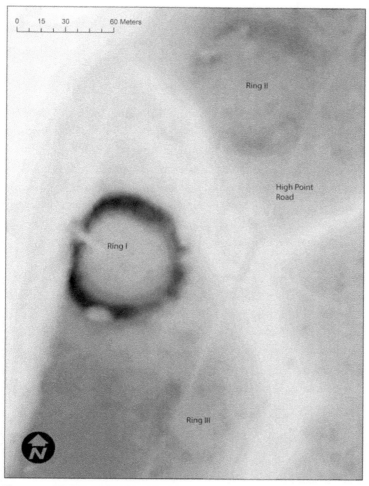

Figure 2.1. LiDAR topographic map of the Sapelo Shell Ring Complex, showing the three rings at the site.

The theoretical perspective that I take is rooted in collective action (Blanton and Fargher 2008, 2016), with an explicit focus on how ecology articulates with questions surrounding human cooperation and power relations at multiple scales (Thompson 2014). As Blanton and Fargher (2016:Locations 249–252) point out, cooperation research tends to focus on small groups, and more is needed for larger-scale formulations where cooperation is much more difficult. They suggest a need for more research on states from this perspective; however, I would also argue that more work on nonstate societies is needed to examine the nested problems of cooperation (i.e., beyond the single village or coresident group). I will address cooperator problems at both the village and the landscape scale. My aim here is to demonstrate that early Georgia Coast villages developed institutions and norms that emphasized a high degree of cooperation because of the nature and distribution of resources, how travel was facilitated around the landscape, and the frequent nature of community interactions in different settings.

Shell Rings as Villages

Before moving to address how Georgia coastal villages interacted and cooperated, I must address what exactly constitutes villages in this region. Shell rings are a common site type found throughout the coastal American Southeast (Russo and Heide 2001, 2003). The vast majority of the research projects on these sites are along the Georgia, South Carolina, and northeast Florida coasts (e.g., Saunders and Russo 2002; Sanger 2015a, 2015b; Saunders 2004; Thompson et al. 2004; Thompson 2006, 2007). These sites are arcuate deposits of shellfish and other terrestrial and aquatic faunal remains, associated with bone, shell, lithic, and early pottery (Saunders and Russo 2011; Thompson and Worth 2011). Thompson and Worth (2011) summarize some of the models that suggest that these sites were seasonal gathering points for mounding and periodic feasts (Saunders 2004); habitation sites where some portion of the population lived and where ceremonial feasts in the pursuit of prestige were held (Russo 2004); and year-round egalitarian villages (Trinkley 1985; DePratter 1980). The details of these arguments have been presented elsewhere (see DePratter 1980, 2010; Russo 2004; Saunders 2004; Thompson and Worth 2011; Thompson and Andrus 2011; Turck and Thompson 2016); however, I explore some of the more important points of these past studies below.

In order to account for the variability offered in the shell ring models, I suggested a slightly different perspective, the developmental model, which allowed for the main function (e.g., habitation, to habitation/ceremonial, to a solely ceremonial site) to shift over time (Thompson 2007). I was clear in this model that researchers should not view it as a unilinear process and that not all shell rings in a given landscape would follow such a pattern. In fact, it could be that most of these sites represent habitation sites, with only a few receiving any type of ceremonial elaborations (e.g., mounding of shellfish along the ring). After all, when we look to later periods in the American Southeast (e.g., Mississippian period), we see a landscape populated with villages and civic-ceremonial centers with mounds, with the latter's early history as a village. Would not such a diverse landscape make sense for the Late Archaic, albeit in a much more muted way in terms of the archaeological record?

The vast majority of the researchers who consider shell rings to be solely monumental feasting sites do so because they believe that the size and scope of these sites imply something more than simple habitation (Saunders 2004). The reasoning behind this rather qualitative perspective is the thought that shells accumulate quickly, and Saunders (2004) cites evidence of radiocarbon dates from the top and bottom of shell deposits being statistically contemporaneous as evidence for this perspective. This, however, is highly problematic in the case that Saunders cites, for several reasons. The major issues include the use of oyster for dating, which has issues regarding the uptake of older carbon (see Cherkinsky et al. 2014); most of the dates themselves have large standard deviations (i.e., 70 years); and, finally, we have no close marine reservoir correction for this area (see Thompson and Krus 2018). In summary, the temporal resolution of these radiocarbon dates in this case is not commensurate with the question being asked. To address this issue subsequent research at shell rings has sought to examine the temporality of midden/mound formation using season of collection data. This line of evidence also provides information on whether shell rings were occupied year-round.

To date, it would seem that the data supports a perspective that at least some portion of the population lived at shell rings throughout the year, constituting a coresident population. Numerous studies using faunal assemblages—including presence/absence indicators of fishes, growth band analysis on hard clam (*Mercenaria* spp.), and oxygen isotope analysis on clams and oysters (*Crassostrea virginica*)—indicate year-round occupation of shell rings (Colaninno 2012a, 2012b; Marrinan 2010; Russo 1998; Thompson 2006; Thompson and Andrus 2011). To date, the best empirical evidence for mounding of shell, possibly from feasting, at these sites comes from Ring I at the Sapelo Shell Ring Complex, where shellfish primarily collected during the colder months of the year were deposited in single events (Thompson and Andrus 2011). However, as Thompson and Andrus (2011) caution, this may not be the result of feasting, but rather from the mass processing of oysters and clams for surplus production and trade, which we know that later groups did along the eastern coast (see Waselkov 1987:108).

The empirical evidence for several shell rings in Georgia seems to point to year-round occupation and a gradual accumulation as a result of daily refuse, strongly suggesting that these rings were indeed the location of villages (Thompson and Andrus 2011). While some have pointed out that large shell rings would be an impediment to daily life because of their height (e.g., Saunders 2014:50), some of which are over 3 m, I find this to be poor reasoning for two reasons. First, people lived on top of shell mounds far larger than these in other areas of the Southeast (Thompson et al. 2016), and second, the vast majority of shell rings were not all that tall to begin with, with many under 1 m at their highest point and an average height of 1.8 meters for the Georgia and South Carolina rings (Russo 2014:23). Many of these are often broad and gently sloping in places like Ring I at Sapelo. In addition, some so-called rings are often open on one side or have segmented shell deposits. Ring III at Sapelo exhibits this pattern, and, I argue, given the relatively dense pottery in the nonshell sites along the ring along with some associated features (e.g., post molds), that these represent former house/domestic locations and that the primary function of Ring III was residential (Thompson 2006, 2007). Bolstering this argument is the stable isotope data from Ring III that indicates that mollusks were collected and deposited year-round with opposing seasons of collection located within the same 10 cm level (Thompson and Andrus 2011).

Saunders (2014:55) states, "Archaic ceremonial centers are supposed to look like village sites, only village sites on a grand scale; these sites are intermediaries between individual houses and villages, and the cosmos, which looks like a ceremonial center or a village or a house, only larger." She says this to offer support for shell rings as ceremonial sites. The question that follows is what to do if Archaic village and/or habitation sites look as if shell rings are solely ceremonial. Many archaeologists, myself included (Thompson 2006), assumed that there was a larger settlement system in place during the Late Archaic that included vast numbers of shell sheet middens and other nonshell sites. However, recent work by Turck and Thompson (2016) calls this into question. In a recent reanalysis of radiocarbon dates from the entire Georgia Coast, we found that these nonshell sites tend to postdate the early Late Archaic, and only appear after shell rings are abandoned as a site type during a terminal Late Archaic period. For the early Late Archaic, shell rings and large shell middens are, by far, the most common, and indeed possibly the only, site type (Turck and Thompson 2016:52).

Collective Action at Shell Ring Villages

By now it should be clear that while I allow for some shell rings to take on a *more* ceremonial function, I, for the most part, view them as village sites. This does not mean, however, that I think all activities were mundane, ecologically related, or restricted to the processing of daily foodstuffs. After all, even in some of the smallest villages there are feasts, rituals, ceremonies, and special events (e.g., births, marriages, rites of passage, initiation, and the like). In fact, I think it is safe to assume that such activities occurred at shell ring villages. Such events would have helped to not only cement fidelity of place (i.e., the village) (Turck and Thompson 2016:52; see also Thompson 2010) but also to reinforce relationships and the identity of the coresident community (i.e., as villagers).

Daily life in villages and ceremonial events required coordination and provisioning. Moore and I (Thompson and Moore 2015) considered the nature of such provisioning at shell rings in terms of surplus production. In that publication, we differentiated two different kinds of surplus: anticipated and opportunistic. In terms of presenting a collective action problem, it is the former of these that likely more frequently required cooperation at the village scale. Anticipated surplus production is highly structured in time and space and can be predicted with regards to both, and as a result creates a greater commitment to certain places on the landscape (Thompson and Moore 2015:248–249).

The greater cooperation for anticipated surplus production activities links in to the type of resources exploited by these communities. In this case, unlike other incipient agricultural villages, shell ring villages exploited a vast estuary and island landscape. The majority of the faunal remains found at these sites are small and medium-size finfishes, with herrings and shads, sea catfishes, mullets, and drums being the most ubiquitous (Colaninno 2010:221; Marrinan 2010). As Colaninno (2010:189) points out, her findings of small fish size for five Georgia Coast shell rings is consistent with ethnographic research that indicates that smaller-bodied fauna that reproduce frequently and in large numbers yield predictable high returns (see also Winterhalder and Lu 1997). These findings have led both Marrinan (2010) and Colaninno (2010:221) especially to suggest that shell ring occupants practiced mass capture technologies in the form of woven fine grain nets and likely fish traps and weirs. Clans or some other form of group with redistricted affiliation may have owned such weirs; however, it is difficult to speculate about this at this point.

Thomas (2008:122–131) notes that ethnohistoric sources indicate the use of fish weirs on the Georgia Coast. Although we have not located them archaeologically in the area, given Colaninno's recent work (2010, 2012a, 2012b), I believe that it would be safe to assume that these were in operation during the Late Archaic. Such facilities, if managed by individual villages, would have represented significant labor investments and upkeep, necessitating collaboration and cooperation among villagers. Mass captures during specific times of the year would have also financed feasts and attendant rituals in the village. The emplacement of fish weir facilities also likely gave certain villages rights, establishing a type of "aquatic landesque capital" (*sensu* Marquardt and Crumley 1987) to fishing areas in the estuaries (see Reitz 2014).

In addition to the communal labor involved in the production and technology of fishing, the layout of villages also likely downplayed and suppressed free riders and agents in pursuit of social prestige through control and management of surplus production. While Russo (2004) and Sassaman and Heckenberger (2004) suggest hierarchal social relations for shell ring inhabitants, empirical support is currently lacking for such notions (see DePratter 2010 for a critique). Russo's (2004, 2014) view of feasting and concomitant transegalitarian social relationships is perhaps the better developed of the two; however, Colaninno's (2010, 2012b:358) testing of this postulate—that big men lived along certain portions of the ring, usually the point with the highest shell deposits—was not supported by the distribution of vertebrate faunal remains. And while this does not discount the idea that certain individuals controlled production (see Russo 2014), it appears that where these resources are concerned ring inhabitants had "similar access to resources, technologies, and processing methods," suggesting that people "were socially equal when using vertebrate resources" (Colaninno 2012b:358). Thus, it appears that if individuals were involved in some degree of management of feasts, they had little "agency" in terms of the manipulation and management of communal resources to use them, or misuse them, as the case may be for their own prestige and benefit (see Blanton and Fargher 2016:Locations 734–735). There seems to be no excludable resources in Colaninno's analysis. In other words, these estuarine resources are the "public goods" of these early villages referred to by collective action researchers (Carballo 2012:Locations 262–264; see also Hardin 2015).

While some differences likely existed among shell ring inhabitants and were expressed during times that surpluses were produced for feasts, it does not appear that they had the agency to create any lasting social differences at the individual level (see the discussion by Pluckhahn 2010, 2012 for Woodland period plaza and attendant ethnohistoric evidence). It may be that, as Thompson and Moore (2015:257) argue, feasts and any ritual disposal of the food remains (e.g., mounding of shell) was likely part of the event itself and was "the collective cooperation that ties individual and groups together." Such ties were possibly reinforced through daily life as the circular layout of shell rings around a central plaza focused all life inward toward the center of the village (see Cobb 2005 for another perspective). Such places were not only the locations of dances, feasts, and rituals, but there is also ample evidence for daily life and processing (Sanger 2015b; Sanger and Thomas 2010; Thompson 2006, 2007). Like many other early circular village societies, such a layout may have served to downplay social distinctions, creating a kind of village panopticon discouraging individualizing behaviors and acts (see also Creese 2014; Sanger 2015b). For shell rings of the Georgia and South Carolina coasts, plazas were quite small, with shell ring diameters measuring, on average, 69 m (Russo 2014:23, Table 3.2); presumably, houses and activities would have been easily visible to all living along the ring.

Cooperating Villages, Habitat Exploitation, and the Shell Ring Landscape

Perhaps the largest gap in discussions of shell ring inhabitants is how such people ranged across the landscape. When we look at the survey data and the faunal record from shell ring sites, it is clear that the marsh estuarine system, the habitat located behind the barrier islands, was exploited most frequently, although this too is quite variable (Figure 2.2) (Pennings et al. 2012). If shell ring villages populated the landscape, then people from different communities would have encountered each other on a regular basis in the estuaries (Turck and Thompson 2016). The ties and structures that governed these encounters would require rules of engagement and access to resources, thus presenting a collective action issue of what constitutes public goods and who has access to which resources (e.g., shell beds, fishing spots) at the intervillage level.

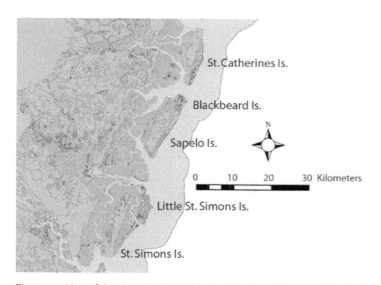

Figure 2.2. Map of the Georgia Coast showing Sapelo and surrounding barrier islands and back barrier marsh estuarine landscape.

As Cummings (2013:Locations 739–741) notes, sedentary hunter-gatherers often forage "beyond the immediate area of the village, thus maintaining access to, and knowledge of, a broader area." This is certainly the case for the Georgia Coast, as Thompson and Turck (2010) and Thompson et al. (2013) found ample evidence for use of the back barrier landscape in the form of sites and artifact scatters dating to all time periods of Native occupation. In addition, it is clear from the species list from shell ring sites that while the vast majority of the fish are estuarine, freshwater fish are present in the middens (Colaninno 2010, 2011, 2012; Reitz 1988, 2014). Marrinan's (2010:89, Table 4.7) analysis of the invertebrates from the Cannons Point Shell Ring, which includes *Littorina irrorata, Busycon carica, Anadara ovalis, Tagelus plebius, Mercenaria mercenaria, Crassostrea virginica, Geukensia demissa,* and *Crytopleura costata,* among others, indicates species taken from a wide range of habitats.

As a way of attempting to quantify habitat exploitation among Late Archaic fisher-hunter-gatherers, Andrus and Thompson (2012) conducted a reanalysis of the oxygen isotope data from the Sapelo Island Shell Ring complex. The data from this study suggests that both oysters and clams were taken from a wide variety of salinity habitats. And, while definitive areas of habitat collection cannot be identified, collection areas would have to be, assuming a relative salinity gradient, in the uppermost portions of the sounds, located some 20 km away. This result was unsurprising to us because canoe travel and the twice-daily tides would have easily facilitated such movement across great distances (Andrus and Thompson 2012:224; see also DePratter 2010:248 for a twentieth-century example). We suggest that, in part, the reason why shell ring inhabitants exploited diverse habitats was to not overexploit any one shell bed and thus was a type of "management" of such resources (Andrus and Thompson 2012:225; Thompson 2013).

There appear to be two collective action problems present if the above narrative fits shell rings. The first is that people from different communities would have encountered one another. Although we do not have a clear idea on the composition of task groups engaged in relations of production, likely this would have included diverse members of the community (i.e., men, women, and children of various ages) participating in gathering and fishing activities (see Marrinan 2010 and Thomas 2008 for thoughts on gender relations). Thus, it would seem that there would need to be some array of mechanisms for conflict resolution among villages 20 km or closer. In addition, there must have also been rules to govern the overexploitation of resources, or else we would see evidence of overexploitation in terms of diminishing oyster size over time. To date, it does not appear that Late Archaic peoples were overexploiting oyster according to our recent study from the Ossabaw Shell Ring (Lulewicz et al. 2017).

Turck and Thompson (2016; see also Thompson and Moore 2015) propose that one way intervillage social relations were maintained on the Georgia Coast was through intervillage rituals and ceremonies (see Roscoe 2009 for another example of this). Thus, "while the central focus of shell rings was domestic life, the recurrent hosting of ceremonies and rituals would have helped suppress conflict over resources, as well as reaffirm rules concerning the use of resource areas (i.e., which were exclusively controlled by a single group as opposed to those that were held in common)" (Turck and Thompson 2016:52; see also Sanger 2015b). These periodic gatherings not only likely cemented symbolic ties but also created perhaps more long-lasting ones among communities. For example, the villages of the Yanomamo of South America are constantly fissioning and changing membership so that kin are living in distant villages (Chagnon 1988:990; Blanton and Fargher 2016:Locations 546–549). Shell ring villages likely did this as well. I also suggest that the people occupying shell rings practiced village exogamy, due to the postulated low populations of such communities (see Thompson and Moore 2015; see also Birch and Williamson, this volume, for another example). Such practices could help solve these encounter issues in the back-barrier region, as well as facilitate communication regarding shellfishing and fishing rights and access discussed above.

Conclusion

In this chapter I argue that the vast majority of shell rings represent coresidential village communities. I identify several types of collective action problems that the formation of villages likely presented to shell ring inhabitants at both the village and landscape scales. I suggest that there were several solutions to these problems, none of which required top-down hierarchical control. Instead, I present a narrative that explains the functioning of these villages as a highly cooperative, self-organizing system, rooted in local and regional interaction through rituals and the maintenance of collective mass capture facilities and fishing technology, and management of resources in the context of surplus production to support village life.

The shell rings of the Georgia and South Carolina coasts represent some of the earliest villages in the Eastern Woodlands. This, of course, is significant; however, this is even more of an interesting phenomenon when we consider how rapidly this took place. Although I have not discussed the temporal beginnings (see Turck and Thompson 2016) of shell ring villages, research by Turck (2012) indicates that this occurred rapidly as new populations moved into the region. Thus, not only did a new way of life emerge in this area, it did so as a whole host of contemporaneous villages at roughly the same time. If this truly is the case, then the mechanisms and networks that sustained these shell ring villages emerged rapidly along with this rapid infilling of the landscape, until their decline at the end of the early Late Archaic, when seemingly new forms of living together emerged (Turck and Thompson 2016:52; see Kowalewski 2006 for details on such processes).

On a final note, researchers have spent the last two decades attempting to ferret out the nature of hierarchical relationships among groups of so-called complex hunter-gatherers (e.g., Arnold 1996; Hayden 1995; Gibson and Carr 2004; Russo 2004; Sassaman and Heckenberger 2004). We have seemingly forgotten that it takes real work to organize into larger cooperative groups (see Kowalewski 2013; Cobb, this volume). This work of getting along not only occurs at the village level but also must be mediated and maintained across vast networks of complex social relationships that were situated, at least in the current example in this chapter, in a highly fluctuating ecosystem with diverse habitats sensitive to human and climatic disturbance (see Thompson and Turck 2009). This, in my view, is the real power of villages, not located in the individual pursuit of prestige, but rather in the collective agency of these groups to negotiate the complex social and environmental landscape that being villagers entails.

Acknowledgments

This research was supported, in part, by a grant in association with the Georgia Coastal Ecosystems LTER project and two National Science Foundation grants (NSF grant OCE-0620959; OCE-123714). The Georgia Department of Natural Resources (GDNR), the Sapelo Island National Estuarine Research Reserve, Department of Anthropology at The Ohio State University, Department of Anthropology at the University of West Florida, and the Department of Anthropology at the University of Georgia provided additional support. Several individuals were instrumental in supporting our fieldwork and include David Crass, Dorset Hurley, Fred Hay, Bryan Tucker, and Buddy Sullivan. The author has benefited immensely from conversations with Chester DePratter, John Turck, Matt Sanger, Matt Napolitano, and David Hurst Thomas regarding the Late Archaic shell rings. Finally, I am grateful to Charlie Cobb, David Anderson, Jennifer Birch, John Turck, Warren DeBoer, and Philip Carr, whose comments and critiques greatly improved this chapter.

References Cited

Andrus, C. Fred T., and Victor D. Thompson
2012   Determining the Habitats of Mollusk Collection at the Sapelo Island Shell Ring Complex, USA Using Oxygen Isotope Sclerochronology. *Journal of Archaeological Science* 39:215–228.

Arnold, Jeanne E.

1996   Understanding the Evolution of Intermediate Societies. In *Emergent Complexity: The Evolution of Intermediate Societies*, 1–12. Archaeological Series 9. International Monographs in Prehistory, Ann Arbor, MI.

Bandy, Matthew S.

2010   Population Growth, Village Fissioning, and Alternative Early Village Trajectories. In *Becoming Villagers: Comparing Early Village Societies*, edited by M. S. Bandy and J. Fox, 19–38. University of Arizona Press, Tucson.

Bandy, Matthew S., and Jake R. Fox, eds.

2010   *Becoming Villagers: Comparing Early Village Societies.* University of Arizona Press, Tucson.

Birch, Jennifer

2013   Between Villages and Cities: Settlement Aggregation in Cross-Cultural Perspective. In *From Prehistoric Villages to Cities: Settlement Aggregation and Community Transformation*, edited by J. Birch, 1–22. Routledge, New York.

Blanton, Richard, and Lane Fargher

2008   *Collective Action in the Formation of Pre-modern States.* Springer, New York.

2016   *How Humans Cooperate: Confronting the Challenges of Collective Action.* University Press of Colorado, Boulder.

Carballo, David M.

2012   Cultural and Evolutionary Dynamics of Cooperation in Archaeological Perspective. In *Cooperation and Collective Action: Archaeological Perspectives*, edited by D. M. Carballo, 3–32. University Press of Colorado, Boulder.

Chagnon, Napoleon A.

1988   Life Histories, Blood Revenge, and Warfare in a Tribal Population. *Science* 239 (4843): 985.

Cherkinsky, Alexander, Thomas J. Pluckhahn, and Victor D. Thompson

2014   Variation in Radiocarbon Age Determinations from the Crystal River Archaeological Site, Florida. *Radiocarbon* 56(2): 801–810.

Cobb, Charles R

2005   Archaeology and the "Savage Slot": Displacement and Emplacement in the Premodern World. *American Anthropologist* 107(4): 563–574.

Colaninno, Carol Elizabeth

2010   Zooarchaeological Analysis of Vertebrate Remains from Five Late Archaic Shell Rings on the Georgia Coast, USA. Ph.D. diss., University of Georgia.

2011   Examining Ichthyofaunal Remains for Evidence of Fishing Technologies Employed in Georgia Estuaries during the Late Archaic Period. *Southeastern Archaeology* 30(2): 337–350.

2012a   Evidence for Year-round Occupation at Late Archaic Shell Rings of the Georgia Coast: Data from Oxygen Isotopic Profiles and Seasonally Sensitive Vertebrate Fauna. In *Seasonality and Human Mobility along the Georgia Bight*, edited by E. J. Reitz, I. R. Quitmyer, and D. H. Thomas, 83–102. Anthropological Papers of the American Museum of Natural History No. 97, New York.

2012b   Evaluating Formational Models for Late Archaic Shell Rings of the Southeastern United States Using Vertebrate Fauna from the St. Catherines Shell Ring, St. Catherines Island, Georgia. *Journal of Island and Coastal Archaeology* 7(3): 338–362.

Creese, John

2014   Village Layout and Social Experience: A Comparative Study from the Northeast Woodlands. *Midcontinental Journal of Archaeology* 39:1–29.

Cummings, Vicki

2013   *The Anthropology of Hunter-Gatherers: Key Themes for Archaeologists.* Bloomsbury Academic Press, London.

DePratter, Chester B

1980   Shellmound Archaic on the Georgia Coast. M.A. thesis, University of Georgia.

2010   Thoughts on the Late Archaic–Early Woodland Transition on the Georgia and South Carolina Coasts. In *Trend, Tradition, and Turmoil: What Happened to the Southeastern Archaic?: Proceedings of the Third Caldwell Conference, St. Catherines Island, Georgia,* edited by D. H. Thomas and M. C. Sanger 247–252. Anthropological Papers of the American Museum of Natural History No. 93, New York.

Gibson, Jon L., and Philip J. Carr

2004   *Signs of Power: The Rise of Cultural Complexity in the Southeast.* University of Alabama Press, Tuscaloosa.

Hardin, Russell

2015   *Collective Action.* Routledge, New York.

Hayden, Brian

1995   Pathways to Power. In *Foundations of Social Inequality,* edited by D. T. Price and G. Geinman, 15–86. Plenum Press, New York.

Kowalewski, Stephen A

2006   Coalescent Societies. In *Light on the Path: The Anthropology and History of the Southeastern Indians,* 94–122. University of Alabama Press, Tuscaloosa.

2013   The Work of Making Community. In *From Prehistoric Villages to Cities: Settlement Aggregation and Community Transformation,* edited by Jennifer Birch, 201–218. Routledge, New York.

Lulewicz, Isabelle H., Victor D. Thompson, Justin Cramb, and Bryan Tucker

2017   Oyster Paleoecology and Native America Subsistence Practices on Ossabaw Island, Georgia, U.S.A. *Journal of Archaeological Science: Reports* 15:282–289.

Marquardt, William H., and Carole L. Crumley

1987   Theoretical Issues in the Analysis of Spatial Patterning. In *Regional Dynamics: Burgundian Landscapes in Historical Perspective,* edited by C. L. Crumley and W. H. Marquardt, 1–18. Academic Press, San Diego, CA.

Marrinan, Rochelle A.

2010   Two Late Archaic Period Shell Rings, St. Simon's Island, Georgia. In *Trend, Tradition, and Turmoil: What Happened to the Southeastern Archaic?,* edited by D. H. Thomas and M. C. Sanger, 71–102. Anthropological Papers of the American Museum of Natural History No. 93, New York.

Pennings, Steven, Merryl Alber, Clark Alexander, Melissa Booth, Adrian Burd, Wei-Jun Cai, Christopher Craft, Chester DePratter, Daniela DiIorio, James T. Hollibaugh, Chuck Hopkinson, Samantha Joye, Christof Meile, Billy Moore, Brian Silliman, Victor D. Thompson, and John Wares

2012   Wetland Habitats of North America: Ecology and Conservation. In *South Atlantic Tidal Wetlands,* edited by D. Batzer and A. Baldwin, 45–61. University of California Press, Berkeley.

Pluckhahn, Thomas J

2010   The Sacred and the Secular Revisited: The Essential Tensions of Early Village Society in the Southeastern United States. In *Becoming Villagers: Comparing Early Village Societies*, edited by M. Bandy and J. Fox, 100–118. University of Colorado Press, Boulder.

2012   Cooperation and Competition among Late Woodland Households at Kolomoki, Georgia. In *Cooperative and Collective Action: Archaeological Perspectives*, edited by D. Carballo, 175–196. University Press of Colorado, Denver.

Pluckhahn, Thomas J., and Victor D. Thompson

2018   *The Archaeology of Village Life at Crystal River*. University Press of Florida, Gainesville.

Price, Douglas T., and James A. Brown, eds.

1985   *Prehistoric Hunter-Gatherers: The Emergence of Cultural Complexity*. Academic Press, New York.

Reitz, Elizabeth J.

1988   Evidence for Coastal Adaptations in Georgia and South Carolina. *Archaeology of Eastern North America* 16:137–158.

2014   Continuity and Resilience in the Central Georgia Bight (USA) Fishery between 2760 BC and AD 1580. *Journal of Archaeological Science* 41:716–731.

Rocek, Thomas R., and Ofer Bar-Yosef, eds.

1998   *Seasonality and Sedentism: Archaeological Perspectives from Old and New World Sites*. Peabody Museum Press, Harvard University, Cambridge, MA.

Roscoe, Paul

2009   Social Signaling and the Organization of Small-scale Society: The Case of Contact-Era New Guinea. *Journal of Archaeological Method and Theory* 16(2): 69–116.

Russo, Michael

1998   Measuring Sedentism with Fauna: Archaic Cultures along the Southwest Florida Coast. In *Seasonality and Sedentism: Archaeological Perspectives from Old and New World Sites*, edited by T. R. Rocek and O. Bar-Yosef, 143–164. Peabody Museum Press, Harvard University, Cambridge, MA.

2004   Measuring Shell Rings for Social Inequality. In *Signs of Power: The Rise of Cultural Complexity in the Southeast*, edited by J. L. Gibson and P. J. Carr, 26–70. University of Alabama Press, Tuscaloosa.

2014   Ringed Shell Features of the Southeast United States. In *The Cultural Dynamics of Shell-Matrix Sites*, edited by M. Roksandic, S. M. de Souza, S. Eggers, M. Burchell, and D. Klokler, 21–39. University of New Mexico Press, Albuquerque.

Russo, Michael, and Gregory Heide

2001   Shell Rings of the Southeast US. *Antiquity* 75(289): 491–492.

2003   *Mapping the Sewee Shell Ring*. Report submitted to the Francis Marion and Sumter National Forests, Columbia, SC.

Sanger, Matthew C.

2015a   Determining Depositional Events within Shell Deposits Using Computer Vision and Photogrammetry. *Journal of Archaeological Science* 53:482–491.

2015b   Life in the Round: Shell Rings of the Georgia Bight. Ph.D. diss., Columbia University.

Sanger, Matthew C., and David Hurst Thomas

2010   The Two Rings of St. Catherines Island: Some Preliminary Results from the St. Catherines and McQueen Shell Rings. In *Trend, Tradition, and Turmoil: What Happened to the Southeastern Archaic?*, edited by D. H. Thomas and M. C. Sanger, 45–102. Anthropological Papers of the American Museum of Natural History No. 93, New York.

Sassaman, Kenneth

2004   Complex Hunter-Gatherers in Evolution and History: A North American Perspective. *Journal of Archaeological Research* 12(3): 227–280.

Sassaman, Kenneth E., and Michael J. Heckenberger

2004   Crossing the Symbolic Rubicon in the Southeast. In *Signs of Power: The Rise of Cultural Complexity in the Southeast*, edited by J. L. Gibson and P. J. Carr, 214–233. University of Alabama Press, Tuscaloosa.

Saunders, Rebecca

2004   The Stratigraphic Sequence at Rollins Shell Ring: Implications for Ring Function. *Florida Anthropologist* 57(4): 249–268.

2014   Shell Rings of the Lower Atlantic Coast of the United States. In *The Cultural Dynamics of Shell-Matrix Sites*, edited by M. Roksandic, S. M. de Souza, S. Eggers, M. Burchell, and D. Klokler, 41–55. University of New Mexico Press, Albuquerque.

Saunders, Rebecca, and Michael Russo

2002   *The Fig Island Complex (38CH42): Coastal Adaptation and the Question of Ring Function in the Late Archaic.* Report prepared for the South Carolina Department of Archives and History, Columbia.

2011   Coastal Shell Middens in Florida: A View from the Archaic Period. *Quaternary International* 239(1): 38–50.

Thomas, David Hurst

2008   Synthesis: The Aboriginal Landscape of St. Catherines Island. In *Native American Landscapes of St. Catherines Island, Georgia III*, edited by D. H. Thomas, 990–1042. Anthropological Papers of the American Museum of Natural History No. 88, New York.

Thompson, Victor D.

2006   Questioning Complexity: The Prehistoric Hunter-Gatherers of Sapelo Island, Georgia. Ph.D. diss., University of Kentucky.

2007   Articulating Activity Areas and Formation Processes at the Sapelo Island Shell Ring Complex. *Southeastern Archaeology* 26(1): 91–107.

2010   The Rhythms of Space-Time and the Making of Monuments and Places during the Archaic. In *Trend, Tradition, and Turmoil: What Happened to the Southeastern Archaic?*, edited by D. H. Thomas and M. C. Sanger, 217–235. Anthropological Papers of the American Museum of Natural History No. 93, New York.

2013   Whispers on the Landscape. In *The Archaeology and Historical Ecology of Small Scale Economies*, edited by V. D. Thompson and J. C. Waggoner, 1–13. University Press of Florida, Gainesville.

2014   What I Believe: Reflections on Historical and Political Ecology as Research Frameworks in Southeastern Archaeology. *Southeastern Archaeology* 33(2): 246–254.

Thompson, Victor D., and C. Fred T. Andrus

2011   Evaluating Mobility, Monumentality, and Feasting at the Sapelo Island Shell Ring Complex. *American Antiquity* 76(2): 315–343.

Thompson, Victor D., and Anthony Krus

2018   Contemplating the History and Future of Radiocarbon Dating in the American Southeast. *Southeastern Archaeology*, http://dx.doi.org/10.1080/0734578X. 2017.1364600.

Thompson, Victor D., and Christopher R. Moore

2015   The Sociality of Surplus among Late Archaic Hunter-Gatherers of Coastal Georgia. In *Surplus: The Politics of Production and Strategies of Everyday Life*, edited by C. T. Morehart and K. De Lucia, 245–266. University of Colorado Press, Bolder.

Thompson, Victor D., and John A. Turck

2009   Adaptive Cycles of Coastal Hunter-Gatherers. *American Antiquity* 74(2): 255–278.

2010   Island Archaeology and the Native American Economies (2500 B.C.–A.D. 1700) of the Georgia Coast, USA. *Journal of Field Archaeology* 74:255–278.

Thompson, Victor D., and John E. Worth

2011   Dwellers by the Sea: Native American Adaptations along the Southern Coasts of Eastern North America. *Journal of Archaeological Research* 19(1): 51–101.

Thompson, Victor D., William H. Marquardt, Alexander Cherkinsky, Amanda D. Roberts Thompson, Karen J. Walker, Lee A. Newsom, and Michael Savarese

2016   From Shell Midden to Midden-Mound: The Geoarchaeology of Mound Key, an Anthropogenic Island in Southwest Florida, USA. *PlOS ONE* 11(4): e0154611.

Thompson, Victor D., Matthew D. Reynolds, Bryan Haley, Richard Jefferies, Jay K. Johnson, and Laura Humphries

2004   The Sapelo Shell Ring Complex: Shallow Geophysics on a Georgia Sea Island. *Southeastern Archaeology* 23:192–201.

Thompson, Victor D., John A. Turck, and Chester B. DePratter

2013   Cumulative Actions and the Historical Ecology of Islands along the Georgia Coast. In *The Archaeology and Historical Ecology of Small Scale Economies*, edited by V. D. Thompson and J. C. Waggoner Jr., 79–95. University Press of Florida, Gainesville.

Trinkley, Michael B.

1985   The Form and Function of South Carolina's Early Woodland Shell Rings. In *Structure and Process in Southeastern Archaeology*, 102–118. University of Alabama Press, Tuscaloosa.

Turck, John A.

2012   Where Were All of the Coastally Adapted People during the Middle Archaic Period in Georgia, USA? *Journal of Island and Coastal Archaeology* 7(3): 404–424.

Turck, John A., and Victor D. Thompson

2016   Revisiting the Resilience of Late Archaic Hunter-Gatherers along the Georgia Coast. *Journal of Anthropological Archaeology* 43:39–55.

Waselkov, Gregory A.

1987   Shellfish Gathering and Shell Midden Archaeology. *Advances in Archaeological Method and Theory* 10:93–210.

Winterhalder, Bruce, and Flora Lu

1997   A Forager Resource Population Ecology Model and Implications for Indigenous Conservation. *Conservation Biology* 11(6): 1354–1364.

3

Powers of Place in the Predestined Middle Woodland Village

NEILL WALLIS

Early villages likely presented a conundrum for prospective community members. Although a village may offer some benefits to its denizens, such as protection from violence and facilitation of trade, the drawbacks are numerous. Larger communities may necessitate that people work harder, intensifying production to feed more people, finding ways to manage waste and environmental degradation on a larger scale, and maintaining social mechanisms—including emergent positions of rank—for quelling inevitable intracommunity disputes (e.g., Kohler 2012; Roscoe 2009; Thompson and Birch, this volume). On the whole, village life may well have seemed unappealing for small groups whose mobility had previously circumvented many of these challenges. The reasons for acquiescing to these compromises must have been truly compelling.

This chapter considers the role of site placement and landscape features in persuading people to inhabit villages and accept the new social structures and other challenges of larger communities. In southern Georgia and northern Florida, between ca. AD 100 and 500, small communities of probably fewer than a few dozen people congregated into larger permanent villages sometimes comprised of hundreds of residents (Figure 3.1). These were not the first villages in the region (e.g., Thompson, this volume), but they were novel developments for the aggregating populations that had lived in small and dispersed mobile groups for more than a millennium. The larger villages were almost uniformly circular or "U-shaped" in plan, and some included mounds with similar (or identical) placements within the sites. Thus, not only did people increasingly aggregate throughout the Middle Woodland period, but they also chose to replicate the same basic community pattern and, presumably, the same social and power relations reinforced by this site layout.

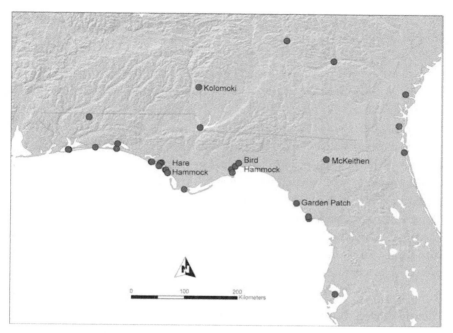

Figure 3.1. Locations of circular and U-shaped Middle Woodland villages. Based in part on Pluckhahn 2010; Russo et al. 2006; Stephenson et al. 2002.

Regardless of specific causal factors for Middle Woodland village aggregation in this region, which are currently unknown (Pluckhahn 2010), the shared spatial layout of the resulting communities manifested an organizational strategy that spanned a variety of social contexts at differing scales. This widespread replication of form could simply reflect the village as a sociogram, with the circular and U-shaped community layouts inscribing existing social and political structures onto the landscape. Indeed, the built environment must have been preceded by the cognitive perception of its organization (Birch 2012; Rapoport 1994). Recognition of premeditated village construction could explain much of the duplication in plans that we see archaeologically, as aggregation and accompanying social and political transformations swept the region and led to replication of a similar sociogram. This narrative conforms to anthropological expectations: scalar stress associated with increasing residential populations is ameliorated by decreasing the number of organizational units via extended families, clans, moieties, and sodalities, and these units may be reflected in the spatial grammar of villages (Johnson 1982; Kent 1991; Lévi-Strauss 1963:132–163). However, the historical origins of this particular solution to the aggregation problem require more explanation. Why did the first villagers in more than 50 generations choose this specific village configuration among other possibilities?

In the case of Middle Woodland inhabitants of northern Florida and southern Georgia, the answer may relate to a deep-seated tradition of geomancy in which "natural" features were the basis for divination and portended relationships among people and the cosmos (e.g., Allen et al. 2016; Ruggles 2015:2239–2240; Sassaman 2016). Using the Garden Patch site on the northern Gulf Coast as a case study, I argue that the presettlement landscape and the cosmic alignments of its features legitimated the founding of larger communities and the ways they were organized. In this sense, the size, orientation, and social structure of the village at Garden Patch, and other similar Middle Woodland villages, could have been "predestined" by autochthonous landscape features that framed the founding of the village and subsequent dwelling within it. Thus, in the founding of the first large Middle Woodland communities, the misgivings of prospective villagers could have been overcome by a cosmic legitimacy recognized in particular places.

Village Aggregation in the Middle Woodland Deep South

Evidence for common drivers of settlement aggregation such as population increase, adoption of agriculture, or widespread intercommunity conflict is lacking (Hutchinson 2004; Hutchinson et al. 1998), necessitating other explanations for why people would be compelled to tolerate the distinctive economic, logistical, and social challenges of larger communities (Kohler 2012; Kowalewski 2013; Thompson and Birch, this volume). One possibility is that major population centers were advantageously positioned as exchange gateways that facilitated access to the expansive exchange networks of the Middle Woodland (e.g., Anderson 1998; but see Pluckhahn 2003:10). In addition, the association of the largest villages in this region with major monumental construction projects and feasting deposits indicates that ritual practice was a mechanism for bringing people together (Pluckhahn 2010:104). This is an unsurprising correlation: ritual is commonly associated with aggregation of disparate populations, even on a temporary basis, and may reduce scalar stress by fostering communication and consensus through actions that are redundant and rehearsed (Adler and Wilshusen 1990; Johnson 1982; Rappaport 1979; Turner 1969). In the North American Southeast, integrative facilities and their attendant rituals had a deep history of providing order for periodic, large-scale gatherings of mobile hunter-gatherers (e.g., Claassen 2010; Gilmore 2015; Kidder 2011; Randall 2015).

Millennia-old traditions of temporary gatherings provided the framework for successfully navigating intercommunity interactions. This framework included integrative ceremonial practices such as mound building and feasting, circular and U-shaped spaces that guided participants, and, likely, extended kin, fictive kin, and nonkin units of social organization. How this legacy was translated into a process by which individual centers became residential communities and endured for generations remains poorly understood. The earliest villages in many other parts of the world are characterized by significant instability that led to frequent fissioning, likely because communities had not yet developed social institutions to resolve disputes among larger and more diverse groups of people (e.g., Bandy and Fox 2010; Kohler and Varien 2010). In contrast, some Middle Woodland newly coalescent societies in northern Florida and southern Georgia seem to have been characterized by marked stability and order for several centuries.

This persistent order seems to have begun with advanced planning for community initiation. At Kolomoki, which spans a square kilometer and is by far the largest of such sites, much of the grand community plan was inscribed early in the site's history by the placement of burials, middens, and mounds (Pluckhahn 2003:183–196; Pluckhahn et al. 2018; West et al., this volume). Recent dating across the site shows that three site features established the main site axis one or two centuries before the U-shaped village appears to have been established (Pluckhahn et al. 2018). These early events include deposition of midden and graves below the eventual location of Mound D, construction of Mound E, and, possibly, initial construction of Mound A by the early fifth century (see Figure 3.2). Kolomoki is not unusual in this regard. Cemeteries appear to have been a primary method of community inscription for generations in the region, dating back at least to the Late Archaic (e.g., Sassaman 2016). Recent AMS dating of osteological assemblages shows that the burial mounds at many of the major Middle Woodland communities on the Gulf Coast, such as Crystal River, Shell Mound/Palmetto Mound, and Shired Island/Hughes Island Mound, were initiated as cemeteries during the Early Woodland period, possibly as much as five centuries prior to significant village occupation (Donop and Wallis 2016).

At Garden Patch, burials also were emplaced early in the site history at the locations of future mounds (Wallis and McFadden 2016). The burials have not been directly dated, but wooden structures associated with the same premound ground surface yielded fourth century AD calibrated date ranges that seem to slightly predate settlement of the U-shaped village (Wallis et al. 2015). Soon after these reference points for the site plan were demarcated by burials and structures, the entire layout was inhabited by a full contingent of residents. The same rapid settlement history may be true at smaller village sites as well, such as at many "ring middens" in the Florida panhandle (e.g., Russo, Dengel, and Shanks 2014; Russo et al. 2014; Russo et al. 2017). At many sites it seems that after some form of initiation event, a new community was formed almost instantaneously, with very clear ideas of village size and organization from the beginning. There was no gradual, organic growth at some of these places. Rather, it is as if these communities gathered together elsewhere and descended upon the site with blueprints and work orders in hand, oftentimes guided by landmarks established by existing cemeteries. In some cases these sites persisted for hundreds of years with little or no change to their layout. This is certainly the case at Garden Patch, where 23 AMS assays across the site show the U-shaped village was occupied from ca. cal AD 415 to 615 (Wallis et al. 2015:513).

These realizations about Woodland sites foreshadow what Cobb and Butler (2016:16) call the "Calvinist quality" of later Mississippian sites, where the scale and layout of the community were determined prior to construction of any mounds. But in northern Florida and southern Georgia, Woodland communities like Kolomoki and Garden Patch arguably were completely novel social experiments, unprecedented in scale and organization. Regardless of the ultimate reasons why people aggregated in villages, the village layout seems to have anticipated the inherent tensions of a novel social organization in which many unrelated people lived together. If Middle Woodland villages were organized by ranked lineages and clans as well as new social institutions that crosscut kin groups, such as sodalities (e.g., Johnson 1982; Kohler and Varien 2010; Pluckhahn 2003), perhaps highly organized village spaces—possibly modeled in part after Archaic gathering centers—helped to codify these novel arrangements and successfully overcome the tendency toward fissioning with each intracommunity dispute. This chapter describes some of the constraints and opportunities that might have been associated with living in U-shaped villages, especially those that incorporated mounds at civic-ceremonial centers.

This chapter also considers the origins of this particular village arrangement in the Middle Woodland period. Although there are precedents for circular and U-shaped communities in the Late Archaic (e.g., Russo and Heide 2001; Thompson, this volume), Middle Woodland communities were not bound by this tradition, as evidenced by a few alternative iterations within the region (e.g., Pluckhahn et al. 2015; Sassaman et al. 2016). As described in the next section, the commonalities among U-shaped villages extend beyond the shape of the habitation outline to mound placement and their cosmic alignments. This cosmogram—the idea for how villages were organized—was written into the landscape prior to village aggregation, at least in some cases. Evidence from the Garden Patch site shows that the configuration of preoccupation landscape features was appropriated by a newly aggregated community as a model of village settlement. I argue that this was a profound event that could have naturalized the new community's social structure, perhaps achieved through the "revelation" of mythical truths already inscribed in the landscape (e.g., Barrett 1999:255–256). Following this line of reasoning, the ritual practices that seem to have drawn people together at villages did so by affirming a preexisting cosmic logic and justification for new community structures of social rank and difference. In this way, the village at Garden Patch was unavoidable, or at least must have seemed so to the inhabitants. Given the similarity of Garden Patch to several other sites, I consider the implications of this idea for understanding the origins of Middle Woodland village societies and associated power structures in northern Florida and southern Georgia.

Common Features of Middle Woodland Villages in the Deep South

U-shaped Village Plans

Dozens of "ring middens" have been documented at Woodland sites in Georgia and northern Florida (Russo et al. 2006; Russo, Dengel, and Shanks 2014; Russo et al. 2014; Stephenson et al. 2002). These come in a variety of sizes and shapes, but many are U-shaped, longer on one axis than the other and open at one end. This configuration is assumed to reflect the layout of houses surrounding a midden-free central plaza. Unlike their Late Archaic counterparts, Woodland ring middens typically are low relief, half a meter high at most. At some sites, such as Garden Patch, the configuration of midden is associated with ubiquitous architectural evidence—a virtual minefield of postholes that leave little doubt that these middens are associated with the living areas of a village.

What does the U-shaped layout signify, and how did it influence social interactions and social structure? As with circular configurations more often discussed by archaeologists, the U-shaped settlement could serve to reinforce collective group identity and cohesion, spatially defining an "in" group and all others that are "out" (Rautman 2016). At the same time, the U-shape, perhaps more than the circle, embodies significant possibilities for formalizing within-group difference. By definition, not all points on the "U" are equal. As Russo (2004) has argued in his discussion of Late Archaic shell rings, the part of the "U" facing the opening is privileged because it has no counterpart. Furthermore, a "U" has two sides mirroring one another that, through comparison of height and shape, can easily emphasize difference. The potential differences among parts of the U-shaped village were especially pronounced by constructed mounds that marked key locations in some Woodland sites. At some sites such as McKeithen (Milanich et al. 1997) and Hare Hammock (Russo et al. 2014), distinctive concentrations of Weeden Island "elite wares" also indicate consistent differences across the village, representing either spatially segregated practices or differential access to certain kinds of vessels, or both.

In the context of widespread village aggregation during the Middle Woodland period, the U-shaped village may be a kind of sociogram, demarcating social and political structure within a community (Gallivan, this volume). Some form of dual reciprocal organization that structured the relationships among newly co-resident lineages on either side of the village is tempting to suggest, perhaps with a sodality or other nonkin group occupying the apex (e.g., Knight 1998, 2016; Lévi-Strauss 1963:132–163; Russo et al. 2011:122–128). Whatever the specifics of organization, the U-shaped village undeniably formalized social relationships among its residents. Moreover, the configuration probably served to reinforce social structure through constant monitoring by its inhabitants, socializing the body and mind (Gallivan, this volume; Thompson, this volume). Presumably every building was visible to every other one within the village and thus subject to constant social surveillance. As Graves and Van Keuren (2011:271) describe for circular Pueblo villages in the American Southwest, the potential of such a configuration is to create what amounts to a "reverse panopticon" in which the community "watched and monitored and exerted discipline over itself" (see also Creese 2013; Potter and Perry 2000; Rautman 2014; Thompson, this volume). Maintenance of the power configurations manifested in the U-shaped village was a job for everyone. Rather than the deliberate plot of particular individuals or groups seeking power, the panoptic surveillance enabled by the U-shaped village may have been an unanticipated consequence of village settlement that allowed for changes in the ways power was conceptualized and enacted (Graves and Van Keuren 2011:272).

Mounds within Villages

Most U-shaped villages do not include mounds within their plans. More common is for one burial mound to be located adjacent to the village or a short distance away (Russo, Dengel, and Shanks 2014; Russo et al. 2014). But the larger village sites incorporated mounds into the village layout. At sites such as McKeithen, Kolomoki, and Garden Patch, where village layouts are well defined by intensive survey, mounds were placed in distinctive locations. At all three of these sites, mounds sit at the apex of the "U" shape, opposite the village opening (Figure 3.2). At McKeithen and Garden Patch, this was the location of a platform mound, which in the former case was interpreted as the surface for a charnel facility (Milanich et al. 1997). At Kolomoki, the largest burial mound (Mound D) was built at this location. At both McKeithen and Garden Patch, but not at Kolomoki, a residential mound occupies one side of the U-shaped village and sits opposite a burial mound on the other side. At Garden Patch and Kolomoki, but not at McKeithen, three mounds occupy the opening of the U-shaped village. Although there

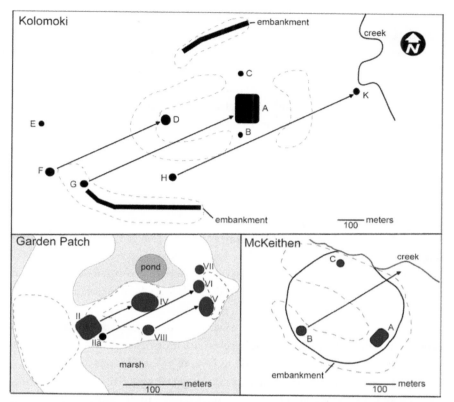

Figure 3.2. Simplified site plans at Kolomoki, Garden Patch, and McKeithen (adapted from Milanich et al. 1997; Pluckhahn 2003, 2010; Wallis et al. 2015). Midden is depicted by dashed lines, mounds are solid black, and arrows point in the approximate direction of the summer solstice sunrise.

is variation among these sites, mounds delimited the layout of each residential site in consistent ways that accentuated and stabilized differences among various parts of the U-shaped village configuration.

Cosmic Alignments

Villages and the mounds that they contained often have solar alignments. Typically, these alignments are to summer and winter solstice sunrises and sunsets. Solitary burial mounds are often located northwest of small, U-shaped villages, the direction of the summer solstice sunset (Russo et al. 2014:136). A line from McKeithen Mound B toward the summer solstice sunrise perfectly bisects the distance between the other two mounds (Milanich et al. 1997). Garden Patch and Kolomoki have alignments between several mound pairs that mark the same solstice event (see more details below). These alignments likely had a strong naturalizing effect, binding incontrovertible cosmic forces to the village layouts and associated social structures. This concern with cosmic alignment as a framework for the social is akin to what some Mesoamericanists call "cosmovision," where natural features are incorporated strategically into civic plans and demonstrate a ruler's control over the associated forces (Ashmore 2008:170). In the Woodland case, it is the community plan that maps onto the cosmos, thereby naturalizing its physical and social structure.

Village Beginnings

In order to achieve these spatial configurations, advanced planning was necessary. Specifically, the landmarks established by mounds seem to have anticipated and directed the village settlements emplaced among them. At well-dated sites such as Garden Patch, we find that the village layout was established rapidly and remained unchanged for nearly three centuries (Wallis et al. 2015). Where did these conceptual designs originate?

Garden Patch offers an intriguing answer. In comparison to other multimound centers, the site is compact, including seven mounds of sand, or sand and shell, that surround an area about 200 by 100 m (Figure 3.3). Midden is distributed in a U-shaped configuration among the mounds on the western half of the site (Wallis and McFadden 2014; Wallis et al. 2015). A much smaller midden also exists just east of the three mounds on the eastern end of the site.

Many of the site's features comprise a dualistic arrangement. On the site's northern boundary is a freshwater pond with potable water. On the opposite, southern side of the site is a tidal saltwater marsh inlet similar in size to the freshwater pond. The mounds at these locations accentuate this dualism. The north side of the village surmounts the largest mound at the site. On the southern, opposite side, the village occupation terminates at the smallest mound at the site, a burial mound. These dualisms—north/south, fresh/salt, habitation/mortuary, high/low—could have provided ample material to support differences observed between opposite sides of the village, which would have extended to its residents. The potential of the U-shaped village to demarcate difference seems to have been accentuated by the configuration at Garden Patch, and these differences could have been one basis for establishing and reaffirming social rank.

Occupying the apex of the U-shaped village—the position of privilege that has no counterpart—is a platform mound and an adjacent low, dome-shaped mound. The privilege of this position is in fact corroborated by several superlatives: the highest density and greatest diversity of fauna compared to other

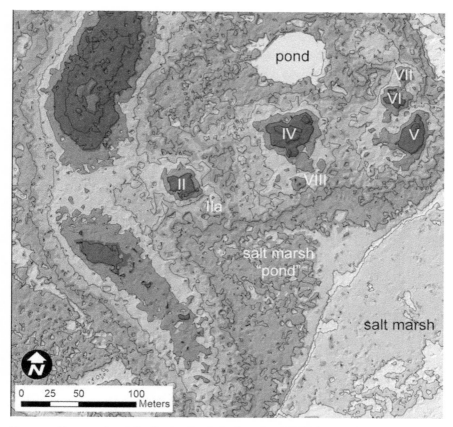

Figure 3.3. Topography of the Garden Patch site based on LiDAR data, with mounds labeled. Contour interval is 50 cm.

excavated areas of the site, and Swift Creek pottery that is entirely nonlocal (Singleton 2015; Wallis et al. 2016). Opposite these two mounds at the apex of the U-shaped village, and beyond its opening, are three mounds, the southernmost a burial mound and the others of unknown function. As already mentioned, some of these mounds have cosmic alignments (Figure 3.2). From each of the two mounds at the apex of the U-shaped village, the summer solstice sunrise occurs over another mound (Mound II to Mound IV; Mound IIa to Mound VI). The two confirmed burial mounds at the site (Mound VIII and Mound V) are connected to each other in the same way. The direction of the winter solstice sunset is nearly reciprocal to that of the summer solstice sunrise and might have been equally, or more, important (Bill Romain, personal communication, 2014). Notably, much of the natural landscape around the Garden Patch site generally follows this same orientation, including the freshwater marsh connected to the freshwater pond, the shoreline adjacent to the salt marsh, and the nearby Horseshoe Point extending into the Gulf of Mexico.

Recent fieldwork reveals that much of this site configuration existed prior to human occupation. Sediment cores date the origin of the freshwater pond to the third century BC, or earlier, and the salt marsh emerged by the first century BC (McFadden and Wallis 2018). At least some of the mounds at Garden Patch (and perhaps all) began as natural rises within the underlying Pleistocene dune formation. Excavations show that Mound II and Mound V both began as small rises at least half a meter above the surrounding terrain prior to human occupation (Wallis and McFadden 2014). Likewise, Mound IV was already a formidable mound rising roughly 3 m above what would later become the adjacent plaza. These natural landmarks provided the framework for the village plan. At Mound II and Mound V—the western and eastern edges of the site, respectively—sometime between cal AD 325 and 375 large structures were erected on the small rises (Wallis et al. 2015). At Mound V, and possibly Mound II, burials were interred in this surface as well. Concurrently, people began living across the entire elevated surface provided by Mound IV, as well as the rest of the U-shaped village configuration. At least by AD 425, sand and shell were added to Mound II and Mound V. "Mound" IV was never truly constructed, but through accumulation of midden and soil development eventually grew as much as a meter taller on its northern and eastern sides (much like Late Archaic shell rings, e.g., Thompson 2007).

In summary, all of the features we have investigated that delimit the Garden Patch site plan began as natural, cosmically aligned features that preceded the village. This discovery has important implications for understanding how Middle Woodland villages became structured as they were. At Garden Patch, the spatial arrangement of the village was not a cognitive model imposed upon a blank canvas. Instead, preexisting features dictated village layout and the placement of important monuments and structures. Given the lack of any precedent for villages in the region, this spatial arrangement may have become a determinative force in the fledgling community. If this was the case, the founding of the site included an important element of discovery. The existence of the site layout prior to its occupation would have been conducive to origin stories that referenced a deep past. Indeed, prior to village aggregation, burials might have already demarcated important features at locales like Garden Patch, indicating a deep history of engagement with cosmically aligned landscape topographies. Whatever the case, the important point is that the way the new community organized itself could have been learned from the landscape as it was revealed by these preexisting features, whose existence was probably explained in mythological terms (e.g., Bradley 2000:36). If this is true, the effect could have been to naturalize the social structure manifested by the form of the village and inextricably bind it to cosmic forces.

Garden Patch and Kolomoki Comparisons

Striking similarities to other Middle Woodland sites may indicate that the significance of Garden Patch's founding extended beyond the site itself. For instance, the general layout shares some important similarities with the much better known Woodland center of Kolomoki. Ignoring Mounds E and K on the outskirts of the site, the configuration of the seven most central mounds at Kolomoki is essentially the same as at Garden Patch (Figure 3.2). At both sites, on the eastern end three mounds sit on a north–south line. In the center of the site, two mounds are located opposite one another. On the western end, two mounds adjacent to one another form a southeast–northwest line. The seven mounds at these sites share the same overall orientation, with the long axis of the sites oriented roughly 15 degrees north of east.

The distribution of village midden appears very similar between the two sites, with both featuring a U-shaped configuration opening toward the east and facing three mounds that are backed by more midden on the eastern edge of the site. One difference is that Kolomoki has two "ring" middens: an early, smaller configuration surrounding the central mounds of the complex, and a late (post–AD 650?), larger layout that encompasses the outermost mounds (West et al., this volume). Neither the early nor the late configuration of midden at Kolomoki is identical to that at Garden Patch when viewed from the landmarks of the mounds. Moreover, the scale of the two villages is much different, with the area of Kolomoki's early and late ring middens roughly four and ten times that of Garden Patch, respectively.

The layouts of these two sites also share alignments to the summer solstice sunrise (or winter solstice sunset). These alignments include Mound II to Mound IV at Garden Patch, equivalent to Mound F to Mound D at Kolomoki; Mound XI to Mound VI at Garden Patch, equivalent to Mound G to Mound A at Kolomoki; and Mound VIII to Mound VI at Garden Patch, equivalent to Mound H to Mound K at Kolomoki.[1]

Although the sites are much different in scale, these similarities indicate that they were built according to the same principles, if not an identical, preconceived plan. Given the mid–AD 300s modeled date range for the features that frame the site parameters at Garden Patch (Wallis et al. 2015), and the centuries-later construction estimates for many of the equivalent mounds at Kolomoki (Pluckhahn et al. 2017), the former may have preceded the full realization of the latter. Kolomoki may have been the grander social experiment in its size and ambition, but Garden Patch may have provided source material for the village layout and social structure. Aspects of the same grammar may have extended to other villages and mound centers in a variety of ways (e.g., Milanich et al. 1997; Pluckhahn and Thompson 2013; Russo et al. 2014), but these comparisons are beyond the scope of the current chapter.

The Predestined Village

Whatever the ultimate reasons for the growing size of settlements in the Middle Woodland, new social collectives would have been challenged by the inherent tensions between an egalitarian ethos of smaller residential communities and emergent inequalities of larger cohabitating units. The spatial configurations of Middle Woodland village settlements and their mounds seem to have inscribed new social structures to ameliorate uncertainty and conflict (Pluckhahn 2010). Perhaps the village layout studded by mounds of various sizes prescribed a dual organization in which certain lineages or other kin-based collectives were ranked higher than others, while the practices of sodalities were focused on the village apex platforms or burial mounds. In any case, the widespread acceptance of the village arrangement and corresponding social structure could have emerged through subtle shifts in deep-seated interpretations of the existing landscape. This appears to have been the case at Garden Patch, a Middle Woodland village that exhibited the ultimate aura of inevitability, drawing on a U-shaped social model that dated back millennia (e.g., Russo and Heide 2001) and attaching it to ancient landscape features that harnessed the powers of the cosmos. In the case of Garden Patch, and perhaps other sites as of yet less thoroughly investigated, the transformation of village spaces was not predicated upon physical modifications of the landscape as much as it was shifting interpretations of existing features (Barrett 1999:256) and their articulation with configurations of social relationships among newly coresident groups.

The natural features at Garden Patch were not causative agents in the emergence of large permanent villages or incipient social inequality. A large coalescent group and some kernel of its organization must have originated sometime before the initial founding of the site as a village, or else its native interpretation as a sociogram would never have been possible. I am suggesting that the power dynamics within newly formed communities were inherently unstable, and that this place on the landscape presented an uncanny and awe-inspiring reflection of what this new society should be. Sanctioned by nonhuman forces such as the heavens and the ancestors, the site could have offered reassurance to villagers that a ranked social structure was the only way forward. While it is unlikely that the composition of the social units was unchanging over the subsequent two or three centuries of village occupation, the notion that a village needed these institutions—perhaps ranked lineages and sodalities—could have been nearly permanently established by their apparently preternatural origins. If this interpretation is correct, it could explain how emergent social rank and positions of leadership gained the legitimacy needed to overcome the volatility inherent to new village societies.

Acknowledgments

Many thanks to Victor Thompson and Jennifer Birch for inviting me to contribute to this volume and for useful comments that improved this chapter. Two anonymous reviewers helped hone the chapter as well. Bill Romain shared his unpublished assessments of solstice alignments at Garden Patch and several other sites and hopefully does not regret his generosity after seeing what I have done with them. If there remain any errors in fact or inference, only I am to blame.

Note

1. The latter alignment at Kolomoki extends outside the seven-mound configuration shared by the two sites.

References Cited

Adler, Michael A., and Richard H. Wilshusen

1990   Large-Scale Integrative Facilities in Tribal Societies: Cross-Cultural and Southwestern US Examples. *World Archaeology* 22:133–146.

Allen, Michael J., Ben Chan, Ros Cleal, Charles French, Peter Marshall, Joshua Pollard, Rebecca Pullen, Colin Richards, Clive Ruggles, David Robinson, Jim Rylatt, Julian Thomas, Kate Welham, and Mike Parker Pearson

2016   Stonehenge's Avenue and "Bluestonehenge." *Antiquity* 90:991–1008.

Anderson, David G.

1998   Swift Creek in Regional Perspective. In *A World Engraved: Archaeology of the Swift Creek Culture*, edited by M. Williams and D. T. Elliot, 274–300. University of Alabama Press, Tuscaloosa.

Ashmore, Wendy

2008   Visions of the Cosmos: Ceremonial Landscapes and Civic Plans. In *Handbook of Landscape Archaeology*, edited by D. Bruno and J. Thomas, 167–175. Left Coast Press, Walnut Creek, CA.

Bandy, Matthew S., and Jake R. Fox

2010   Becoming Villagers: The Evolution of Early Village Societies. In *Becoming Villagers: Comparing Early Village Societies*, edited by Matthew S. Bandy and Jake R. Fox, 1–18. University of Arizona Press, Tucson.

Barrett, John C.

1999   The Mythical Landscapes of the British Iron Age. In *Archaeologies of Landscape: Con-*

temporary Perspectives, edited by W. Ashmore and A. B. Knapp, 253–265. Blackwell Publishing, Malden, MA.

Birch, Jennifer

2012   Coalescent Communities: Settlement Aggregation and Social Integration in Iroquoian Ontario. *American Antiquity* 77(4): 646–670.

Bradley, Richard

2000   *An Archaeology of Natural Places.* Routledge, New York.

Claassen, Cheryl

2010   *Feasting with Shellfish in the Southern Ohio Valley: Archaic Sacred Sites and Rituals.* University of Tennessee Press, Knoxville.

Cobb, Charlie R., and Brian M. Butler

2016   Mississippian Plazas, Performances, and Portable Histories. *Journal of Archaeological Method and Theory* 1–27.

Creese, John L.

2013   Rethinking Early Village Development in Southern Ontario: Toward a History of Place-Making. *Canadian Journal of Archaeology* 37:185–218.

Donop, Mark C., and Neill J. Wallis

2016   Deptford, Diagnostics, and the Dead. Paper presented at the Sixty-Eighth Annual Florida Anthropological Society (FAS) Meeting, Jupiter, FL.

Gilmore, Zackary I.

2015   *Gathering at Silver Glen: Community and History in Late Archaic Florida.* University Press of Florida, Gainesville.

Graves, William M., and Scott Van Keuren

2011   Ancestral Pueblo Villages and the Panoptic Gaze of the Commune. *Cambridge Archaeological Journal* 21(2): 263–282.

Hutchinson, Dale L.

2004   *Bioarchaeology of the Florida Gulf Coast: Adaptation, Conflict, and Change.* University Press of Florida, Gainesville.

Hutchinson, Dale L., Clark Spencer Larsen, Margaret J. Schoeninger, and Lynette Norr

1998   Regional Variation in the Pattern of Maize Adoption and Use in Florida and Georgia. *American Antiquity* 63(3): 397–416.

Johnson, Gregory A.

1982   Organizational Structure and Scalar Stress. In *Theory and Explanation in Archaeology,* edited by Colin Renfrew, Michael Rowlands, and Barbara Segraves, 389–421. Academic Press, New York.

Kent, Susan

1991   Partitioning Space: Cross-Cultural Factors Influencing Domestic Spatial Segmentation. *Environment and Behavior* 23:438–473.

Kidder, Tristam R.

2011   Transforming Hunter-Gatherer History at Poverty Point. In *Hunter-Gatherer Archaeology as Historical Process,* edited by Kenneth E. Sassaman and Donald H. Holly, 95–119. University of Arizona Press, Tucson.

Knight, Vernon J., Jr.

1998   Moundville as a Diagrammatic Ceremonial Center. In *Archaeology of the Moundville Chiefdom,* edited by V. J. Knight Jr. and V. P. Steponaitis, 44–62. Smithsonian Institution Press, Washington, DC.

2016   Social Archaeology of Monumental Spaces at Moundville. In *Rethinking Moundville and Its Hinterland*, edited by V. P. Steponaitis and C. M. Scarry, 23–43. University Press of Florida, Gainesville.

Kohler, Timothy A.

2012   The Rise and Collapse of Villages in the Central Mesa Verde Region. In *Emergence and Collapse of Early Villages: Models of Central Mesa Verde Archaeology*, edited by T. A. Kohler and M. D. Varien, 247–262. University of California Press, Berkeley.

Kohler, Timothy A., and Mark D. Varien

2010   A Scale Model of Seven Hundred Years of Farming Settlements in Southwestern Colorado. In *Becoming Villagers: Comparing Early Village Societies*, edited by Mathew S. Bandy and Jake R. Fox, 37–61. University of Arizona Press, Tucson.

Kowalewski, Stephen A.

2013   The Work of Making Community. In *From Prehistoric Villages to Cities: Settlement Aggregation and Community Transformation*, edited by Jennifer Birch, 201–218. Routledge, New York.

Lévi-Strauss, Claude

1963   *Structural Anthropology*. Basic Books, New York.

McFadden, Paulette S., and Neill J. Wallis

2018   *Horseshoe Cove Survey 2015: Archaeological Investigations of the Garden Patch (8DI4) Landscape*. Miscellaneous Report, Division of Anthropology, Florida Museum of Natural History, University of Florida, Gainesville.

Milanich, Jerald T., Ann S. Cordell, Vernon J. Knight Jr., Timothy A. Kohler, and Brenda J. Sigler-Lavelle

1997   *Archaeology of Northern Florida, A.D. 200–900: The McKeithen Weeden Island Culture*. University Press of Florida, Gainesville.

Pluckhahn, Thomas J.

2003   *Kolomoki: Settlement, Ceremony, and Status in the Deep South, A.D. 350 to 750*. University of Alabama Press, Tuscaloosa.

2010   The Sacred and the Secular Revisited: The Essential Tensions of Early Village Societies in the Southeastern U.S. In *Becoming Villagers: Comparing Early Village Societies*, edited by M. Brandy and J. Fox, 100–118. University of Arizona Press, Tucson.

Pluckhahn, Thomas J., and Victor D. Thompson

2013   Constituting Similarity and Difference in the Deep South: The Ritual and Domestic Landscapes of Kolomoki, Crystal River, and Fort Center. In *Early and Middle Woodland Landscapes of the Southeast*, edited by Alice P. Wright and Edward R. Henry, 181–195. University Press of Florida, Gainesville.

Pluckhahn, Thomas J., Martin Menz, Shaun E. West, and Neill J. Wallis

2018   A New History of Community Formation and Change at Kolomoki (9ER1). *American Antiquity* 83(2): 320–344.

Pluckhahn, Thomas J., Victor D. Thompson, and Alexander Cherkinsky

2015   The Temporality of Shell-bearing Landscapes at Crystal River, Florida. *Journal of Anthropological Archaeology* 37:19–36.

Potter, James M., and Elizabeth M. Perry

2000   Ritual as a Power Resource in the American Southwest. In *Alternative Leadership Strategies in the Prehispanic Southwest*, edited by B. J. Mills, 60–78. University of Arizona Press, Tucson.

Randall, Asa R.

2015   *Constructing Histories: Archaic Freshwater Shell Mounds and Social Landscapes of the St. Johns River, Florida*. University Press of Florida, Gainesville.

Rapoport, Amos

1994   Social Organization and the Built Environment. In *Companion Encyclopedia of Anthropology: Humanity, Culture, and Social Life*, edited by Tim Ingold, 460–502. Routledge, London.

Rappaport, Roy A.

1979   *Ecology, Meaning and Religion*. North Atlantic Books, Berkeley, CA.

Rautman, Alison E.

2014   *Constructing Community: The Archaeology of Early Villages in Central New Mexico*. University of Arizona Press, Tucson.

2016   "Circling the Wagons" and Community Formation: Interpreting Circular Villages in the Archaeological Record. *World Archaeology* 48(1): 125–143.

Roscoe, Paul

2009   Social Signaling and the Organization of Small-Scale Society: The Case of Contact-Era New Guinea. *Journal of Archaeological Method and Theory* 16:69–116.

Ruggles, Clive L. N.

2015   Archaeoastronomy in Polynesia. In *Handbook of Archaeoastronomy and Ethnoastronomy*, edited by Clive L. N. Ruggles, 2231–2245. Springer, New York.

Russo, Michael

2004   Measuring Shell Rings for Social Inequality. In *Signs of Power: The Rise of Cultural Complexity in the Southeast*, edited by J. L. Gibson and P. J. Carr, 26–70. University of Alabama Press, Tuscaloosa.

Russo, Michael, and Gregory Heide

2001   Shell Rings of the Southeast US. *Antiquity* 75:491–492.

Russo, Michael, Craig Dengel, and Jeffrey Shanks

2014   Northwest Florida Woodland Mounds and Middens: The Sacred and Not So Secular. In *New Histories of Pre-Columbian Florida*, edited by N. J. Wallis and A. R. Randall, 121–142. University Press of Florida, Gainesville.

Russo, Michael, Craig Dengel, Jeffrey Shanks, and Andrew McFeaters

2014   *Archaeological Determinations of Boundaries and Cultural Affiliations at the Hare Hammock 8BY31 Site*. Report on file, Southeast Archaeological Center, National Park Service.

Russo, Michael, Craig Dengel, Jeffrey Shanks, and Thadra Stanton

2011   *Baker's and Strange's Mounds and Middens: Woodland Occupations on Tyndall Air Force Base*. Report submitted to Tyndall Air Force Base, Panama City, FL.

Russo, Michael, Margo Schwadron, and Emily M. Yates

2006   *Final Report, Archaeological Investigations of the Bayview Site (8BY137): A Weeden Island Ring Midden*. Report submitted to Tyndall Air Force Base, Panama City, FL.

Russo, Michael, Jeffrey Shanks, Andrew McFeaters, Thadra Stanton

2017   *Archaeological Testing and Mapping at Byrd Hammock, 8WA30*. Report on file, Southeast Archaeological Center, National Park Service.

Sassaman, Kenneth E.

2016   A Constellation of Practice in the Experience of Sea-Level Rise. In *Knowledge in Mo-*

tion: *Constellations of Learning across Time and Place*, edited by Andrew P. Roddick and Ann B. Stahl, 271–298. University of Arizona Press, Tucson.

Sassaman, Kenneth E., Neill Wallis, Paulette McFadden, Ginessa Mahar, Jessica Jenkins, Mark Donop, Micah P. Monés, Andrea Palmiotto, Anthony Boucher, Joshua M. Goodwin, and Cristina I. Oliveira

2016   Keeping Pace with Rising Sea: The First 6 Years of the Lower Suwannee Archaeological Survey, Gulf Coastal Florida. *Journal of Island and Coastal Archaeology* 12(2): 1–27.

Singleton, Hayley M.

2015   *Subsistence and Ceremony: A Zooarchaeological Study at the Garden Patch Site (8DI4).* MA non-thesis paper, Department of Anthropology, University of Florida, Gainesville.

Stephenson, Keith, Judith A. Bense, and Frankie Snow

2002   Aspects of Deptford and Swift Creek on the South Atlantic and Gulf Coastal Plains. In *The Woodland Southeast*, edited by D. G. Anderson and R. C. Mainfort, 318–351. University of Alabama Press, Tuscaloosa.

Thompson, Victor D.

2007   Articulating Activity Areas and Formation Processes at the Sapelo Island Shell Ring Complex. *Southeastern Archaeology* 26(1): 91–107.

Turner, Victor

1969   *The Ritual Process.* Aldine Publishing, Chicago.

Wallis, Neill J., and Paulette S. McFadden

2014   *Suwannee Valley Archaeological Field School 2013: The Garden Patch Site (8DI4).* Miscellaneous Report No. 64, Division of Anthropology, Florida Museum of Natural History, University of Florida, Gainesville.

2016   Recovering the Forgotten Woodland Mound Excavations at Garden Patch (8DI4). *Southeastern Archaeology* 35:194–212.

Wallis, Neill J., Paulette S. McFadden, and Hayley M. Singleton

2015   Radiocarbon Dating the Pace of Monument Construction and Village Aggregation at Garden Patch: A Ceremonial Center on the Florida Gulf Coast. *Journal of Archaeological Science: Reports* 2:507–516.

Wallis, Neill J., Thomas J. Pluckhahn, and Michael D. Glascock

2016   Sourcing Interaction Networks of the American Southeast: NAA of Swift Creek Complicated Stamped Pottery. *American Antiquity* 81(4): 717–736.

4

Size Matters

Kolomoki (9ER1) and the Power of the Hypertrophic Village

SHAUN E. WEST, THOMAS J. PLUCKHAHN, AND MARTIN MENZ

By definition and etymology, the term "village" refers to a cluster or collection of houses, smaller than a town or city but larger than a hamlet (Darvill 2003:456; Oxford University Press 2016; see also Thompson and Birch, this volume). Explicit within this typical definition is the dimension of size, and archaeologists have thus usually classified settlements as villages based on the areal extent of material remains. However, the definition of a village as a "cluster" or "collection" of houses also implies a certain density, and this dimension adds to the conceptual burden as the houses within a single village may be separated by spaces used for agricultural fields, plazas, or monuments. The struggle over variability in the density of house remains within villages is indicated by the rather tortured terminology employed in some of our most seminal settlement pattern studies. For the Virú Valley, Gordon Willey (1953:7) identified at least three categories of villages: the "scattered small-house village," the "agglutinated village," and the "compound village." William Sanders (1965:50) separated the villages in his survey of the Teotihuacán Valley into three types: the "scattered village," the "compact low-density village," and the "high-density compact village." Jeffrey Parsons (1971:22) settled for four varieties of village in his survey of Texcoco: "small nucleated village," "large nucleated village," "small dispersed village," and "large dispersed village." Willey, at least, and probably not alone, was well aware of the arbitrary nature of these definitions:

> A past inhabitant of Virú approaching his home, in a compact cluster of similar homes, might have thought of the whole as his "village." As such it was a unit of space and structure with meaning for him. But did he consider the similar house cluster 200 meters distant as "his village" or "another village"? Similarly, he must have had certain thoughts about the pyramidal mound

500 meters down the quebrada, but we do not know if he conceived of it as part of "his village," or a part of someone else's village, or an isolated entity. Perhaps he did all of these, quite naturally, in the different compartments of his consciousness. The significant thing is that there are different orders of function. In some contexts the house is meaningful, in others the immediate cluster of houses, and so on, through larger communities. Certainly, for some purposes the whole of Virú must have been considered as a single settlement unit. . . . We can, then, only approximate what was once meaningful in our functional classification. (Willey 1953:6)

We take this chapter as an opportunity to introduce yet another term—the hypertrophic village—to the already confusing lexicon. By "hypertrophic," we mean a village of deliberately exaggerated size, as the moniker has been occasionally employed to describe anomalously large or ornate examples of otherwise relatively mundane classes of artifacts, typically with the implication that the objects would be poorly

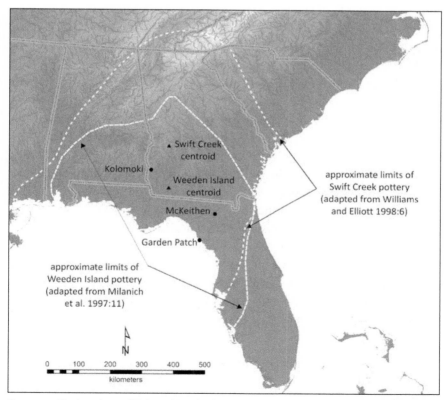

Figure 4.1. The locations of Kolomoki and other sites mentioned in the text and the distributions of the Swift Creek and Weeden Island pottery traditions.

suited for any utilitarian purpose (e.g., Anderson 2012:101; Clark 1996:193; Dye 2009:62; Emerson and McElrath 2009:33; Gilmore 2016:117; Malinowski 1934:193; Marceaux and Dye 2007:167–168; McElrath et al. 2009:347; Pauketat 1997:7; Sassaman 2005:83–87; Sassaman and Randall 2007:196). For example, in what may be the original use of the term in reference to material culture, Malinowski (1934:193) described the tendency among the native people of Papua New Guinea to craft objects that are "strikingly big, or strikingly well-finished, or of a strikingly fine material, even though in the process the article were to become unwieldy, breakable, and good for nothing else but display." We offer the designation not as a functional classification, but instead as a closer approximation of the meaning that may have attuned to particularly large villages by the sort of villager described by Willey (1953). We also use the expression with the aim of ascribing agency to both the residents of hypertrophic villages and the villages themselves, the latter point drawing on Kidder's (2011:110–111) observation that "to many indigenous peoples, the landscape is a real thing with power to influence events and actions."

We use the term "hypertrophic village" specifically in reference to the Kolomoki site (9ER1) in the lower Chattahoochee Valley of southwestern Georgia (Figure 4.1), occupied during the Middle and Late Woodland periods (ca. 200 BC to AD 1050). As summarized in the section that follows, recent work by Pluckhahn (2003, 2010a, 2011, 2015), Menz (2015), and West (2016) (see also Pluckhahn et al. 2018) significantly revises our understanding of the development of the village at Kolomoki, and suggests that a shift from a relatively compact to a hypertrophic village began around the sixth century AD and culminated a century or two later. The power of Kolomoki's hypertrophic village, we argue, lies within the sprawl of the settlement. The wide spacing between sections of the village both enabled and constrained social cohesion, and may have afforded the community at Kolomoki unrivaled symbolic power. Looking to recent work at other sites by our colleagues, we suggest that the construction of Kolomoki's hypertrophic village was likely related to concomitant settlement shifts taking place throughout the region in the mid-to-late seventh century AD. We begin with a brief overview of previous understandings of village development at Kolomoki, follow this with the results of our new investigations, and then discuss the significance of the hypertrophic village and the possible extension of the term more widely.

Previous Understandings of Kolomoki's Village

The unique scale of Kolomoki was established as early as the middle 1800s when the number, size, and extent of its mounds were first mapped by antiquarians and archaeologists (e.g., Jones 1873; McKinley 1873; Palmer 1884; Pickett 1851; White 1854). Later work by William Sears (1951a, 1951b, 1953, 1956) revealed the elaborate nature of Kolomoki's burial mounds, but his excavations in the village were underreported. Sears's treatment of the site was further flawed by his mis-classification and inversion of the ceramic chronology, which forced the domi-nant occupation into the Mississippian period when large villages with platform mounds became more common in the region (Knight and Schnell 2004; Pluck-hahn 2003, 2007, 2010b; Sears 1992; Trowell 1998).

Pluckhahn's (2003) site-wide investigations began nearly a half century later. Systematic testing of the off-mound areas revealed the expansive extent of the site's residential debris (Figure 4.2). Whereas previous depictions by Sears (1953:Figure 82, 1956:Figure 21) suggested that Kolomoki's village was focused on the site's central plaza, Pluckhahn (2003) demonstrated that this "near-plaza" artifact scatter (or "inner village," as we refer to it here) was paralleled by a larger, and generally denser ring of residential debris nearly a kilometer in diameter (which we refer to as the "outer village"). Subsequent excavations in

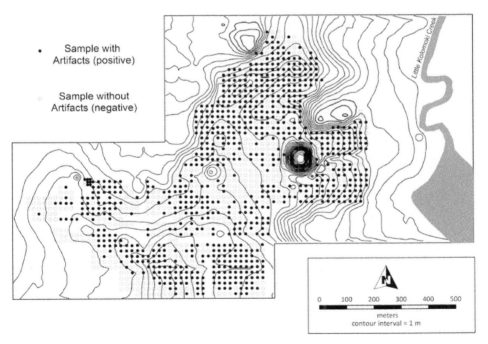

Figure 4.2. Pluckhahn's systematic sitewide grid. Note that samples are generally spaced in 20 m intervals and are comprised of 30 cm diameter shovel tests (n=1,084) and 4 m diameter "dog leash" surface collections (n=225) (Pluckhahn 2003:91). Figure adapted from Pluckhahn (2003:Figure 4.1).

the northern arc of the outer village revealed numerous features and at least one semisubterranean house, indicating that this was an area of intensive, probably year-round habitation (Pluckhahn 2003:130–139, 148–165). Based on a relative ceramic chronology that assumed a gradual shift from Swift Creek to Weeden Island pottery, and supplemented by several radiocarbon dates, Pluckhahn (2003:183–219) described four 100-year phases of village occupation covering the interval from AD 350 to 750. The inner and outer rings were assumed to have formed early in the site's history, concomitant with the construction of the site's two burial mounds (Mounds D and E). Ceramic changes, dated to around AD 550, marked a shift from the formal, circular village plan to a more haphazard arrangement that coincided with a decline in mound construction.

An additional block excavation just south of Mound A was carried out by Pluckhahn between 2006 and 2008 to investigate an area of relatively late occupation at Kolomoki (see Pluckhahn 2010a, 2011, 2013, 2015). This excavation complicated Pluckhahn's (2003) previous assessment of the site's chronology. Specifically, radiocarbon dates suggested that the ceramic changes occurred later and at a more rapid pace than previously assumed; comparisons with other dated contexts suggested a somewhat sudden increase in the relative frequency and variety of Weeden Island pottery around AD 750. The Block D excavation also indicated that the occupation of Kolomoki persisted a century or so later than previously assumed (Pluckhahn 2011:179–209).

New Insights on Kolomoki's Village

Pluckhahn's Block D excavations, coupled with new assessments of the regional chronology (see Smith 2009; Smith and Neiman 2007), made it apparent that the occupational history of Kolomoki's village was in need of refinement. Toward this end, Menz (2015) and West (2016) began a field program within the heretofore little-investigated southern arc of the outer village. In addition to retrieving ten new AMS dates (six from the southern arc of the outer village), the materials generated by our program also served to illuminate contrasts between sections of Kolomoki's residential areas. Comparisons of ceramic densities, pit and post feature frequency and volume, and macrobotanical assemblages corroborated Pluckhahn's (2003:120, 122) original assessment of the southern arc as an area of more seasonal occupation relative to its northern counterpart (West 2016). Patterned differences in distributions of lithic raw materials and reduction strategies between the northern and southern arcs of the outer village have also been identified (Menz 2015), and aspects of mound symbolism represent opposition between north and south that mirrors the village arcs (Pluckhahn 2003).

These and other disparities suggest Kolomoki's outer village was composed of a socially heterogeneous community, one that recent research also indicates was a prominent node in regional networks of exchange (Wallis, Cordell, et al. 2016; Wallis, Pluckhahn, and Glascock 2016).

Our new AMS dates were combined with nine trapped charge assays recently obtained by Pluckhahn and Neill Wallis, and 12 radiometric determinations generated from previous projects at the site (see Pluckhahn 2003:Table 2.3, 2011:Table 7-1) to construct a Bayesian model of occupation for Kolomoki's village. Here we provide only a cursory description of the new village chronology; more thorough descriptions of the details of our model can be found elsewhere (see Pluckhahn et al. 2018 or West 2016:139–148 for a previous version).

Based on our model, we now think that the earliest occupation at Kolomoki began in the second or third century AD. The nature of this occupation, however, is at present poorly understood. Dates adhering to this early and lengthy interval represent five assays scattered across the site, with locations within the vicinity of Mound D being most strongly represented (Figure 4.3). During Phase I, Kolomoki may have been used mainly for ceremonial purposes, perhaps with scattered habitations, but lacking a formal village plan. Alternatively, the inner village may have been established during this phase, though is perhaps simply underrepresented in our batch of dates.

Phase II, beginning sometime around the sixth or seventh century AD, provides stronger evidence for the initiation of a formal residential plan within the inner village. Pluckhahn's (2003:108, 120) previous investigations appeared to indicate less permanent settlement of this inner ring, though the richness of the midden below Mound D (see Sears 1953, 1956:9) suggests the possibility that the remainder of this habitation area may have been severely eroded from intensive agriculture in the nineteenth century. It is also possible that the material remains here were remodeled by later activities, including the use of midden for mound fill (Caldwell 1978:96) or to construct portions of the site's enclosures. Notably, Phase II also contains dates from two isolated contexts in the northern and southern arcs of the outer village. In any case, based on these dates and the pottery recovered from shovel tests, we now suspect that Kolomoki's village during Phase II conformed to a ring, probably open toward the east, that minimally fronted the site's central plaza. Radiocarbon dates suggest that the construction of Mound E might have been coincident with this early village (Crane 1956; Pluckhahn 2003:Table 2.3).

This inner village measured around 300 m wide by at least 400 m long, and defined a plaza about 150 m wide and 250 m long. It was anchored at its western end by a burial mound (Mound D), and may have been defined at the other end by a

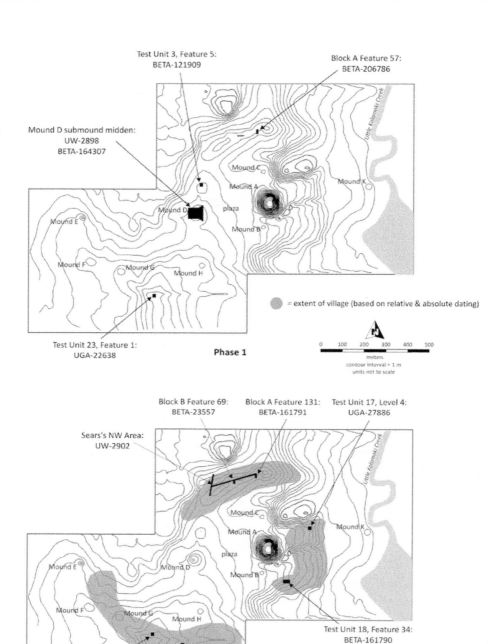

Figure 4.3. The approximate extent of Kolomoki's village areas corresponding to our revised chronology.

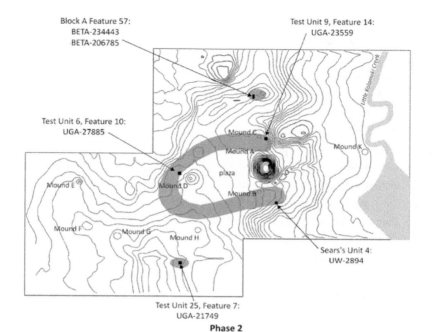

Block A Feature 57:
BETA-234443
BETA-206785

Test Unit 9, Feature 14:
UGA-23559

Test Unit 6, Feature 10:
UGA-27885

Mound C

Mound A

plaza

Mound E

Mound D

Mound B

Mound F

Mound G

Mound H

Mound K

Sears's Unit 4:
UW-2894

Test Unit 25, Feature 7:
UGA-21749

Phase 2

= extent of village (based on relative & absolute dating)

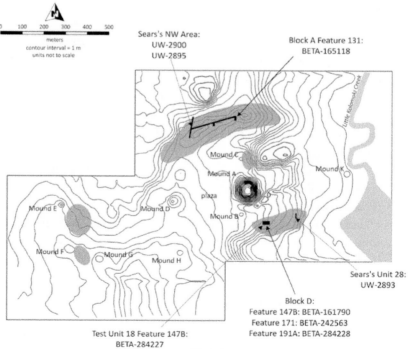

N

0   100   200   300   400   500

meters
contour interval = 1 m
units not to scale

Sears's NW Area:
UW-2900
UW-2895

Block A Feature 131:
BETA-165118

Mound C

Mound A

plaza

Mound E

Mound D

Mound B

Mound F

Mound G

Mound H

Mound K

Sears's Unit 28:
UW-2893

Block D:
Feature 147B: BETA-161790
Feature 171: BETA-242563
Feature 191A: BETA-284228

Test Unit 18 Feature 147B:
BETA-284227

Phase 4

platform mound (Mound A). In form, this village was similar to the ring middens found throughout the region. In size, however, it was already at least three times larger than the average Swift Creek villages of its time (see Russo et al. 2011:27; Stephenson et al. 2002:342; Willey 1949:368).

Around the turn of the eighth century AD, corresponding with our Phase III, the village plan conformed to a much larger discontinuous ring, now largely open toward the west. During this interval, the inner village appears to have fallen into disuse as the two opposing arcs of the outer village were fully established along with an intermediate area of occupation east of Mound A. The northern and southern arcs are each at least 500 m long by 50 m wide. The eastern arc is roughly 300 m long and around 100 m wide. Together, the arcs define an area of around 850 m in diameter. Weeden Island villages are generally larger than their Swift Creek counterparts; examples in north and northwest Florida typically range from around 100 to 250 m in extent (Milanich et al. 1997; Russo et al. 2011). The McKeithen site in north Florida, perhaps the best-documented Weeden Island village, is around 450 m in diameter (Milanich et al. 1997). Kolomoki's outer village was thus more than three times the size of a typical Weeden Island village, and roughly twice the size of its closest peer.

Mounds A and D may have been constructed or enlarged in association with this period of village expansion. The most recent TL date for ceramics associated with the pottery cache in Mound D provides a terminus post quem (TPQ) of AD 570 to 870 (Pluckhahn et al. 2018). A recent radiocarbon date on charcoal recovered by Edward Palmer from the upper levels of Mound A provides a TPQ of cal AD 680 to 770. Consistent with the hypertrophic nature of the village during this phase, Mound D was arguably the largest and most elaborate Weeden Island burial mound in the region (Sears 1953, 1956), while Mound A represented the largest Woodland-period platform mound in eastern North America (Wood and Pluckhahn 2017).

The final interval, Phase IV, represents another puzzling period in our revised chronology. During the eighth or ninth centuries AD, sections of the outer village remained occupied, though seemingly to a substantially less extent. The majority of dates assigned to this interval were retrieved primarily from excavations just southeast of Mound A, though a few dates from this phase are also associated with the northern arc of the outer village.

Kolomoki as a Hypertrophic Village

A certain amount of "empty" space is inherent to all Swift Creek and Weeden Island ring middens, in that these villages are, by definition, centered on plazas. But the habitation areas that define Kolomoki's outer village encompass not only an oversized plaza but also the relatively substantial open areas between the inner and outer villages. In terms of topography and proximity to resources—much of the southern arc of the outer village is located well removed from the nearest water source—there seem to be no compelling reasons that the arcs of the outer village needed to be separated by such vast distances. We believe Kolomoki's village suggests a degree of exaggeration of size consistent with the term "hypertrophic." In keeping with the use of this expression in reference to oversized artifacts, we suggest that the hypertrophic village at Kolomoki did not function in the same sense as villages of typical size.

Birch (2013:6, following Kolb and Snead 1997) has observed that political economic perspectives tend to ascribe three basic functions to communities: "social reproduction, subsistence production, and self-identification or group association." We doubt that the hypertrophic village at Kolomoki operated effectively with regard to social reproduction or subsistence production. At an average walking pace of around 1.4 m (4.5 ft)/second (Carey 2005), crossing between the northern and southern arcs of the outer village would have required a 10-minute walk. This would seem to have been an impediment to face-to-face communication or cooperation in daily activities, especially as compared to the more ubiquitous compact Middle Woodland villages in the region. Further, the distance between these arcs is about four times the normal intelligible outdoor range of the human voice (at around 180 m) (Guinness World Records 2016). Visual communication would have also been a challenge; human-scale objects are reportedly resolvable from a distance of just under 3 km (Wolchover 2012), so while it would have been possible for villagers on the opposing arcs to see each other, it likely would have been difficult to identify who they were or what they were doing. These constraints on everyday interaction suggest to us that the hypertrophic village plan was not intended to promote social reproduction or cooperative subsistence production at the village level. Indeed, we wonder if the size of the village was intended to limit interaction, perhaps primarily to special occasions.

Still, the formal opposition of the northern and southern arcs of the outer village across the central plaza and east–west axis of mounds is a powerful signal that the hypertrophic village at Kolomoki was intended to promote self-identification and group association. Sassaman and Randall (2007:208) argue that hypertrophic bannerstones "were designed to make an emphatic statement about cultural identity" in the centuries leading up to the Classic Stallings ethnogenesis. The relative abundance of elaborated bannerstone forms indicates that the Stallings Island site was "a locus of traditionalism, not in the sense of conservative, unchanging cultural practice, but rather in the elaboration of tradition to emphatically assert difference with an emergent 'other.'" Similarly, Johnson and Brookes (1989) observe that oversized Benton points appear to have been coincident with a network of exchange in Fort Payne Chert during the Late Archaic period in the middle Tennessee and upper Tombigbee drainages. They relate the occurrence of this network to an increase in sedentism and social boundedness.

It is not clear why the Phase III residents of Kolomoki's hypertrophic village felt it necessary to make such a bold declaration of identity, but recent work suggests that they were not alone, as a number of circular villages in the surrounding region appear to have undergone significant alterations or relocations during the mid-to-late seventh century AD. On the west coast of the Florida peninsula, Wallis and colleagues (Wallis and McFadden 2013, 2014, 2016; Wallis et al. 2015) have documented a change in the orientation of the circular village at the Garden Patch site. As demonstrated by Russo and colleagues (2009, 2011, 2014) in the Florida panhandle, smaller Swift Creek ring middens were abandoned as larger new ones were established nearby.

The scale of both the residential plan and the central plaza suggests that Kolomoki held a role as a sort of regional hub, a notion supported by the labor that would have been required to complete Mounds A and D (Pluckhahn 2003:Table 7.3; Sears 1956:93). In this light, and with the apparent power of hypertrophic artifacts to serve as markers of social identity, it is worth noting the location of Kolomoki near the northern and southern bounds of the Weeden Island and Swift Creek pottery traditions, respectively (see Figure 4.1). Consistent with recent models of community formation at later mound centers such as Cahokia, where the coming together of diverse ethnicities is emphasized (e.g., Alt 2002, 2006; Emerson and Hargrave 2000; Pauketat 2003, 2007), perhaps Kolomoki's hypertrophic village provided a mechanism that allowed people of different regions to participate in the creation of a pan-regional identity, while also acknowledging and preserving their disparities. Physical separation between the more permanent residents in the northern arc of the outer village and those that resided more seasonally toward the south may have been an active strategy for lessening tensions among different factions, even as the formality of the layout sent a message of social solidarity.

As a corollary to the notion of group identity, we suggest that Kolomoki's hypertrophic village may have had agentive qualities both real and imagined. Regarding the former, we think it likely that the residents of Kolomoki's village were attributed a certain amount of regional prestige, simply from their association with the oversized settlement. Superlatives such as "largest" and "most elaborate" were presumably as attractive in the past as they are today. Kolomoki's size and elaboration may have afforded it a standing comparable to the "old, beloved white towns" of the historic Creek, which were ascribed special status because of their age (see Hudson 1976:238–239). While discussing regional dynamics, Milanich and colleagues (1997:43) allude to a similar idea: "Kolomoki's reputation among Weeden Island peoples must have dwarfed those of McKeithen and Aspalaga" (two of the larger Weeden Island sites in the region). Perhaps as Kolomoki's size increased, so too would have the draw of people, similar to our modern fascination with big cities, because they are *big cities*.

With regards to its symbolic agency, we suggest that aspects of Kolomoki's site plan represent common cosmological themes writ large on the landscape. Specifically, the village plan mirrors the concentric circles common to Swift Creek pottery, interpreted by Snow (1998) as representative of the sun circle. As Snow (1998:82–52) notes, the sun symbol was frequently substituted as an eye in Swift Creek depictions of human and animals faces, and is reminiscent of the Choctaw belief "that the Sun watched them with its great blazing eye, and so long as the eye was on them they were all right, but if the eye was not on them they were doomed" (Hudson 1976:126). The central mound axis also calls to mind the later (Mississippian and historic era) cosmological progression from above the world (the Mound A platform on the east) to this world (the plaza in the center) to the underworld (the Mound D burial facility on the west) (see also West and Menz 2015). Whether or not associations such as these originated at Kolomoki or the smaller ring middens in the surrounding region is unclear based on current dating. However, these themes were certainly more fully elaborated at Kolomoki; the symbolic power of the hypertrophic village was probably similarly outsized.

Potential Examples of Other Hypertrophic Villages

We do not present the hypertrophic village as a functional or classificatory type to be generalized, but as a concept to be explored. As is apparent in several of the chapters in this volume, it seems clear that villages elsewhere in time and space might have been deliberately exaggerated in size in a similar manner to Kolomoki, and especially in cases where social identities and boundaries were likewise in flux. Additional potential instances of hypertrophic villages can be found, for example, in the North American midcontinent, where Krause (2001:198) has described the "less than cohesive placement of lodges and their low average density per palisade-enclosed space" for Initial Coalescent settlements of the Plains Village tradition. Krause further summarizes differing interpretations for the peculiar village and palisade plan: some suggest it was an ad hoc response to warfare by dispersed households, while others view it as "a conscious attempt to retain the basic elements of Central Plains community in the face of an unfamiliar and potentially hostile social environment" (2001:198).

The later, ethnographically documented settlements of the Great Plains might also provide an appropriate context for the concept of the hypertrophic village. For the Cheyenne, Hoebel (1960:6) described summer-solstice aggregations of "eight hundred to a thousand tipis . . . raised in a great open circle, in the form of the new moon." The Arrow Renewal ceremony associated with these aggregations was described by Hoebel (1960:11) as "the great symbolic integrator of the tribe, ritually demonstrating that the tribe . . . is more than the sum of its parts." Hoebel provides no images of these aggregations, but photographs from other sources suggest considerable spacing between tipis and much unoccupied space (e.g., Lenny and Sawyers 2016).

From much farther afield, the Trypillia "Mega-sites" of Ukraine—dating to the interval from around 4000 to 3200 BC (Chapman et al. 2014)—are another possible example. These settlements of up to several kilometers in length are generally much larger than Kolomoki, and demonstrate greater density of habitations, but also share certain broad structural similarities, including their concentric "circuits" of habitations separated by open spaces and surrounding a central, vast open space, similar to Kolomoki's plaza areas.

Finally, another parallel may be drawn with the Ilahita village near the Sepik River of northeastern New Guinea, which Tuzin (2001) describes as a settlement of much greater size than those typical of the region. Ilahita is notable for its composition of numerous spatially separated and semiautonomous "wards" integrated through ritual practice and common village identity (Tuzin 2001:72–75). Variable concentrations of different artifact types throughout the proposed village arc at Kolomoki may represent different clusters of households within the village (Menz 2015:84), similar to the wards identified by Tuzin at Ilahita.

Willey (1953:6) wondered if a past inhabitant of the Virú Valley would have considered the residents of households several hundred meters distant from their own as members of the same village. We share his conclusion that this hypothetical villager could have conceived the answer as both yes and no. At one level, the size of the hypertrophic village at Kolomoki must have constrained the sort of daily interactions critical to the social reproduction of the community. But on another level, the formal structure of the hypertrophic village was a statement of shared identity, and the size and cosmological associations communicated power to both the residents of this village and the dozens of smaller but similarly structured villages throughout the region.

Acknowledgments

Funding for our work at Kolomoki has been supported by grants from the National Geographic Society, the Society for Georgia Archaeology, a John S. Freeman Award from the Department of Anthropology at the University of South Florida, and awards from local chapters of the Florida Anthropological Society, including the Time Sifters Archaeological Society of Sarasota and the Warm Mineral Springs/Little Salt Spring Archaeological Society of North Port. We thank the Georgia Department of Natural Resources; Kolomoki Mounds State Historic Park; the U.S. Army Corps of Engineers; the Jenkins, Moore, and Whitehead families; the Smithsonian Institution; and the University of Georgia Laboratory of Archaeology for permission to work at Kolomoki and for access to previous collections from the site. Great gratitude goes to our many volunteers for assistance with the South Village fieldwork. Many thanks also go to Neill Wallis and Michael Russo and his colleagues at the Southeast Archeological Center for graciously sharing their work. Finally, we thank Jennifer Birch and Victor Thompson for inviting us to participate in the SEAC session that inspired this volume, David Anderson and Charlie Cobb for their comments on our paper in the session, and two anonymous reviewers of this chapter for helpful insights.

References Cited

Alt, Susan M.

2002   Identities, Traditions, and Diversity in Cahokia's Uplands. *Midcontinental Journal of Archaeology* 27(2): 217–236.

2006   The Power of Diversity: The Roles of Migration and Hybridity in Culture Change. In *Leadership and Polity in Mississippian Society*, edited by B. M. Butler and P. D. Welch, 289–308. Center for Archaeological Investigations, Occasional Paper 33, Southern Illinois University, Carbondale.

Anderson, David G.

2012   Pleistocene Settlement in the East. In *The Oxford Handbook of North American Archaeology*, edited by Timothy R. Pauketat, 96–107. Oxford University Press, New York.

Birch, Jennifer

2013   Between Villages and Cities: Settlement Aggregation in Cross-Cultural Perspective. In *From Prehistoric Villages to Cities: Settlement Aggregation and Community Transformation*, edited by Jennifer Birch, 1–22. Routledge, New York.

Caldwell, Joseph R.

1978   *Report of the Excavations at Fairchild's Landing and Hare's landing, Seminole County, Georgia*, edited by Betty Smith. Department of Anthropology, University of Georgia, Athens. Report prepared for the National Park Service.

Carey, Nick

2005   *Establishing Pedestrian Walking Speeds. Portland State University, ITE Student Chapter, Portland, OR.* Submitted to Parsons Brinckerhoff, Albuquerque, NM.

Chapman, John, Mikhail Yu Videiko, Duncan Hale, Bisserka Gaydarska, Natalia Burdo, Knut Rassmann, Carsten Mischka, Johannes Müller, Aleksey Korvin-Piotrovskiy, and Volodymyr Kruts

2014   The Second Phase of the Trypillia Mega-Site Methodological Revolution: A New Research Agenda. *European Journal of Archaeology* 17(3): 369–406.

Clark, John E.

1996   Craft Specialization and Olmec Civilization. In *Craft Specialization and Social Evolution: In Memory of V. Gordon Childe,* edited by Bernard Wailes, 187–199. University Museum of Archaeology and Anthropology–University of Pennsylvania, Philadelphia.

Crane, H. R.

1956   University of Michigan Radiocarbon Dates I. *Science* 124:664–665.

Darvill, Timothy

2003   *Oxford Concise Dictionary of Archaeology.* Oxford University Press, New York.

Dye, David H.

2009   *War Paths, Peace Paths: An Archaeology of Cooperation and Conflict in Native Eastern North America.* AltaMira Press, New York.

Emerson, Thomas E., and Eve Hargrave

2000   Strangers in Paradise? Recognizing Ethnic Mortuary Diversity on the Fringes of Cahokia. *Southeastern Archaeology* 19(1): 1–23.

Emerson, Thomas E., and Dale L. McElrath

2009   The Eastern Woodlands Archaic and the Tyranny of Theory. In *Archaic Societies: Diversity and Complexity across the Midcontinent,* edited by Thomas E. Emerson, Dale L. McElrath, and Andrew C. Fortier, 23–38. State University of New York Press, Albany.

Gilmore, Zachary I.

2016   *Gathering at Silver Glen: Community and History in Late Archaic Florida.* University Press of Florida, Gainesville.

Guinness World Records

2016   Farthest Distance Travelled by a Human Voice. http://www.guinnessworld records.com/world-records/farthest-distance-travelled-by-a-human-voice.

Hoebel, E. Adamson

1960   *The Cheyennes: Indians of the Great Plains.* Holt, Rhinehart and Winston, New York.

Hudson, Charles

1976   *The Southeastern Indians.* University of Tennessee Press, Knoxville.

Johnson, Jay K., and Samuel O. Brookes

1989   Benton Points, Turkey Tails, and Cache Blades: Middle Archaic Exchange in the Midsouth. *Southeastern Archaeology* 8(2): 134–145.

Jones, C. C.

1873   *Antiquities of the Southern Indians.* Appleton, New York.

Kidder, Tristram R.

2011   Transforming Hunter-Gatherer History at Poverty Point. In *Hunter-Gatherer Archaeology as Historical Process,* edited by Kenneth E. Sassaman and Donald H. Holly Jr., 95–119. University of Arizona Press, Tucson.

Knight, Vernon James, Jr., and Frank T. Schnell

2004   Silence Over Kolomoki: A Curious Episode in the History of Southeastern Archae-
        ology. *Southeastern Archaeology* 23(1): 1–11.

Kolb, Michael J., and James E. Snead

1997   It's a Small World After All: Comparative Analyses of Community Organization in
        Archaeology. *American Antiquity* 62(4):609–628.

Krause, Richard A.

2001   Plains Village Tradition: Coalescent. In *Handbook of North American Indians*, Vol.
        13, *Plains, Part 1*, edited by Raymond J. DeMallie, 196–206. William C. Sturtevant,
        general editor. Smithsonian Institution, Washington, DC.

Lenny, William J., and William L. Sawyers

2016   *Cheyenne Village on Canadian River.* https://www.flickr.com/photos/pennmuse-
        um/4185744542.

Malinowski, Bronislaw

1934   Stone Implements in Eastern New Guinea. In *Essays Presented to C. G. Seligman*,
        edited by E. E. Evans-Pritchard, Raymond Firth, Bronislaw Malinowski, and Isaac
        Schapera, 189–196. Kegan Paul, Trench, Trubner, London.

Marceaux, Shawn, and David H. Dye

2007   Hightower Anthropomorphic Marine Shell Gorgets and Duck River Sword-Form
        Flint Bifaces: Middle Mississippian Ritual Regalia in the Southern Appalachians.
        In *Southeastern Ceremonial Complex: Chronology, Content, Context*, edited by Adam
        King, 165–184. University of Alabama Press, Tuscaloosa.

McElrath, Dale L., Andrew C. Fortier, Brad Koldehoff, and Thomas E. Emerson

2009   The American Bottom: An Archaic Cultural Crossroads. In *Archaic Societies: Diver-
        sity and Complexity across the Midcontinent*, edited by Thomas E. Emerson, Dale L.
        McElrath, and Andrew C. Fortier, 317–376. State University of New York Press, Al-
        bany.

McKinley, William

1873   *Mounds in Georgia.* Smithsonian Annual Report for 1872, Washington, DC.

Menz, Martin

2015   Like Blood from a Stone: Teasing Out Social Difference from Lithic Production De-
        bris at Kolomoki (9ER1). Master's thesis, University of South Florida.

Milanich, Jerald T., Ann S. Cordell, Vernon J. Knight Jr., Timothy A. Kohler, and Brenda J.
        Sigler-Lavelle

1997   *Archaeology of Northern Florida, A.D. 200–900.* University Press of Florida, Gaines-
        ville.

Oxford University Press

2016   Village. https://en.oxforddictionaries.com/definition/village.

Palmer, Edward

1884   *Mercier Mounds, Early County, Georgia.* Report prepared for the Bureau of Ethnol-
        ogy Mound Survey, Smithsonian Institution. On file at the National Anthropological
        Archives, American Museum of Natural History, Smithsonian Institution, Washing-
        ton, DC.

Parsons, Jeffrey R.

1971   *Prehistoric Settlement Patterns of the Texcoco Region, Mexico.* Memoir 3, Museum of
        Anthropology, University of Michigan.

Pauketat, Timothy R.

1997   Specialization, Political Symbols, and the Crafty Elite of Cahokia. *Southeastern Archaeology* 16(1): 1–15.

2003   Resettled Farmers and the Making of a Mississippian Polity. *American Antiquity* 68(1): 39–66.

2007   *Chiefdoms and Other Archaeological Delusions.* AltaMira Press, New York.

Pickett, A. J.

1851   *History of Alabama and Incidentially of Georgia and Mississippi.* Birmingham Magazine Company, Birmingham, AL.

Pluckhahn, Thomas J.

2003   *Kolomoki: Settlement, Ceremony, and Status in the Deep South, A.D. 350 to 750.* University of Alabama Press, Tuscaloosa.

2007   "The Mounds Themselves Might Be Perfectly Happy in Their Surroundings": The "Kolomoki Problem" in Notes and Letters. *Florida Anthropologist* 60(2–3): 63–76.

2010a   "Gulfization" Revisited: Household Change in the Late Woodland Period at Kolomoki (9ER1). *Early Georgia* 38(2): 207–220.

2010b   Practicing Complexity (Past and Present) at Kolomoki. In *Ancient Complexities: New Perspectives in Precolumbian North America,* edited by Susan M. Alt, 52–72. University of Utah Press, Salt Lake City.

2011   *Households Making History: Household Change in the Late Woodland Period at Kolomoki (9ER1).* Department of Anthropology, University of South Florida, Tampa. Submitted to Georgia Department of Natural Resources, Atlanta.

2013   Cooperation and Competition among Late Woodland Households at Kolomoki, Georgia. In *Cooperation and Collective Action: Archaeological Perspectives,* edited by David M. Carballo, 175–196. University Press of Colorado, Boulder.

2015   Households Making History: An Eventful Temporality of the Late Woodland Period at Kolomoki (9ER1). In *The Enigma of the Event: Moments of Consequence in the Ancient Southeast,* edited by Zackary I. Gilmore and Jason M. O'Donoughue, 93–118. University of Alabama Press, Tuscaloosa.

Pluckhahn, Thomas J., Martin Menz, Shaun E. West, and Neill J. Wallis

2018   A Revised Chronology for Natural and Imagined Communities at Kolomoki (9ER1). *American Antiquity,* in press.

Russo, Michael, Craig Dengel, Jeffrey Shanks, and Andrew McFeaters

2014   *Archaeological Determinations of Boundaries and Cultural Affiliations at the Hare Hammock 8By31 Site.* National Park Service, Southeast Archeological Center, Tallahassee, FL. Submitted to Tyndall Air Force Base, Panama City, FL.

Russo, Michael, Craig Dengel, Jeffrey H. Shanks, and Thadra Stanton

2011   *Baker's and Strange's Mounds and Middens: Woodland Occupations on Tyndall Air Force Base.* National Park Service, Southeast Archeological Center, Tallahassee, FL. Submitted to Tyndall Air Force Base, Panama City, FL.

Russo, Michael, Carla Hadden, and Craig Dengel

2009   *Archeological Investigations of Mounds and Ring Middens at Hare Hammock, Tyndall Air Force Base.* National Park Service, Southeast Archeological Center, Tallahassee, FL. Submitted to Tyndall Air Force Base, Panama City, FL.

Sanders, William T.
1965   The Cultural Ecology of the Teotihuacán Valley. Ph.D. diss., Pennsylvania State University.

Sassaman, Kenneth E.
2005   Structure and Practice in the Archaic Southeast. In *North American Archaeology*, edited by Timothy R. Pauketat and Diana DiPaolo Loren, 79–107. Blackwell Studies in Global Archaeology, Vol. 5, edited by Lynn Meskell and Rosemary A. Joyce, Blackwell Publishing, Malden, MA.

Sassaman, Kenneth E., and Asa R. Randall
2007   The Cultural History of Bannerstones in the Savannah River Valley. *Southeastern Archaeology* 26:196–211.

Sears, William H.
1951a   *Excavations at Kolomoki: Season I—1948*. University of Georgia Press, Athens.
1951b   *Excavations at Kolomoki: Season II—1950*. University of Georgia Press, Athens.
1953   *Excavations at Kolomoki: Seasons III and IV—Mound D*. University of Georgia Press, Athens.
1956   *Excavations at Kolomoki: Final Report*. University of Georgia Press, Athens.
1992   Mea Culpa. *Southeastern Archaeology* 11(1): 66–71.

Smith, Karen Y.
2009   Middle and Late Woodland Period Cultural Transmission, Residential Mobility, and Aggregation in the Deep South. Ph.D. diss., University of Missouri.

Smith, Karen Y., and Fraser D. Neiman
2007   Frequency Seriation, Correspondence Analysis, and Woodland Period Ceramic Assemblage Variation in the Deep South. *Southeastern Archaeology* 26(1): 47–72.

Snow, Frankie
1998   Swift Creek Design Investigations: The Hartford Case. In *A World Engraved: Archaeology of the Swift Creek Culture*, edited by Mark Williams and Daniel T. Elliott, 61–98. University of Alabama Press, Tuscaloosa.

Stephenson, Keith, Judith A. Bense, and Frankie Snow
2002   Aspects of Deptford and Swift Creek on the South Atlantic and Gulf Coastal Plains. In *The Woodland Southeast*, edited by David G. Anderson and Robert C. Mainfort Jr., 318–351. University of Alabama Press, Tuscaloosa.

Trowell, Christopher T.
1998   A Kolomoki Chronicle: The History of a Plantation, a State Park, and the Archaeological Search for Kolomoki's Prehistory. *Early Georgia* 26(1): 12–81.

Tuzin, Donald
2001   *Social Complexity in the Making: A Case Study among the Arapesh of New Guinea*. Routledge, London.

Wallis, Neill J., and Paulette S. McFadden
2013   *Archaeological Investigations at the Garden Patch Site (8DI4), Dixie County, Florida*. Miscellaneous Report No. 63, Division of Anthropology, Florida Museum of Natural History, University of Florida, Gainesville.
2014   *Suwannee Valley Archaeological Field School 2013: The Garden Patch Site (8DI4)*. Miscellaneous Report No. 64, Division of Anthropology, Florida Museum of Natural History, University of Florida, Gainesville.

2016   Recovering the Forgotten Woodland Mound Excavations at Garden Patch (8DI4). *Southeastern Archaeology*, DOI:10.1080/0734578X.2015.1106211.

Wallis, Neill J., Ann S. Cordell, Erin Harris-Parks, Mark C. Donop, and Kristen Hall

2016   Provenance of Weeden Island "Sacred" and "Prestige" Vessels: Implications for Specialized Ritual Craft production. *Southeastern Archaeology* 36(2): 131–141.

Wallis, Neill J., Paulette S. McFadden, and Hayley M. Singleton

2015   Radiocarbon Dating the Pace of Monument Construction and Village Aggregation at Garden Patch: A Ceremonial Center on the Florida Gulf Coast. *Journal of Archaeological Science: Reports* 2:507–516.

Wallis, Neill J., Thomas J. Pluckhahn, and Michael D. Glascock

2016   Sourcing Interaction Networks of the American Southeast: Neutron Activation Analysis of Swift Creek Complicated Stamped Pottery. *American Antiquity* 81(4): 717–736.

West, Shaun E.

2016   Investigating Early Village Community Formation and Development at Kolomoki (9ER1). Master's thesis, University of South Florida.

West, Shaun E., and Martin Menz

2015   Mythologizing Monumentality: A Kolomoki-Creek Connection? Paper presented at the 72nd Annual Meeting of the Southeastern Archaeological Conference, Nashville, TN. https://www.academia.edu/30794510/Mythologizing_Monumentality_A_Kolomoki-Creek_Connection.

White, George

1854   *Historical Collections of Georgia*. Pudney & Russell, New York.

Willey, Gordon R.

1949   *Archaeology of the Florida Gulf Coast*. University of Florida Press, Gainesville.

1953   *Prehistoric Settlement Patterns in the Virú Valley, Peru*. Bulletin No. 155, Bureau of American Ethnology, Washington, DC.

Wolchover, Natalie

2012   How Far Can the Human Eye See? http://www.livescience.com/33895-human-eye.html.

Wood, Jared M., and Thomas J. Pluckhahn

2017   Terra Incognita: Terrestrial LiDAR Documentation of Mound A at Kolomoki (9ER1). *Southeastern Archaeology*, 37(2):95–111.

5

When Villages Do Not Form

A Case Study from the Piedmont Village Tradition–Mississippian
Borderlands, AD 1200–1600

ERIC E. JONES

This chapter explores factors that influenced the absence of village formation
among Piedmont Village Tradition (PVT) households in the upper Yadkin River
valley. This occurred in an area and at a time when other nearby PVT groups were
coalescing and hierarchically organized societies with Mississippian characteristics were emerging in and migrating into the area. In these cases, the resultant
settlement form was the village, as defined by Thompson and Birch (this volume)
as a permanent, multifamily residential cluster with emphasis on interhousehold
interaction. For the PVT communities in the Eno, Haw, and Dan River valleys,
this took the form of a ring of 6–12 houses surrounding a central cleared space
and surrounded by a palisade (Davis and Ward 1991; Dickens et al. 1987; Simpkins
1985; Ward and Davis 1993). This new settlement form suggests a change in social
organization toward household interdependence and cooperation. For Mississippians in the lower Yadkin/Pee Dee River valley and the upper and lower Catawba River valleys, settlements contained clusters of houses sometimes around
a single mound (Boudreaux 2007; Moore 2002; Oliver 1992). The upper Yadkin
River valley, located between these areas of village-dwellers, continued a trend
of dispersed household settlements with little evidence of cooperative structures
or interhousehold interdependence (Jones et al. 2012; Woodall 1984, 1990, 1999,
2009). This research attempts to explain this distinct pattern in the context of the
broader village formation occurring.

Previous research has offered explanations for the distribution of PVT (Jones
and Ellis 2016) and Mississippian settlements (Jones 2015, 2017a) and for specific settlement changes in the upper Yadkin River valley during AD 800–1600
(Jones 2017b). My goal here is to combine existing regional and subregional

settlement pattern results with new intrasettlement data to build a multiscalar model to explain the lack of coalescence in the upper Yadkin River valley. This works builds off of Rogers's (1995) sociosettlement research, agreeing with her that this valley was occupied by heterarchical societies, but also diverges and follows ideas by Woodall (1984) and Mikell (1987) that households and communities were more permanent and the people more sedentary.

The results suggest that the spatial distribution of PVT and Mississippian villages resulted from the confluence of environmental and resource variability across the landscape, location of overland trails facilitating interaction, and temporal and spatial trends in intergroup violence. This helps to explain why the PVT-Mississippian boundary formed where it did along the upper Yadkin River valley. Exploring the theme of power relations between communities, I propose that PVT and Mississippian villages with varying value systems and sociopolitical organizations benefited from a political buffer zone between them, but one through which economic activities could still operate. These circumstances and environmental conditions in the upper Yadkin River valley favored a dispersed settlement pattern that would not stress resources or pose political threats but one where people could still participate in informal regional economic networks.

Background

In this research, I focus on the northern end of the Piedmont Southeast, in modern North Carolina and Virginia. The PVT is the archaeological culture assigned to the egalitarian, semisedentary, swidden agricultural, and likely Siouan-speaking societies that lived in this area during 200 BC–AD 1700 (Dickens et al. 1987; Ward and Davis 1993; Rogers 1995; Woodall 1990). Most archaeological research on the PVT has focused on the Dan, Eno, Haw, and Yadkin River valleys in North Carolina and Virginia. From AD 800 to 1300, PVT settlements were either single households or clusters of two to four households usually located in floodplains and arranged parallel to rivers (Davis and Ward 1991; Dickens et al. 1987; Simpkins 1985; Ward and Davis 1993; Woodall 1984, 1990, 1999, 2009). Each of the four main valleys has between 10 and 30 sites that fit this description, with several having been excavated in each valley (Dickens et al. 1987; Ward and Davis 1993; Woodall 1990). Survey projects have compared surface artifact patterns and assemblage characteristics from unexcavated sites to excavated sites to create settlement size and function typologies and chronologies (Barnette 1978; Jones et al. 2012; Simpkins 1985). The one notable difference between these valleys is that the Dan River appears to have had a significantly larger population (Ward and Davis 1993:418).

During the fourteenth and fifteenth centuries, sites such as Mitchum (Haw), Wall (Eno), and William Klutz (Dan) show that dispersed settlements began co-alescing into villages: circular arrangements of 8–15 households surrounded by a palisade (Figure 5.1). In the Haw and Eno Valleys, some households continued living in dispersed settlements. In the Dan River valley, very few dispersed settle-ments remained after coalescence (Ward and Davis 1993), and sites such as Up-per Saratown show evidence of communal spaces and community-wide ritual and feasting (Eastman 1999; VanDerwarker 2007; Ward 1980; Wilson 1985).

Extensive surveys and site-level excavations throughout the upper Yadkin River valley have identified approximately 30 late Middle Woodland and Late Woodland sites (Barnette 1978; Jones et al. 2012; Woodall 1990). Up to AD 1300, settlement sites in the upper Yadkin River valley look similar to dispersed settlements in the Dan, Haw, and Eno Valleys (Dickens et al. 1987; Ward and Davis 1993). Later sites that have been excavated, such as Porter (Woodall 1999), T. Jones (Woodall 2009), and Redtail (described below), do not show features consistent with planned communities of multiple households, or villages.

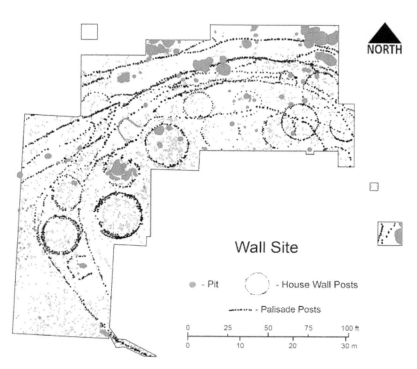

Figure 5.1. Wall site excavation plan, 1938–2016. Courtesy of the Research Laboratories of Archaeology, University of North Carolina, Chapel Hill.

The first evidence of Mississippian sociopolitical systems in the Piedmont is dated to approximately AD 1100 at Town Creek, which is located in the lower Yadkin/Pee Dee River drainage basin. Several related settlement sites, such as Teal, Leak, and Payne, were established over the next 300 years, with later sites being located farther north (Oliver 1992). In the upper and lower Catawba River valleys, denser settlements with Mississippian characteristics begin to appear around AD 1200. These tend to be single-mound sites with resident populations. A small number even begin to appear farther upstream along the upper Yadkin River, not far from the T. Jones settlement (Moore 2002). Villages with Mississippian characteristics also form in the adjacent mountain areas of Virginia (King and Meyers 2002; Meyers 2002; Jeffries, this volume). Hierarchically organized villages without Mississippian characteristics formed to the north and east around a similar time (Gallivan, this volume). Thus, the inhabitants of the upper Yadkin River valley show a distinct settlement pattern and sociopolitical organization in this region.

Methods

This work synthesizes an existing regional settlement pattern dataset with new intrasite settlement data to create a multiscalar model for the upper Yadkin River valley. The regional dataset is from a settlement ecology analysis of PVT and Mississippian sites throughout the northern Piedmont that sought to describe and explain the factors that influenced settlement location choice (Jones 2015; Jones 2017a, 2017b; Jones and Ellis 2016). Those works compiled upper Yadkin River valley PVT site locations from Woodall's regional surveys (Woodall 1984, 1990) and conducted follow-up surveys that distinguished Woodall's sites by date and size (Jones et al. 2012). PVT site locations in the Dan, Eno, and Haw River valleys came from The Research Laboratories in Archaeology at the University of North Carolina–Chapel Hill, from state archaeology and historic preservation offices in North Carolina and Virginia, and from Simpkins (1985), Dickens et al. (1987), Davis and Ward (1991), and Ward and Davis (1993). Mississippian locations also came from state archaeology and historic preservation offices in North Carolina and Virginia and from Moore (2002). Figure 5.2 is a map of the region showing these site locations.

In those works, I estimated past landscapes using digital elevation maps and early-to-mid-twentieth-century USGS-recorded sediment properties. Sediment texture analyses at the Redtail site (31Yd173) show similar sediment texture profiles on the levee across strata containing archaeological remains, suggesting that similar fluvial and alluvial processes have been occurring from AD 1300 until today.

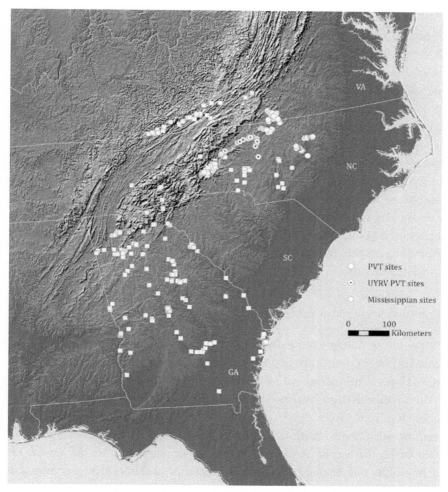

Figure 5.2. Map of the Piedmont Southeast, showing the location of Piedmont Village Tradition and Mississippian settlement sites discussed in this chapter.

I assumed similar continuity throughout this portion of the valley. In a Geographic Information System (GIS), I collected measurements within 2 km catchments of the areas of particular sediment texture types, counts and areas of wetlands, and number of streams. I also measured distances to overland trails using digitized historic maps (Mouzon 1775; Myer 1971) and documents and created viewsheds for each settlement site. Finally, I compared settlements to sets of randomly placed points and to each other using discriminant function analysis to distinguish observed from expected geographic patterns. Using the proximity principle, I assumed identified spatial correlations indicated settlement location preferences.

The intrasite data comes from the Redtail site (31Yd173), supplemented by published data from five sites (Woodall 1984, 1990, 1999, 2009) in the upper Yadkin River valley. Excavations at the Redtail site—with the assistance of undergraduate researchers—have uncovered a 10 × 20 m dark sediment lens. Within this lens, we identified, excavated, and measured morphological characteristics of over 400 post molds. Adjacent to that lens, we uncovered an 8 × 8 m area populated by pit features of varying size and depth and with variable remains inside (Figure 5.3). To date, several mentored undergraduate research projects have analyzed a number of components of the site, including the sediment profile through hydrometer analysis to examine environmental changes and the landscape, zooarchaeological analysis of animal diversity to identify seasonality, the spatial patterning of post molds using GIS to identify structures, sediment organic content through loss on ignition (LOI) testing to identify areas of intensive human activity, and the patterning of lithic and ceramic artifacts to determine spatial arrangement of past intrasite activities.

Regional Settlement Ecology

In the upper Yadkin River valley, settlements are farther from trails and are located in larger floodplains. In the Dan River valley, communities preferred locations closer to tributaries, with fewer forested wetlands, farther from other settlements, and with larger but fewer wetlands. In the Haw River valley, communities chose locations with a higher slope in their catchments. In the Eno River valley, communities chose locations farther from trails (Jones and Ellis 2016). In all four cases, there appears to be an avoidance of neighbors or concerns about defensibility influencing settlement. The Yadkin and Dan settlements were also influenced by the location of productive farming and foraging areas.

Mississippian sites in North Carolina correlate with larger floodplains, larger wetlands, larger viewsheds, and more diverse sediment drainage types within their catchments. Sites in Virginia have more tributaries, lower slope, smaller floodplains, and less well-drained sediment. Sites in Georgia have larger floodplains, larger and more wetlands, more diverse sediment drainage types, and less slope, and are closer to trails. The settlement sites in North Carolina and Georgia show similar preferences. In Virginia, the sites are located in the mountains instead of Piedmont, likely contributing to these differences (Jones 2017b).

When I compared Mississippian and upper Yadkin River valley PVT settlements in North Carolina directly, I found that Mississippian settlements were farther from trail nodes, have larger wetlands, and have larger viewsheds. They also had better tree-growing sediments, less loam, and less well-drained sediments

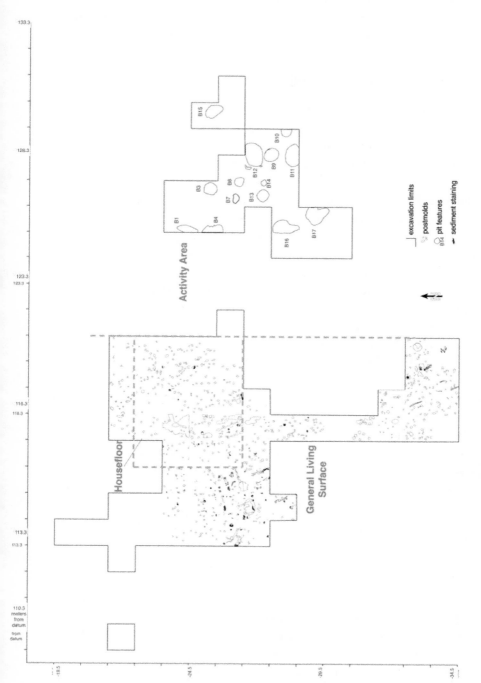

Figure 5.3. Map of post mold and pit feature distribution at the Redtail site (31Yd173).

(Jones 2015). Finally, the general landscape around Mississippian settlements, when compared to that around PVT settlements, tended to have more diverse sediments and better sediments for tree growth (Jones 2015).

Subregional Settlement Ecology

Within each of the PVT-occupied valleys, there are some variations with regard to date and settlement size, as interpreted by surface assemblage spatial distribution and composition (Jones et al. 2012; Jones and Ellis 2016). In the upper Yadkin River valley, the largest settlements were in larger floodplains with better tree growth. Smaller settlements were farther from trails. In the Dan River valley, the largest settlements were far from other settlements, were closer to tributaries, were farther from overland trails, had less well-drained sediment, and had fewer forested wetlands nearby. In the Haw River valley, larger settlements had more loam sediments and better tree-growing sediments nearby. In the Eno River valley, larger settlements had more solar radiation, fewer tributaries, and more well-drained sediments nearby. Smaller settlements were farther from trails (Jones and Ellis 2016). In each case, subsistence needs appear to be important for larger settlements, and smaller settlements were less concerned with interaction.

I also examined changes that occurred after AD 1200, which was the date for the earliest evidence for coalescence among PVT communities (Jones 2017a). In the upper Yadkin River valley, settlements shifted upstream after AD 1200. Settlements tend to be smaller after this date. They maintain similar settlement location preferences, but the upstream areas have less of those preferences (e.g., smaller floodplains, less loam, fewer wetlands). In the Dan River valley, later settlements were located in more productive agricultural and forest areas. In the Haw River valley, later settlements were in larger floodplains, in locations with more slope, and in locations with lower solar radiation. In the Eno River valley, later settlements had less visibility of trails, were located in larger floodplains, had more well-drained sediments, and had fewer tributaries around them (Jones and Ellis 2016).

Piedmont Village Tradition Site-Level Patterning

Exact house dimensions or house floors at dispersed PVT settlements occupied before AD 1300 have been difficult to define, primarily because excavations have usually been somewhat limited at each site (Ward and Davis 1993) and houses may have been less substantial. Later coalesced villages, such as Wall, Mitchum, and William Klutz, were the focus of the most intensive research, and thus have better evidence for structure dimensions and settlement arrangement (Dickens et al. 1987; Ward and Davis 1993). These sites display the shift after AD 1300 from linearly arranged households toward settlements with a ring of houses surrounded by a palisade. Similar or larger settlements continued to be built in each of these valleys into the early 1700s.

Surveyed and excavated sites in the upper Yadkin River valley show a different picture. We have yet to identify a site with strong evidence of more than three to four contemporaneous domestic structures or with the aforementioned circular arrangement. The most common features found are pits, post molds, and burials. Post mold patterns and living surfaces (i.e., likely house floors) have been identified at several sites, but usually there are no more than three contemporaneous examples at any one location. Larger sites appear to have been reoccupied several times throughout the Middle and Late Woodland and occupied year-round, leaving behind a complex, partially overlapping stratigraphy of living surfaces (Woodall 1990:113). Some sites with multiple households appear to have been created by a single household shifting across the floodplain (Woodall 1990:113).

The Redtail site dates to AD 1300–1400 (Jones 2017a) and likely had two to three households. We are in the early stages of analysis, but one appears to have been located in a 4 × 5 m area within the cluster of post molds in the northwestern block displayed in Figure 5.3. In the field, we defined that area as a house floor based on a darker sediment color. We then tested several variables in relation to this hypothesis. Analyses of post molds failed to reveal any patterning based on depth, diameter, or density of post molds, which is not surprising if the structure was repaired and rebuilt frequently over the 100-year occupation. We next divided the excavated areas of the site into hypothesized house floor, general living surface, and activity area, as shown in Figure 5.3. We compared the concentrations of lithics and ceramics to the organic content in the sediment, with the idea that a house floor would have fewer artifacts but higher organic content. Across all three areas, we examined 50 percent of the units with regard to ceramics and 42 percent with regard to lithics. The results show lower ceramic and lithic artifact counts between the house floor and the other two areas (Table 5.1). The average organic content is also higher in the house floor area, at an average of 1.10 percent, compared to the generalized living area, which is 0.91 percent.

We conclude that this area of the site was a single household with a cluster of associated shallow pit features located approximately 3 m southeast of the house floor. The pit features ranged in composition, suggesting a range of functions including storage/trash pits, hearths, and cooking pits. Subsurface testing of the surrounding floodplain found an additional area with post mold clustering, suggesting there was potentially one to two more households at this site. However, we are not certain of their chronological relationship at this time. Most of the surveyed

Table 5.1. Average lithic and ceramic counts from units in the three functional areas of the Redtail site

Site Area	Avg. Lithic Count per unit	Avg. Ceramic Count per unit	Comparison to House Floor	Comparison to General Living Surface	Comparison to Activity Area
House Floor	11.00	10.50		0.038/0.058	0.079/0.002
General Living Surface	18.44	15.63	0.038/0.058		0.643/0.021
Activity Area	21.33	35.33	0.079/0.002	0.643/0.021	

Note: The comparisons are p-values from t-tests comparing the raw numbers from units examined. The first number is the lithic result; the second is the ceramic result.

sites in the upper Yadkin River valley dating to AD 1200–1600 show similar surface assemblage characteristics to Redtail with similar modern agricultural use histories (Jones 2017a), which suggests that there were a number of similar settlements, either with two to three contemporaneous households or a single household moving along a floodplain over time. In either scenario, the settlement trajectory is very different from that in other PVT areas. The period of AD 1300–1400 in those other locations is a distinct period of village formation.

Examining the artifact assemblages across upper Yadkin River valley sites shows people and ideas were not isolated or restricted to the valley. High percentages of nonlocal lithics are found at several sites—rhyolite at Donnaha and Hardy and chert (originating from Mississippian-occupied areas) at T. Jones and Porter (Rogers 1993; Woodall 1984, 1999, 2009). Pottery styles within the valley show similarities to adjacent areas in temper and design (Woodall 1984, 1999, 2009). Finally, mortuary analyses also showed a small number of Mississippian-style burials and associated artifacts at the T. Jones and Porter sites (Woodall 1999, 2009).

Discussion

With these results, a multiscalar and multicausal settlement model for the Piedmont begins to take form. Mississippian polities emerged and persisted in areas with diverse sediments and productive agricultural and forest resources (Jones 2015, 2017b), supporting previous hypotheses by Beck and Moore (2002) that proposed locations that promoted large and sedentary populations were those that saw the emergence of Mississippian polities. In North Carolina, these locations seem to be more prevalent at the edges of the Piedmont, where the Coastal Plain and Piedmont join to the southeast and where the Appalachian Mountains and Piedmont meet to the west. This suggests some environmental factors in the location of their formation and for the extent of expansion. However, there were a large number of Mississippian settlements in the Georgia Piedmont with similar locational preferences, and there were similar-sized and sedentary PVT villages in the Piedmont, so environmental factors are likely not the only cause.

In the Haw and Eno River valleys, population growth and warfare are the likeliest explanations for village formation. Competition with Iroquoian neighbors for territory likely caused warfare (Dickens et al. 1987; Simpkins 1985), impacted settlement shifts to defensible locations, and precipitated the construction of compact settlements surrounded by palisades (Jones and Ellis 2016). In the Dan River valley, communities were also building fortifications, and population sizes and density appear to have been the highest among PVT areas (Ward and Davis 1993:418). These two factors may explain why this is the one area where dispersed settlement completely ceases after coalescence begins. The later, larger communities were choosing the most productive agricultural and foraging resource areas in the valley. Perhaps congregating in these locations and abandoning dispersed settlements were the best strategies for simultaneously feeding and protecting these larger populations.

In the upper Yadkin River valley, we see similarities to other PVT areas before AD 1300 with settlement location choice, subsistence (Jones 2017a), and population growth (Woodall 1990). Like most PVT communities, those in the upper Yadkin River valley were engaged in subregional economic networks and possibly even regional networks as well. Thus, the majority of communities were not isolated from their PVT neighbors. However, while coalescence was occurring in other PVT areas, it appears Yadkin Valley settlements were shifting upstream and remaining small and dispersed (Jones 2017a). It does not appear to have been associated with a shift in resource use or ecology, as settlement location choice did not change after the migration.

Unlike in the Dan, Eno, and Haw Valleys, warfare may have had the opposite effect on settlement in the upper Yadkin River valley, causing the observed migration and dispersal. I have argued elsewhere (Jones and Ellis 2016) that the power balance (i.e., similar community sizes and sociopolitical organization) between PVT communities in the Haw, Eno, and Dan Valleys and their neighbors may have encouraged competition, and the power imbalance between PVT communities in the upper Yadkin River valley and their Mississippian neighbors may have discouraged it from the former's perspective.

Thus, the upper Yadkin River valley settlement pattern may have formed as a result of a complex suite of ecological and sociopolitical factors. The lower ecological diversity in the valley—evidenced by less diverse sediment types and less productive sediments with regard to forest productivity—may have discouraged sustained population growth after AD 1200 and the establishment of denser population clusters (i.e., villages). The aforementioned migration upstream coincided with the establishment of Town Creek and the northward expansion of related settlements. These smaller communities may have been easy targets for raids by larger, expansion-minded Mississippian communities to the south. If communities were abandoning sections of the valley, what prevented Mississippian communities from expanding farther into the Piedmont?

I propose that the PVT villages in the Dan, Haw, and Eno Valleys were significant impediments to this expansion. PVT communities coalesced just as Mississippian polities were migrating into and forming in the area. As a result, these new compact PVT settlements accustomed to warfare may have unknowingly created a substantial obstacle to further Mississippian expansion. Any conflict that did occur had the chance of being costly for both sides. Conversely, the settlements in the upper Yadkin River valley were not imposing obstacles if the Redtail site is indicative of the typical community at this time. The remaining important question is why there was no Mississippian expansion into the upper Yadkin River valley? Several factors may have played a role in the placement of the Mississippian boundary to the west and south of this valley. These same factors may have encouraged a lack of coalescence in the upper Yadkin River valley that was rare in the eastern Woodlands at this time.

First, having a geographic space between the larger Mississippian and PVT communities may have been intentional to avoid conflict. As Mississippian polities avoided expanding too close to the larger PVT communities, the upper Yadkin River valley and its small, nonthreatening communities became a de facto buffer zone. Second, if the Yadkin Valley was unable to support larger or denser populations, it may have simply been undesirable to any group other than those living in small communities. Finally, it is important to not paint a picture in which Yadkin Valley communities were simply reacting to their surroundings. Taking into account the presence of nonlocal lithic materials from both PVT- and Mississippian-occupied areas, ceramic styles similar to both areas, and the evidence of Mississippian-style burials at later sites, they may have been an important part of economic networks. They occupied an important location through which material goods, such as lithic material and shell (Thomas 1996), moved throughout the region and between PVT and Mississippian communities, likely through down-the-line exchange.

Thus, the forces that encouraged village formation in the other three PVT-inhabited valleys never materialized in the upper Yadkin River valley. Communities did not have incentives to coalesce for defense or because populations were rapidly growing. In fact, it may have been to their benefit to remain small and dispersed. They would have been harder to find by Mississippians and less likely to be perceived as competition for resources. Life may have remained much the same in the upper Yadkin River valley *because* villages were forming around them. Their role in economic networks may have been a reason for the lack of violence toward them. Given the PVT-Mississippian interaction documented at later upper Yadkin River sites (Woodall 1999, 2009), I am inclined to think communities were active agents in their settlement patterns. That is, they were not simply reacting to their Mississippian and PVT neighbors. The shift toward lithic resources in Mississippian-controlled areas over time may be an example of their agency in these interactions. Work is presently examining lithic economic patterns in the Piedmont during this time that may shed even more light on how upper Yadkin River communities created and navigated these interactions.

Conclusion

Starting in AD 1100, the first PVT and Mississippian villages formed in and around the western and southern edges of the Piedmont, respectively. However, the upper Yadkin River valley, which lies between these areas, did not see this same development. My contention is that three factors influenced the patterns there: the geopolitical location of the valley as the boundary between Mississippian and PVT communities; the existence of exchange networks that would have discouraged large, uninhabited areas of the landscape; and the relatively lower ecological diversity in this particular valley. There is still work to be done in the upper Yadkin River valley and throughout the Piedmont to test such a model, including more directed research into what materials were moving through the trade networks and how, into the size and layout of other settlements in the valley, and into more detailed characteristics of the past environment. We may find the upper Yadkin River valley to be a productive place for studying the edges of the Mississippian world and how communities adapt and negotiate the natural, social, political, and economic landscapes between larger communities with more complex sociopolitical organizations.

Acknowledgments

The data used here were produced from fieldwork and analyses funded by an NSF Grant (BCS-1430945). I must thank several Wake Forest undergraduates who have assisted on this work since the beginning of the Yadkin River Settlement Ecology Project in 2010, including Madison Gattis, Thomas Morrison, Andrew Wardner, Sara Frantz, Samantha Yaussy, Peter Ellis, K. Pierce Wright, Charlotte Gable, Irene Kim, Danny Herman, Dowell Harmon, Hadley Scharer, Shannon O'Hanlon, Jacob Daunais, Caroline Watson, Brittany Ezer, David Burch, Grayson O'Saile, Melissa Pouncey, and Maya Krause. Thank you to Ned Woodall, R. P. Stephen Davis Jr., Rhea Rogers, Paul Thacker, and Ken Robinson for sharing your knowledge of the region and sites. LOI results were produced by the University of Tennessee Archaeological Research Laboratory under the direction of Howard Cyr. Although results come solely from this lab, the original idea for the LOI analysis was explored and tested in the Wake Forest University Archaeology Laboratories under the direction of Paul Thacker and carried out by Hadley Scharer. Site locations were provided by the Research Laboratories of Archaeology at the University of North Carolina–Chapel Hill; Susan Myers, Steven Claggett, and Dolores Hall at the North Carolina Office of State Archaeology; Jolene Smith and Michael Pulice at the Virginia Department of Historic Resources; and Jacob Lulewicz. Thank you to Sharon DeWitte for your support, editorial skills, and anthropological expertise.

References Cited

Barnette, Karen L.
1978   Woodland Subsistence-Settlement Patterns in the Great Bend Area, Yadkin River Valley, North Carolina. Master's thesis, Wake Forest University.
Beck, Robin A., Jr., and David G. Moore
2002   The Burke Phase: A Mississippian Frontier in the North Carolina Foothills. *Southeastern Archaeology* 21(2): 192–205.
Boudreaux, Edmond A.
2007   *The Archaeology of Town Creek*. University of Alabama Press, Tuscaloosa.
Davis, R. P. Stephen, and H. Trawick Ward
1991   The Evolution of Siouan Communities in Piedmont North Carolina. *Southeastern Archaeology* 10(1): 40–53.
Dickens, Roy S., Jr., H. Trawick Ward, and R. P. Stephen Davis Jr.
1987   *The Siouan Project: Seasons I and II*. Research Laboratories of Anthropology, Monograph Series No. 1, University of North Carolina, Chapel Hill.
Eastman, Jane M.
1999   The Sara and Dan River Peoples: Siouan Communities in North Carolina's Interior Piedmont from A.D. 1000 to A.D. 1700. Ph.D. diss., University of North Carolina.
Jones, Eric E.
2015   The Settlement Ecology of Middle-Range Societies in the Western North Carolina Piedmont, AD 1000–1600. *North Carolina Archaeology* 64:1–32.
2017a   Significance and Context in GIS-Based Spatial Archaeology: A Case Study from Southeastern North America. *Journal of Archaeological Science* 84C:54–62.

2017b   The Ecology of Shifting Settlement Strategies in the Upper Yadkin River Valley, AD 600–1600. In *Settlement Ecology of the Ancient Americas*, edited by Lucas C. Kellett and Eric E. Jones, 29–56. Routledge Press, London.

Jones, Eric E., and Peter Ellis

2016   Multiscalar Settlement Ecology Study of Piedmont Village Tradition Communities in North Carolina, AD 1000–1600. *Southeastern Archaeology* 35(2): 85–114.

Jones, Eric E., Madison Gattis, Andrew Wardner, Thomas C. Morrison, and Sara Frantz

2012   Exploring Prehistoric Tribal Settlement Ecology in the Southeast: A Case Study from the North Carolina Piedmont. *North American Archaeologist* 33(2): 159–192.

King, Adam, and Maureen Meyers

2002   Exploring the Edges of the Mississippian World. *Southeastern Archaeology* 21(2): 113–116.

Meyers, Maureen

2002   The Mississippian Frontier in Southwestern Virginia. *Southeastern Archaeology* 21(2): 178–191.

Mikell, Gregory A.

1987   The Donnaha Site: Late Woodland Period Subsistence and Ecology. Master's thesis, Wake Forest University.

Moore, David G.

2002   *Catawba Valley Mississippian: Ceramics, Chronology, and Catawba Indians*. University of Alabama Press, Tuscaloosa.

Mouzon, Henry, Jr.

1775   An Accurate Map of North and South Carolina, with their Indian Frontiers. Robert Sayer and J. Bennett, London.

Myer, William E.

1971   *Indian Trails of the Southeast*. Blue & Gray Press, Nashville, TN.

Oliver, Billy L.

1992   Settlements of the Pee Dee Culture. Ph.D. diss., University of North Carolina.

Rogers, Rhea J.

1993   A Re-examination of the Concept of the Tribe: A Case Study from the Upper Yadkin Valley, North Carolina. Ph.D. diss., University of North Carolina.

1995   Tribes as Heterarchy: A Case Study from the Prehistoric Southeastern United States. *Archaeological Papers of the American Anthropological Association* 6(1): 7–16.

Simpkins, Daniel L.

1985   *First Phase Investigations of Late Aboriginal Settlement Systems in the Eno, Haw, and Dan River Drainages, North Carolina*. Research Laboratories of Anthropology, Research Report No. 3, University of North Carolina, Chapel Hill.

Thomas, Larissa

1996   A Study of Shell Beads and Their Social Context in the Mississippian Period: A Case from the Carolina Piedmont and Mountains. *Southeastern Archaeology* 15(1): 29–46.

VanDerwarker, Amber M.

2007   Menus for Families and Feasts: Household and Community Consumption of Plants at Upper Saratown, North Carolina. In *The Archaeology of Food and Identity*, edited by Katheryn C. Twiss, 16–49. Center for Archaeological Investigations, Occasional Paper No. 34, Southern Illinois University, Carbondale.

Ward, H. Trawick

1980   The Spatial Analysis of the Plow Zone Artifact Distributions from Two Village Sites in North Carolina. Ph.D. diss., University of North Carolina.

Ward, H. Trawick, and R. P. Stephen Davis Jr.

1993   *Indian Communities on the North Carolina Piedmont, A.D. 1000 to 1700*. Research Laboratories of Anthropology, Monograph Series No. 2, University of North Carolina, Chapel Hill.

Wilson, Jack H., Jr.

1985   Feature Zones and Feature Fill: More Than Trash. In *Structure and Process in Southeastern Archaeology*, edited by Roy S. Dickens Jr. and H. Trawick Ward, 60–82. University of Alabama Press, Tuscaloosa.

Woodall, J. Ned

1984   *The Donahew Site: 1973, 1975 Excavations*. North Carolina Archaeological Council Publication No. 22.

1990   *Archaeological Investigations in the Yadkin River Valley, 1984–87*. North Carolina Archaeological Council Publication No. 25.

1999   Mississippian Expansion on the Eastern Frontier: One Strategy in the North Carolina Piedmont. *Archaeology of Eastern North America* 27:55–70.

2009   The T. Jones Site: Ecology and Agency in the Upper Yadkin Valley of North Carolina. *North Carolina Archaeology* 58:1–58.

6

Initial Northern Iroquoian Coalescence

JENNIFER BIRCH AND RONALD F. WILLIAMSON

Northern Iroquoian societies experienced two phases of community coalescence. The first, in the late thirteenth and early fourteenth centuries, brought previously semisedentary groups together into the first permanent villages in the Lower Great Lakes region. The second occurred in the late fifteenth and early sixteenth centuries, creating large, heavily palisaded villages that were catalysts for the formation of nations and confederacies. Here, we are primarily concerned with the first "wave" of village formation and the changes in social and power relations that accompanied the transition to sedentism.

In this chapter, we employ the rich corpus of archaeological settlement data available for southern Ontario and New York State to examine the processes associated with village formation. This includes the establishment of maize-based agricultural economies, the emergence of village-communities and the longhouse-based residential pattern, and the development of social institutions that served to integrate village residents within local and regional social networks. These are some of the sociopolitical hallmarks that signal the transformation of local Middle and transitional Woodland populations into a cultural pattern that is historically recognized as Iroquoian (Trigger 1976:91–104). These developments necessitated more complex social and power relations both within and between communities. One key observation is that females, as the primary contributors to the agricultural economies of early villages and keepers of the domestic realm, may have been the principal drivers of the transition to sedentism. Conversely, it could be argued that male taskscapes changed little between the preceding Middle and Late Woodland periods, although males were critical in extending the social networks of households and villages across the region.

Transition to Agriculture

The adoption of an agricultural way of life in the northeastern woodlands was gradual and multilineal, unfolding over many generations across a wide and differentiated landscape (Hart and Lovis 2013; Williamson 1990). Phytolith evidence indicates maize was used more than 2,300 years ago in central New York (Thompson et al. 2004). Isotopic analysis of dentin and enamel of human teeth, together with dental caries in permanent dentition in burials from the Kipp Island site in north-central New York, indicate it was a considerable component of the diet by the middle of the cal. seventh century AD (Hart et al. 2011). Hart and colleagues (2011:38) note, however, that this likely seasonal uptake of maize in the diet had little or no impact on regional settlement patterns. Only centuries later did large nucleated villages appear in the archaeological record.

The earliest evidence for maize in Ontario, in the form of carbonized plant macroremains, comes from sites in the Grand River valley, dated to cal. AD 400–600 (Crawford et al. 1997; Crawford et al. 2009). As in New York, maize initially supplemented rather than dramatically altered traditional Middle Woodland hunting, fishing, and gathering patterns (Hart and Lovis 2013). Isotopic analyses of human bone collagen and carbonate from sites in southern Ontario suggest that maize did not become a nutritional staple until at least AD 1000 (Harrison and Katzenberg 2003:241) and that it likely comprised 10–20 percent of the diet until the end of the thirteenth century (Harrison and Katzenberg 2003:241; Katzenberg et al. 1995; Schwartz et al. 1985), when it came to constitute some 50 percent of the diet (Pfeiffer et al. 2014; Pfeiffer et al. 2016). Current archaeological data suggest a south-to-north dispersal of maize, allowing for the development of cold-adapted varieties (Hart and Lovis 2013). In both Ontario and New York, the incorporation of maize as even a minor component of subsistence regimes corresponded to a major shift to upland well-drained locations amenable to successful maize agriculture by AD 900 (Beales 2014).

When considering evidence for the uptake of maize and its contribution to diet, we must be cognizant of the more ephemeral social practices that appear to have accompanied the transition to farming life. An increasing investment in crops, however minor at first, would have included changes in attachment to place (Creese 2013; Timmins 1997), allocation of labor (Schneider and Gough 1961; Trigger 1976:135), and the production of surpluses for facilitating group ceremonials and feasts (Hayden 2014). Indeed, Bruce Trigger (1976:133) suggested some 40 years ago that the emergence of agricultural economies and early villages was rooted in efforts to maintain the year-round cohesion of social groups, in this case the macroband aggregations of the preceding Middle Woodland, and eliminate the need for winter dispersal. This would have also helped to reduce regional political tensions and brought about greater economic security through shared work parties (Trigger 1976:135–136).

Early Village Life: AD 900–1250

The earliest settlements with evidence for semisedentary habitation have been characterized as transitional between the preceding Middle Woodland and subsequent Late Woodland communities of the region (Crawford et al. 1997; Fox 1990). They appear at approximately AD 1000 in both Ontario and New York. The earliest and best-known examples of these sites occur in floodplain environments and include the Holmedale (Pihl et al. 2008), Auda (Kapches 1987), and Porteous (Stothers 1977) sites in southern Ontario. In New York, at least one house (the smaller House B) at the Maxon-Derby site (Ritchie and Funk 1973) and one house identified at the Port Dickinson site (Prezzano 1992) have been characterized as transitional Middle–Late Woodland (Hart 2000).

These "base camps" featured small, circular or elliptical house structures containing clusters of hearths and pits. Neither in Ontario nor New York did these sites include what we would recognize as a typical Iroquoian longhouse (Hart 2000; Warrick 1996). Large, deep pits were used for storage. The ubiquitous presence of maize on many of the Ontario sites suggests that it was consumed by all social units, even if it was only a minor contributor to the diet.

Between the base settlements of the tenth and eleventh centuries and the appearance of the first year-round villages at the end of the thirteenth century, there is a robust record of evolving early village life. In Ontario, settlement-subsistence patterns are characterized by multiple clusters of geographically discrete, semipermanent settlements, together with smaller camps and special-purpose sites (Timmins 1997; Williamson 1990). There is enough internal differentiation among these site clusters that the transition to village life was clearly a multilinear process, with the adoption of settlement and subsistence strategies and social, political, and economic developments occurring at slightly different times in different subregional localities (Williamson 1990).

Villages of this period include Miller (Kenyon 1968), Van Besien (Noble 1975), Reid (Wright 1978), Elliott (Fox 1986), Tara (Warrick 1992), Ireland (Warrick 1992), Lightfoot (D. R. Poulton and Associates 1996), and Calvert (Timmins 1997) in southern Ontario, and Kelso (Ritchie and Funk 1973), Sackett (Ritchie and Funk 1973), and the later occupation at Maxon-Derby (Ritchie 1965; Hart 2000) in New York (Figure 6.1). These sites are generally small in size, covering approximately 1 acre, or 0.4 ha (Williamson 1990), and encompass multiple structures,

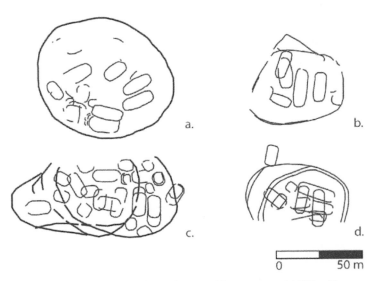

Figure 6.1. Early Iroquoian village plans, ca. AD 1000–1250: (a) Miller (Kenyon 1968); (b) Ireland (Warrick 2000); (c) Elliott (Fox 1986); (d) Calvert (Timmins 1997).

averaging 10–20 m in length and 7 m in width (Warrick 1996). These include the first true longhouse forms, traditionally defined as being at least twice as long as they are wide. Some of the sites were encircled by one or two rows of palisade. It has been argued that these palisades were too flimsy to have been defensive, perhaps serving as fences or windbreaks, but they nevertheless defined a community precinct (Ramsden 1990).

Occupied over a longer period of time than later villages, these communities reflect multiple episodes of rebuilding involving reoccupations over many decades, sometimes for a century or more. For example, Peter Timmins (1997) has reconstructed the occupational history of the Calvert site, showing how it developed from a seasonal hunting camp into a semipermanently occupied village between AD 1150 and 1250. Timmins (1997:227) argues that these long-term occupations suggest that village locations and the hunting territories with which they were associated would have been highly valued and protected. Some regional clusters of sites may have involved two or more contemporary communities that may have shared a hunting territory or other common resource base. Multiple resource extraction camps, occupied in the spring and fall, are often located within 5–10 km of early villages (Timmins 1997; Williamson 1990:312–320). Thus, both at the village level and within the wider catchment in which males and females operated, we see a greater commitment to place-making and territorialisation than is apparent in earlier transitional Middle–Late Woodland settlement forms (Creese 2013; Timmins 1997).

Populations based on site size and hearth counts indicate that the earliest villages comprised approximately 75–150 people (Timmins 1997:199), suggesting that they were derived from late Middle and Transitional Woodland yearly territorial band aggregations (Trigger 1976:134, 1985:86). It is likely that power dynamics in these communities differed little from the preceding Middle Woodland period, consisting of informal family-based decision-making structures, perhaps including individuals who also acted as spokespersons in dealings with neighboring groups (Trigger 1981:24).

Long-distance exchange in this period appears to have been restricted, evidencing the waning of extensive Middle Woodland interactions (Fox 1990:188). Evidence for the importance of local, as opposed to regional, social networks comes from ceramic data. Sequences of ceramic development were quite variable from one region to another, as was the use of specific decorative motifs or techniques (Williamson 1985:289–290). This pattern may be attributed to local endogamy whereby spouses were obtained from other communities within a regional cluster (Timmins 1997:228).

There is no evidence that suggests these first villages marked the incorporation of matrilineal descent and residence patterns (Hart 2001; Williamson 1990). Instead, the development of matrilineal descent, matrilocal residence, maize horticulture, and settled village life appears to have evolved gradually and opportunistically (Hart 2001). Ceramic (Schumacher 2013) and mortuary data (DeLaurier and Spence 2003) both point to variable origins for the female members of some early Iroquoian villages. This suggests the continued but possibly limited practice of patrilocality. In this way, early village populations may have participated in a locally based social network that involved resource procurement, spousal exchanges, defensive alliances, and trading relationships that may have served to "predispose people for the eventual decision to amalgamate into large villages" (Timmins 1997:228).

This phase of early village life, therefore, seems to have been characterized by a flexible and evolving sociopolitical structure, whereby people were free to pursue seasonal subsistence activities in either extended or nuclear family units. Such overall flexibility would explain the variations in house morphology, interior house activity, seasonally intermittent occupations, and diverse burial practices documented for these populations. Until dependence on cultigens resulted in a realignment of work tasks that separated men from women for prolonged periods, residence and descent patterns may have remained patrilocal and largely unchanged from Middle Woodland times (Williamson 1990:318–319; see also Trigger 1976:136), although incipient agricultural economies and commitment to place may have begun to encourage more cooperative behavior among village residents.

Initial Village Coalescence: AD 1250–1350

Beginning in the mid-to-late 1200s, we see the coalescence of larger settlements that were, for the first time, occupied year-round by the entire community. This shift appears to have been accompanied by a region-wide intensification of food production, decreased mobility, and increased levels of cooperation and communication among neighbouring groups (Dodd et a1. 1990; Pearce 1984; Williamson and Robertson 1994). Indeed, the late thirteenth and very early fourteenth centuries seem to represent a hinge-point in Iroquoian cultural development—an "event" (*sensu* Sewell 1996; Beck et al. 2007) or "tipping point" (Cobb, this volume) that, within a generation or two, transformed early Late Woodland peoples into "Iroquoians."

Intensified horticultural production is reflected by a growing emphasis on the placement of villages adjacent to the most suitable soils for agriculture (Williamson 1985:326). Isotopic analyses of human remains indicate that after ca. AD 1300, maize consumption increases to comprise at least half of the Iroquoian diet (Katzenberg et al. 1995; Pfeiffer et al. 2014; Pfeiffer et al. 2016). Changes in the built environment and material culture provide evidence of the social transformations that accompanied this economic shift.

Sites typical of this period include Uren (Wright 1986), Myers Road (Williamson 1998), Roeland (Williamson 1990), Gunby (Rozel 1979), and Antrex (ASI 2010) (Figure 6.2). These now larger villages averaged almost 4 acres (1.5 ha) in extent, or twice the size of the earlier base settlements. Populations are estimated at an average of some 200–500 individuals (Warrick 2008). These larger communities are believed to have been formed through the result of aggregation of previously dispersed groups as opposed to strictly through internal population growth. At the same time, much larger longhouses appear, averaging 30 m in length and reaching lengths of up to 90 m (Warrick 1996). Organizationally, villages featured less rebuilding and structural change than did communities of the previous period and were relocated more frequently, on the order of every 20–40 years (Dodd et al. 1990; Warrick 2008:135). Former village sites were very rarely reoccupied, establishing the community relocation sequences that characterize late precontact Iroquoian archaeology (e.g., Birch and Williamson 2013, 2015; Niemczycki 1984; Snow 1995; Tuck 1971).

Some post–AD 1250 villages are palisaded and defensively situated above steep breaks-in-slope. While the catalyst(s) for initial coalescence has not been clearly defined, one possibility includes aggregation for defense. While it is possible that the source of this threat may have been political instability and conflict among large, complex societies throughout the Midwest and greater Southeast after AD

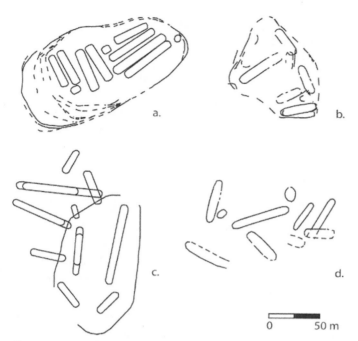

Figure 6.2. Iroquoian village plans, ca. 1250–1350: (*a*) Uren (Wright 1986);
(*b*) Antrex (ASI 2010); (*c*) Myers Road (Williamson 1998); (*d*) Gunby (Rozel 1979).

1200 (Krus 2016; Milner et al. 2013), there is little evidence for direct contact between Mississippian and Iroquoian populations or influence on one another (Jamieson 1992; Williamson and Robertson 1994). Instead, this may reflect tensions between expanding agricultural populations. This may have particularly been so among communities located near the Niagara Frontier, between Lakes Ontario and Erie. Niemczycki (1984) and Emans (2007) have described the rapid nucleation and fortification of villages in western New York as a result of southward population expansion from Ontario beginning after AD 1300, although this hypothesis has yet to be systematically explored.

Social and Political Transformations Accompanying Village Coalescence

Significant social and political developments accompanied initial community coalescence. Primary among these is the development of matrilineal descent and matrilocal residence. Formal leadership and village councils were likely required to facilitate group decision-making, including negotiations over community affairs and the maintenance of external relationships (Pearce 1984:293–304; Trigger

1990:124). Sweeping cultural changes, including mortuary rites, ritual practice focused on semisubterranean sweat lodges, and the elaboration of ceramic pipes and vessels, suggest the expansion of regional interaction and signaling networks between village-communities. In the remainder of this chapter, we explore changes in social and power relations within and between village-communities, with a particular focus on the gendered dynamics involved in this transition. Our focus here is on the ancestral Wendat populations of south-central Ontario, where there is a more robust record of late thirteenth- and early fourteenth-century village life than exists in New York or the St. Lawrence Valley.

Internal Village Dynamics

Rather than viewing the archaeological remains of households and communities as a simple reflection of a social order or cultural template, we must understand how these spaces were constructed through social work—"the labour by which such orders were tenuously composed and ceaselessly tested and contested" (Creese 2016:15).

The populations of the first permanent villages were larger and would have required the development of control mechanisms and decision-making processes (Johnson 1978; Warrick 2000). The increasing importance of communal labor and stored surplus within extended family households is evident in the increasing size of storage vestibules, which tripled in area (Creese 2011:246). Expanding longhouse size suggests the creation of large corporate groups that included one or more households. These larger corporate groups would have served to buffer ing, promoting consensus and cooperation in village-communities (Creese 2011; Hayden 1977; MacDonald 1986). We expect that the rapidity with which coalescence into villages spread across Iroquoia had much to do with the already-developed social institutions and practices that crosscut communities, together with the adoption of new strategies for meeting the challenges and opportunities of village life. One of these institutions was the clan system, the antiquity and stability of which may have facilitated the transition to larger households, and changes in residence patterns, and provided a familiar structuring mechanism for powerful sociopolitical transitions that accompanied the emergence of larger villages. Trigger (1976:109–110) traces the origins of clans back to the preceding Middle Woodland period with the transformation of patrilineal bilateral bands to clan groups, which claimed a common real or fictitious ancestor. This in turn led to band endogamy and enhanced social alliances among neighbouring bands.

One of the most dramatic changes that accompanied village nucleation was the transition to a largely matrilocal residence and a matrilineal descent system

(Hart 2001; Trigger 1976). The importance of female work-groups in horticultural economies has led scholars to link the adoption of matrilocal residence patterns to this transition (Murdock 1949; Ritchie 1965:296; Service 1962; Whallon 1968:236). Indeed, matrilocal residence would have favored inter- and intragenerational continuity in the "perpetuation of agricultural management traditions, innovations, and favourable maize gene complexes under all conditions more strongly than would patrilocal or neolocal residence" (Hart 2001:164). Females, as keepers of agricultural knowledge and anchors of the domestic realm, may have come to possess additional sources of power during the transition to year-round sedentism and an agricultural economy. It is their lives and taskscapes that would have been the most changed with an increasing commitment to village life. As such, we must afford them agency as influential individuals in their kin-groups who may have "pushed the process" of village formation rather than passive receptors of environmental or demographic forces.

The adoption of matrilocality and matrilineality has also been linked to expansion of populations into hostile frontiers (Divale 1984; Jones 2011) insofar as matrilocal residence and village exogamy bolster group solidarity by cultivating crosscutting ties of kinship between dispersed communities within a region. As such, cooperative efforts at the household, village, and regional levels may have more to do with the development of the Iroquoian "cultural pattern" than any one realm of practice on its own.

Regional Dynamics and Ideological Systems

The Iroquoian cultural pattern was characterised by a complex ceremonial cycle that included feasting, gift-giving, and world renewal (Snow 1994; Tooker 1970). Certain of these beliefs and practices will be less archaeologically visible than others. However, others, such as ossuary burial, semisubterranean sweat lodges, and an elaborate pipe-smoking complex, can be traced to the inception of year-round village life in the late thirteenth and fourteenth centuries. In Ontario, Huron-Wendat community-based ossuary burials are found at the turn of the fourteenth century for the first time. These features contain the commingled secondary remains of the dead and represent the majority of individuals who died during settlement tenure of village-communities (Williamson and Steiss 2003). They have been interpreted as representing the transition to the historically documented "feast of the dead," a multiday ceremony involving feasting, gift-giving, mourning, and internment (Wrong 1939). This practice involved both community members and other kin, trading partners, and allies from other communities.

It is also at this time that semisubterranean sweat lodges first appear in the archaeological record (Figure 6.3); they thereafter become ubiquitous (Mac-

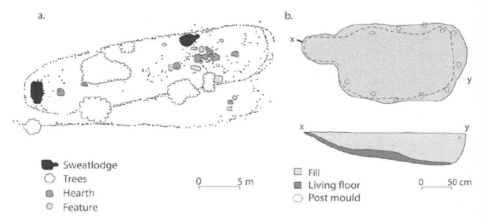

Figure 6.3. Semisubterranean sweat lodges: (*a*) Locations of two sweat lodges in House 4, Antrex site (reproduced after ASI 2010); (*b*) Plan and profile of semisubterranean sweat lodge, Feature 500 from House 9, Myers Road site (Williamson 1998:72).

Donald 1988). These features are "turtle"-shaped, covered structures that were typically excavated into the interiors of longhouses or attached to sidewalls. Items such as pipes and the elements of culturally significant animals, including the great horned owl and bear, have been found on their floors (MacDonald and Williamson 2001; Ramsden et al. 1998). They may have served dual roles as loci of ritual activity as well as venues for unrelated males to convene in common ritual practice, thereby alleviating tensions between males inhabiting matrilocal households and generating, through social and ritual practice, ties between different social groups (MacDonald and Williamson 2001). In this way, the changing built environment creates a "dialectical space" for mitigating social stress (Cobb, this volume).

While pipes and the smoking of tobacco have considerable antiquity in the Eastern Woodlands (Rafferty and Mann 2004), their presence in Iroquoian assemblages increases dramatically after AD 1300. Some feature anthropomorphic and zoomorphic effigies or complex iconographic motifs (Noble 1979; Wonderley 2005). Pipes have been linked to curing societies and other ritual or spiritual practices that accompanied increased interaction among hunters, kinsmen, and trading partners in the context of population growth, expansion, and diplomatic relations. Braun (2012) suggests that pipes may have been made by individuals or small groups for personal use, employing a wide range of materials that were personally or symbolically significant. Braun hypothesizes that this may reflect a shift from more group-oriented ritual practices overseen by shamans or religious specialists, to a more personal or individual practice. That pipes are frequently found intentionally broken in sweat lodges (Braun 2015) links these settings and instruments of practice in meaningful ways.

In terms of ceramics, following the formation of permanent villages there was a general shift from the regional heterogeneity described previously toward increased homogeneity (Williamson and Robertson 1994). This involved rapid and dramatic increases in the manufacture of collared vessels and the use of incised horizontal motifs across most of southern Ontario and central New York State. Incised horizontals may have represented motifs with which women signaled their social networks and membership in the wider Iroquoian cultural arena. Such signaling practices may have been especially important in times of interregional tension or widespread cultural change (Roscoe 2009). Recent social network analysis by Hart and colleagues (2016) has shown that strong network ties existed between Ontario Iroquoian communities in multiple subregions during the late fourteenth century, crosscutting the territories of later nation-based groups.

Concluding Thoughts

In conclusion, the transition to year-round occupation and an agricultural domestic economy was a catalyst for major cultural transformations for Iroquoian societies. The production of surpluses by corporate groups facilitated the means to underwrite the political economy through the hosting of feasts and ceremonials that integrated village members with networks of kin, allies, and trading partners who made up regional networks. In this way, the transition to village life and what we have come to know as the Iroquoian cultural pattern involved both community- and regional-level processes.

This involved transformations in power relations within villages—including the elevation of women's roles in the community through the development of matrilocal residence patterns and, ultimately, matrilineal descent reckoned through the elaboration of the clan system. Women, as the keepers of the domestic realm, would have anchored households, communities, and the domestic economy. Clan exogamy resulted in the extension of kinship and social networks between communities, bolstering societal solidarity by cultivating crosscutting ties of kinship between communities. Indeed, within such a system, men would have been born into one village, married into another, and spent much of their time away from both engaging in hunting, trade, and perhaps war. As such, males may have formed recursive entanglements between their natal villages, villages in which they resided, and the homes of kin and clans dispersed across a wide social landscape. As such, the social and physical labor of males and females, configured through social relations at the village and regional levels, were both critical, in equal measure, for the realization of the Iroquoian world.

References Cited

ASI (Archaeological Services Inc.)
2010   *Report on the Salvage Excavation of the Antrex Site (AjGv-38) City of Mississauga, Regional Municipality of Peel, Ontario*. Report on file, Ontario Ministry of Culture, Toronto.

Beales, Eric
2014   A Critical Analysis of the Adoption of Maize in Southern Ontario and Its Spatial, Demographic, and Ecological Signatures. M.A. thesis, Trent University.

Beck, Robin A., Jr., Douglas J. Bolender, James A. Brown, and Timothy K. Earle
2007   Eventful Archaeology: The Place of Space in Structural Transformation. *Current Anthropology* 48(6): 833–860.

Birch, Jennifer, and Ronald F. Williamson
2013   *The Mantle Site: An Archaeological History of an Ancestral Wendat Community*. AltaMira, Lanham, MD.

2015   Navigating Ancestral Landscapes in the Northern Iroquoian World. *Journal of Anthropological Archaeology* 39:139–150.

Braun, Gregory V.
2012   Petrography as a Technique for Investigating Iroquoian Ceramic Production and Smoking Rituals. *Journal of Archaeological Science* 39:1–10.

2015   Ritual, Materiality, and Memory in an Iroquoian Village. Ph.D. diss., University of Toronto.

Crawford, Gary W., Della Saunders, and David G. Smith
2009   Pre-contact Maize from Ontario, Canada: Context, Chronology, Variation, and Plant Association. In *Histories of Maize: Multidisciplinary Approaches to the Prehistory, Linguistics, Biogeography, Domestication, and Evolution of Maize*, edited by John Staller, Robert H. Tykot, and Bruce F. Benz, 549–559. Left Coast Press, Walnut Creek, CA.

Crawford, Gary W., David G. Smith, and Vandy E. Bowyer
1997   Dating the Entry of Corn (Zea mays) into the Lower Great Lakes Region. *American Antiquity* 62(1): 112–119.

Creese, John L.
2011   *DEYUGHNYONKWARAKDA*—"At the Wood's Edge": The Development of the Iroquoian Village in Southern Ontario, A.D. 900–1500. Ph.D. diss., University of Toronto.

2013   Rethinking Early Village Development in Southern Ontario: Toward a History of Place-Making. *Canadian Journal of Archaeology* 37:185–218.

2016   "Extending the Rafters": The Iroquoian Longhouse as a Sociotechnical System. *Palethnologie* 8:11–30.

DeLaurier, April, and Michael W. Spence
2003   Cranial Genetic Markers: Implications for Postmarital Residence Patterns. In *Bones of the Ancestors: The Archaeology and Osteobiography of the Moatfield Ossuary*, edited

by Ronald F. Williamson and Susan Pfeiffer, 263–294. Mercury Series Archaeology Paper 163, Canadian Museum of Civilization, Gatineau, QC.

Divale, William

1984   *Matrilocal Residence in Pre-Literate Society.* UMI Research Press, Ann Arbor, MI.

Dodd, Christine F., Dana Poulton, Paul A. Lennox, David G. Smith, and Gary Warrick

1990   The Middle Ontario Iroquois Stage. In *Archaeology of Southern Ontario to A.D. 1650,* edited by Christopher J. Ellis and Neal Ferris, 321–360. Occasional Publication of the London Chapter No. 5, Ontario Archaeological Society, London.

D. R. Poulton and Associates

1996   *The 1987–1989 Archaeological Investigations of the Meadow Ridge East Subdivision, Draft Plan 21T-91020, City of Mississauga, Ontario.* Report on file at the Ontario Ministry of Tourism, Culture, and Sport, Toronto.

Emans, Rebecca J.

2007   Tribalization, Ethnic Formation, and Migration on the Allegheny Plateau of Southwestern New York. Ph.D. diss., State University of New York at Buffalo.

Fox, William A.

1986   The Elliott Villages (AfHc-2)—An Introduction. *Kewa* 86(1): 11–17.

1990   The Middle Woodland to Late Woodland Transition. In *The Archaeology of Southern Ontario to A.D. 1650,* edited by Christopher J. Ellis and Neal Ferris, 171–188. Occasional Publication of the London Chapter No. 5, Ontario Archaeological Society, London.

Harrison, Roman G., and M. Anne Katzenberg

2003   Paleodiet Studies Using Stable Carbon Isotopes from Bone Bio Apatite and Collagen: Examples from Southern Ontario and San Nicolas Island, California. *Journal of Anthropological Archaeology* 22:227–244.

Hart, John P.

2000   New Dates from Classic New York Sites: Just How Old Are Those Longhouses? *Northeast Anthropology* 60:1–22.

2001   Maize, Matrilocality, Migration and Northern Iroquoian Evolution. *Journal of Archaeological Method and Theory* 8:151–182.

Hart, John P., and William A. Lovis

2013   Reevaluating What We Know about the Histories of Maize in Northeastern North America: A Review of Current Evidence. *Journal of Archaeological Research* 21:175–216.

Hart, John P., Lisa M. Anderson, and Robert S. Feranec

2011   Additional Evidence for cal. Seventh-Century A.D. Maize Consumption at the Kipp Island Site, New York. In *Current Research in New York State Archaeology: A.D. 700–1300,* edited by Christina B. Rieth and John P. Hart, 27–40. New York State Museum Record 2. University of the State of New York, Albany.

Hart, John P., Termeh Shafie, Jennifer A. Birch, Susan Dermarkar, and Ronald F. Williamson

2016   Nation Building and Social Signaling in Southern Ontario: A.D. 1350–1650. *PLOS ONE* 11(5): e0156178.

Hayden, Brian

1977   Corporate Groups and the Late Ontario Iroquoian Longhouse. *Ontario Archaeology* 28:3–16.

2014   *The Power of Feasts: From Prehistory to the Present.* Cambridge University Press, Cambridge.

Jamieson, Susan M.

1992   Regional Interaction and Ontario Iroquois Evolution. *Canadian Journal of Archaeology* 16:70–88.

Johnson, Gregory

1978   Information Sources and the Development of Decision-Making Organizations. In *Social Archaeology: Beyond Subsistence and Dating,* edited by Charles L. Redman, 87–112. Academic Press, New York.

Jones, Doug

2011   The Matrilocal Tribe: An Organization of Demic Expansion. *Human Nature* 22:177–200.

Kapches, Mima

1987   The Auda Site: An Early Pickering Iroquois Component in Southeastern Ontario. *Archaeology of Eastern North America* 15:155–175.

Katzenberg, M. Anne, Henry Schwarcz, Martin Knyf, and F. Jerome Melbye

1995   Stable Isotope Evidence for Maize Horticulture and Paleodiet in Southern Ontario, Canada. *American Antiquity* 60(2): 335–350.

Kenyon, Walter A.

1968   *The Miller Site.* Art and Archaeology Occasional Paper No. 14, Royal Ontario Museum, Toronto.

Krus, Anthony M.

2016   The Timing of Precolumbian Militarization in the U.S. Midwest and Southeast. *American Antiquity* 81(2): 375–388.

MacDonald, Robert I.

1986   The Coleman Site (AiHd-7): A Late Prehistoric Iroquoian Village in the Waterloo Region. M.A. thesis, Trent University.

1988   Ontario Iroquoian Sweat Lodges. *Ontario Archaeology* 48:17–26.

MacDonald, Robert I., and Ronald F. Williamson

2001   Sweat Lodges and Solidarity: The Archaeology of the Hubbert Site. *Ontario Archaeology* 71:29–78.

Milner, George R., George Chaplin, and Emily Zavodny

2013   Conflict and Societal Change in Late Prehistoric Eastern North America. *Evolutionary Anthropology* 22:96–102.

Murdock, George P.

1949   *Social Structure.* Macmillan, New York.

Niemczycki, Mary Ann P.

1984   *The Origin and Development of the Seneca and Cayuga Tribes of New York State.* Research Records No. 17, Research Division, Rochester Museum and Science Center, Rochester, NY.

Noble, William C.

1975   Van Besien (AfHd-2): A Study in Glen Meyer Development. *Ontario Archaeology* 24:3–95.

1979   Ontario Iroquois Effigy Pipes. *Canadian Journal of Archaeology* 3:69–90

Pearce, Robert

1984   Mapping Middleport: A Case Study in Societal Archaeology. Ph.D. diss., McGill University.

Pfeiffer, Susan, Judith C. Sealy, Ronald F. Williamson, Suzanne Needs-Howarth, and Louis Lesage

2016   Maize, Fish, and Deer: Investigating Dietary Staples among Ancestral Huron-Wendat Villages, as Documented from Tooth Samples. *American Antiquity* 81(3): 515–532.

Pfeiffer, Susan, Ronald F. Williamson, Judith C. Sealy, David G. Smith, and Meradeth H. Snow

2014   Stable Dietary Isotopes and mtDNA from Woodland Period Southern Ontario People: Results from a Tooth Sampling Protocol. *Journal of Archaeological Science* 42:334–345.

Pihl, Robert H., Stephen G. Monckton, David A. Robertson, and Ronald F. Williamson

2008   Settlement and Subsistence Change at the Turn of the First Millennium: The View from the Holmedale Site, Brantford, Ontario. In *Current Northeast Paleoethnobotany II*, edited by John P. Hart, 151–172. New York State Education Department, New York State Museum Bulletin Series No. 512, The University of the State of New York, Albany.

Prezzano, Susan C.

1992   Longhouse, Village, and Palisade: Community Patterns at the Iroquois Southern Door. Ph.D. diss., State University of New York, Binghamton.

Rafferty, Sean M., and Rob Mann, eds.

2004   *Smoking and Culture: The Archaeology of Smoking Pipes in Eastern North America*. University of Tennessee Press, Knoxville.

Ramsden, Carol N., Ronald F. Williamson, Robert I. MacDonald, and Carol Short

1998   Settlement Patterns. In *The Myers Road Site: Archaeology of the Early to Middle Iroquoian Transition*, edited by Ronald F. Williamson, 11–84. Occasional Publication of the London Chapter No. 7, Ontario Archaeological Society, London.

Ramsden, Peter

1990   Death in Winter: Changing Symbolic Patterns in Southern Ontario Prehistory. *Anthropologica* 32:167–181.

Ritchie, William A.

1965   *The Archaeology of New York State*. Natural History Press, New York.

Ritchie, William A., and Robert E. Funk

1973   *Aboriginal Settlement Patterns in the Northeast*. New York State Museum Bulletin 173, The University of the State of New York, Albany.

Roscoe, Paul

2009   Social Signaling and the Organization of Small-Scale Society: The Case of Contact-Era New Guinea. *Journal of Archaeological Method and Theory* 16:69–116.

Rozel, John R.

1979   The Gunby Site and Late Pickering Interactions. M.A. thesis, McMaster University.

Schneider, David M., and Kathleen Gough

1961   *Matrilineal Kinship*. University of California Press, Berkeley.

Schumacher, Jennifer

2013   Exploring Technological Style and Use in the Ontario Early Late Woodland: The Van Besien Site. M.A. thesis, McMaster University.

Schwarz, Henry P., Jerome Melbye, M. Anne Katzenberg, and Martin Knyf

1985 Stable Isotopes in Human Skeletons of Southern Ontario: Reconstructing Palaeo-diet. *Journal of Archaeological Science* 12:187–206.

Service, Elman R.

1962 *Primitive Social Organization: An Evolutionary Perspective*. Random House, New York.

Sewell, William H., Jr.

1996 Three Temporalities: Toward an Eventful Sociology. In *The Historic Turn in the Human Sciences*, edited by Terrence J. McDonald, 245–280. University of Michigan Press, Ann Arbor.

Snow, Dean R.

1994 *The Iroquois*. Taylor and Francis, New York.

1995 *Mohawk Valley Archaeology: The Sites*. Occasional Papers in Anthropology No. 23, Matson Museum of Anthropology, Pennsylvania State University, University Park.

Stothers, David

1977 *The Princess Point Complex*. Archaeological Survey of Canada Mercury Series Paper No. 58, Canadian Museum of Civilization, Ottawa, ON.

Thompson, Robert G., John P. Hart, Hetty Jo Brumbach, and Robert Lusteck

2004 Phytolith Evidence for Twentieth-Century BP Maize in Northern Iroquoia. *Northeast Anthropology* 68:25–39.

Timmins, Peter G.

1997 *The Calvert Site: An Interpretive Framework for the Early Iroquoian Village*. Archaeological Survey of Canada Mercury Series Paper No. 156, Canadian Museum of Civilization, Gatineau, QC.

Tooker, Elizabeth

1970 *The Iroquois Ceremonial of Midwinter*. Syracuse University Press, Syracuse, NY.

Trigger, Bruce G.

1976 *The Children of Aataensic: A History of the Huron People to 1660*. McGill-Queen's University Press, Montreal.

1981 Prehistoric Social and Political Organization: An Iroquoian Case Study. In *Foundations of Northeast Archaeology*, edited by Dean R. Snow, 1–50. Academic Press, New York.

1985 *Natives and Newcomers Canada's "Heroic Age" Reconsidered*. McGill-Queen's University Press, Montreal.

1990 Maintaining Economic Equality in Opposition to Complexity: An Iroquoian Case Study. In *The Evolution of Political Systems: Sociopolitics in Small-Scale Sedentary Societies*, edited by Steadman Upham, 119–145. Cambridge University Press, Cambridge.

Tuck, James A.

1971 *Onondaga Iroquois Prehistory: A Study in Settlement Archaeology*. Syracuse University Press, Syracuse, NY.

Warrick, Gary A.

1992 Ministry of Transportation: Archaeological Investigations in the Central Region. *Annual Archaeological Report, Ontario (New Series)* 2:67–71.

1996 Evolution of the Iroquoian longhouse. In *People Who Lived in Big Houses: Archaeological Perspectives on Large Domestic Structures*, edited by Gary Coupland and Edward B. Banning, 11–26. Monographs in World Archaeology No. 27. Prehistory Press, Madison, WI.

2000 The Precontact Iroquoian Occupation of Southern Ontario. *Journal of World Prehistory* 14(4): 415–466.

2008 *A Population History of the Huron-Petun, A.D. 500–1650*. Cambridge University Press, Cambridge.

Whallon, Robert, Jr.

1968 Investigations of Late Prehistoric Social Organization in New York State. In *New Perspectives in Archaeology*, edited by Sally R. Binford and Lewis R. Binford, 223–244. Aldine, Chicago.

Williamson, Ronald F.

1985 Glen Meyer: A People in Transition. Ph.D. diss., McGill University.

1990 The Early Iroquoian Period of Southern Ontario. In *The Archaeology of Southern Ontario to A.D. 1650*, edited by Christopher J. Ellis and Neal Ferris, 291–320. Occasional Publication of the London Chapter No. 5, Ontario Archaeological Society, London.

Williamson, Ronald F., ed.

1998 *The Myers Road Site: Archaeology of the Early to Middle Iroquoian Transition*. Occasional Publication of the London Chapter No. 7, Ontario Archaeological Society, London.

Williamson, R. F., and David G. Robertson

1994 Peer Polities Beyond the Periphery: Early and Middle Iroquoian Regional Interaction. *Ontario Archaeology* 58:27–40.

Williamson, Ronald F., and Debbie A. Steiss

2003 A History of Iroquoian Burial Practice. In *Bones of the Ancestors: The Archaeology and Osteobiography of the Moatfield Ossuary*, edited by Ronald F. Williamson and Susan Pfeiffer, 89–132. Archaeological Survey of Canada Mercury Series Paper No. 163, Canadian Museum of Civilization, Gatineau, QC.

Wonderley, Anthony

2005 Effigy Pipes, Diplomacy, and Myth: Exploring Interactions between St. Lawrence Iroquoians and Eastern Iroquoians in New York State. *American Antiquity* 70(2): 211–240.

Wright, Milton J.

1978 Excavations at the Glen Meyer Reid Site, Long Point, Lake Erie. *Ontario Archaeology* 29:25–32.

1986 *The Uren Site (AfHd-3): An Analysis and Reappraisal of the Uren Substage Type Site*. Monographs in Ontario Archaeology No. 2, Ontario Archaeological Society, Toronto.

Wrong, George M., ed.

1939 *The Long Journey to the Country of the Hurons by Gabriel Sagard (1632)*. Champlain Society, Toronto.

7

The Path to the Council House

The Development of Mississippian
Communities in Southeast Tennessee

LYNNE P. SULLIVAN

The development of villages in the region now encompassing the Tennessee River Valley from Chattanooga to Knoxville is an ideal case study for several of the research questions posed in chapter 1 of this volume by the editors. A shift from dispersed to nucleated communities, population movements, and processes of coalescence that affected intravillage power dynamics all may be relevant to the "hows and whys" of village formation in southeastern Tennessee. This chapter discusses the unique history of village development in this region with a focus on the establishment of large, nucleated villages near the beginning of the fourteenth century. This time frame also is congruent with the transition during the Mississippian period from the Hiwassee Island phase (AD 1100–1300) to the Dallas phase (AD 1300–1500), but the village formation process in southeast Tennessee may not have been the same as in other Dallas phase subregions (Sullivan and Harle 2010).

Of particular interest here is the power of kin groups in the dynamics of village governance and the circumstances that may have led to the gender-based power structure that Sullivan and Rodning (2001, 2011; see also Sullivan 2001, 2006) have discussed for some early communities in Southern Appalachia. The discussion begins with an overview of the changes in regional settlement patterns from the Late Woodland through the Late Mississippian periods to provide the context in which villages developed in this region. The focus is on developments along the main channel of the Tennessee River, but relevant information from the lower reaches of tributary valleys is mentioned where appropriate.

Burial Mounds, Rotundas, and Platform Mounds of the Terminal Woodland and Early Mississippian Periods

Late Woodland populations resided in seasonal encampments scattered across the southeastern Tennessee region. The only known relatively permanent architectural features for the Late Woodland period are conical burial mounds (Cole 1975; Lewis and Kneberg 1946; Lewis et al. 1995) and large, circular structures, or rotundas (Sullivan and Koerner 2010) (Figure 7.1). Both the burial mounds and the rotundas are best interpreted as communal facilities used by dispersed populations (Sullivan and Koerner 2010). "Household" shell middens were thought by Lewis and Kneberg (1946:36–37; Lewis et al. 1995:27–30) to be locations of residential sites, but no associated structure patterns have been found. Household buildings are presumed to have left no discernable evidence because they were lightly constructed (Lewis and Kneberg 1946:36–37; Lewis et al. 1995:27–30).

The burial mounds, which came into use around AD 700, range from about 1 to 2.5 m in height and from 6 to 15 m in diameter, and often are found in small groups along a major river (Chapman 1987; Cole 1975:83; Lewis et al. 1995:29–30; Schroedl et al. 1990). The most comprehensive analysis to date of the burial mounds was done by Patricia Cole for her thesis at the University of Tennessee in 1975. Her multivariate statistical analysis examined 14 burial mounds from the upper Tennessee, Clinch, and Hiwassee River valleys. Cole's (1975:80–87) results clustered the mounds into northern, central, and southern subregional groupings, showing a pattern of local similarity and areal diversity. Mound construction techniques and associated artifacts were instrumental in forming the geographic clusters, but not the distribution of individual burial practices. Cole (1975:82) concluded that distinct groups, rather than a single, uniform culture, existed in the region during this time frame. Williamson and Roberston's (1994) observations about peer polity interaction in early Iroquoia may provide parallels for this regional occurrence. Cole's findings further suggested that a discrete, egalitarian social group, such as a lineage, sib, or clan, was responsible for each mound. The primary burial in each mound typically was an adult male, and mound demographics are biased toward adults and males, but individuals of all ages and both sexes were interred in the mounds (Cole 1975:73–78).

Both the burial mounds and the rotundas were used well into the Mississippian period, until at least AD 1200 (Sullivan and Koerner 2010). The rotundas, ranging from 8 to 12 m in diameter, typically are single isolated structures and were in use by AD 900. The earlier rotundas were constructed with posts 15 to 20 cm in diameter, spaced about 76 cm apart. Rotundas are known from several areas in the South-

Figure 7.1. Hamilton burial mound and Late Woodland rotunda. (*A, above*) Hiwassee Island site, Meigs County, Tennessee; (*B, below*) DeArmond site, feature 30, Roane County, Tennessee. Photos courtesy of the McClung Museum of Natural History and Culture, WPA/TVA Photo Archives, University of Tennessee, Knoxville.

east during this time frame, including as geographically close as Middle Tennessee (Faulkner 2002) and as distant as the Georgia coast (Thompson 2009). Some earlier rotundas in southeast Tennessee were constructed in places where Mississippian platform mounds were later built (Sullivan and Koerner 2010). Some later rotundas were constructed with wall trenches, and some were built on platform mounds (Lewis and Kneberg 1946; Lewis et al. 1995; Sullivan 2007, 2009, 2016).

The earliest platform mounds in southeast Tennessee were being constructed by AD 1100. These mounds essentially were an addition to the existing Woodland landscape and replaced or enhanced the rotundas (Sullivan 2007, 2016; Sullivan and Koerner 2010). Some early platform mounds began as two low platforms that later were joined into one mound. These early mounds also served dispersed populations living in farmsteads and hamlets, which by this time included more formal, relatively permanent dwellings, but some of which may have continued to be seasonally occupied. Wall trench-style architecture came into use about the same time as platform mounds, but buildings with small, single-set posts also were constructed. Residences were rectangular or square (Sullivan 2007, 2009, 2016).

Multiple buildings typically were constructed on mound summits (Figure 7.2a). The nature of the architecture suggests that these buildings were used for specialized rituals or other community-related events. Buildings on mound summits included partitions, clay platforms, and special hearths. Some buildings were rectangular or square, and some were rotundas. Some of each configuration were of wall trench construction and others of small, single-set posts (Koerner 2005; Lewis and Kneberg 1946:Plates 16 and 17; Lewis et al. 1995:Figures 24.4 and 25.7; Sullivan 2016).

By AD 1200, very clear interregional connections with people to the south, in what is now northern Georgia, were well established and continued through most of the thirteenth century. Pottery motifs, engraved shell gorget styles, and several types of ritual objects are common to both regions (Lewis and Kneberg 1946:Plate 51; Sullivan 2007, 2009, 2016). Some burials were placed in platform mounds with elaborate accompaniments, and the use of burial mounds lessened or ceased. A few people built residences near some of the mounds, but the majority of the population remained in scattered farmsteads and hamlets (Sullivan 2016). The changes in mortuary ritual and clear connections with the Etowah polity are significant, but no evidence has been found that these changes led to the formation of large, nucleated villages in this region.

Late Mississippian Council Houses, Plazas, Household Units, and the Weather

By the end of thirteenth century, there were significant changes that led to the beginnings of large, nucleated villages. The regional population, which had been

Figure 7.2. Platform mound summits of the Hiwassee Island and Dallas phases. (*A, above*) Mound phase E-1 with multiple buildings and dual summits, Hiwassee Island site, Meigs County, Tennessee; (*B, below*) Dallas site, Feature 14, council house with benches, Hamilton County, Tennessee. Photos courtesy of the McClung Museum of Natural History and Culture, WPA/TVA Photo Archives, University of Tennessee, Knoxville.

dispersed for millennia, moved into these large settlements, many of which were fortified (Sullivan 2007, 2016). As part of this transition, new styles of pottery, architecture, and symbolism, as well as significant changes in mortuary practices and new forms of community leadership, were overlaid upon the older and continuing social base of kinship groupings as was represented in the burial mounds.

These changes mark the beginning of the Dallas phase. In several cases, villages were constructed near the earlier platform mounds, and these mounds were incorporated into the village plans, which became relatively formal in arrangement (e.g., the Hiwassee Island site, 40MG31) (Lewis and Kneberg 1946; Sullivan 2016). A new platform mound sometimes was added across a plaza from an earlier one (e.g., the Citico site, 40HA65) (Sullivan 2014, 2016). In other cases, a completely new village was established and a previous mound site was abandoned (e.g., the Dallas site, 40HA1, replaced the Hixon site, 40HA3) (Lewis et al. 1995; Sullivan 2007, 2016).

Residences were now square in plan; were constructed with large, single-set posts; and measured 4.5–7.5 m on a side (Lewis et al. 1995:67–68). A secondary, more lightly constructed building accompanied each more heavily constructed main residence. These "winter" and "summer" houses formed household units, and they often were repaired or rebuilt multiple times at the same locations within the village (Polhemus 1987; Sullivan 1987, 1995). The summer houses were used for outdoor cooking and presumably gatherings in warm weather. Burials were placed in and near these residential structures (Sullivan and Rodning 2011). By AD 1400, the main residences were constructed within house basins, and this style of architecture and the household units were prevalent throughout the Southern Appalachian region (Cable and Reed 2000; Eggiman 2010; Hally 2008; Polhemus 1987; Rodning 2007, 2015; Sullivan 1987; Sullivan and Rodning 2011). These household units are presumed to represent the residences of matrilineal kin groups and compare favorably with those of historically known groups such as the Cherokee in Southern Appalachia (Rodning 2007; Sullivan and Rodning 2001, 2011).

The types of buildings constructed on mound summits also changed from multiple buildings to single, large structures that mimicked the winter houses (Figure 7.2b). In some cases, a bench or seating platform around the interiors suggests that these large buildings (14–15 m square) were places for a number of people to gather to conduct meetings and/or special rituals (Lewis et al. 1995:68–70; Sullivan 1995, 2016). After AD 1400, at some sites these large buildings were not constructed on mounds, but they continued to front a central plaza. Some burials were placed in the platform mounds or, when these mounds were not built, in cemeteries associated with the central plaza (Sullivan 1987, 1995, 2016; Sullivan and Rodning 2001, 2011).

The timing of the beginning of the dramatic transition to large-scale, nucleated village life in southeast Tennessee is significant because it corresponds with Meeks and Anderson's (2013) first period of drought-induced food stress in the central Mississippi Valley from AD 1288 to 1308. This natural disaster was a factor that affected population movements out of that region and population increases elsewhere (Bird et al. 2017; Cobb and Butler 2002). Increases similar to those that affected Middle Tennessee likely spilled into southeast Tennessee (Meeks 2009). The same patterns noted for the Middle Cumberland region of Middle Tennessee during this period are also seen in southeast Tennessee, including the establishment of large, fortified villages. Clues to this in-migration may be seen in artifact style changes that can be linked to similarities with the Middle Cumberland region, including Nashville-style triskele gorgets and Nashville negative-painted pottery (Figure 7.3a, b). Incised pottery, notched applique rims, and strap handles also became prevalent in southeast Tennessee at this time (Sullivan 2007, 2009, 2016). It is worth noting that Emmert (Thomas 1894:Figure 240) found a Middle Cumberland–style ancestor statue (Smith and Miller 2009) in a mound on Long Island in the Tennessee River, near the confluence with the Clinch River and the base of the Cumberland Plateau (Figure 7.3c).

The Hiwassee Island site is one of the few sites in the region where excavations document the transition from the Hiwassee Island phase to the Dallas phase. Lewis and Kneberg (1946:90–102 and Table 19) placed the break for the phases at Level D in the large platform mound. Phase D is the first mound level to include small percentages of Dallas-style incised and modeled pottery in conjunction with Hiwassee Island–style sherds.[1] The first rotunda appears below Level D on mound Level E2 and is single-post construction and about 8 m in diameter. It is accompanied by a wall trench structure on the second summit. A wall trench and some early single-post buildings were present on Level D, including a small, single-post rotunda, 6 m in diameter (Lewis and Kneberg 1946:Plate 18). An AMS date for Building/Feature 27 on Level D places this structure close in time to the critical drought period (Table 7.1; Figure 7.4).

A sequence of palisades, discovered with geophysical survey, at Hiwassee Island is also relevant to the transition from the Hiwassee Island phase to the Dallas phase (Patch et al. 2015). These palisades were further investigated by test excavations in the spring of 2017 (Patch et al. 2017). One feature proved to be a ditch rather than a palisade. Charcoal samples from several of the palisades produced AMS dates in the thirteenth century and document a rapid sequence of palisade construction that correlates with the mound Levels E-1 and D interface (Table 7.1; Figure 7.4). The AMS dating placed construction of the ditch during the early stages of mound construction, but it was filled in the midst of the pali-

Figure 7.3. Middle Cumberland–related artifacts from southeast Tennessee. (*A, above*) Nashville-style shell gorget, Hiwassee Island site, Meigs County, Tennessee; (*B, right*) Nashville Negative Painted bottle, Dallas site, Hamilton County, Tennessee; (*C, below*) Ancestor statue, Long Island site, Roane County, Tennessee. Photos A and B courtesy of the McClung Museum of Natural History and Culture, University of Tennessee, Knoxville; image C from Thomas 1894:Figure 240.

Table 7.1. Hiwassee Island AMS dates from the substructure mound, palisades, and ditch

Context	Date	Calibration 2σ
WPA F. 69 Premound	893±44	AD 1030–1222
2017 F. 1.1 Midden/Ditch (Bottom)	860±30	AD 1049–1256
WPA F. 42 Mound Level E-1	810±40	AD 1160–1277
2017 F. 2.2 Palisade 2 post	800±30	AD 1184–1275
2017 F. 3.2 Palisade 3 post	790±30	AD 1190–1279
2017 F. 1.1 Midden/Ditch (Top)	790±30	AD 1190–1279
2017 F. 4.3 Palisade 4 post	780±30	AD 1210–1281
WPA F. 27 Mound Level D	773±44	AD 1170–1289
2017 F. 3.1 Palisade 3 post	530±30	AD 1320–1440
2017 F. 13.1 Palisade 5 ditch	390±30	AD 1441–1631

Note: Calibrated in Oxcal version 4.3 (Bronk Ramsay 2009) using IntCal 2013 (Reimer et al. 2013).

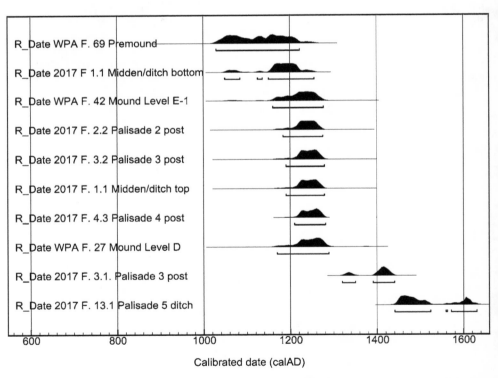

Figure 7.4. Calibrated ranges for Hiwassee Island dates. Brackets indicate 2σ (95.4 percent) confidence interval.

sade construction sequence (Table 7.1; Figure 7.4). This ditch demarcated the platform mound precinct and was intentionally filled in a short period of time with layers of pottery, rock, and shell (Patch et al. 2017).

Hiwassee Island mound Level C includes two large rotundas of wall-trench construction, 10.5–15.25 m in diameter (Lewis and Kneberg 1946:Plate 19). Of relevant interest is the large, circular wall-trench structure, about 20 m in diameter (Beahm 2013:40) excavated by Smith et al. (2012) at the Middle Cumberland Castalian Springs site. According to Beahm (2013:315–316), this Early Thruston phase rotunda was built between AD 1300 and 1320 and was covered over by AD 1350. These dates make the Castalian Springs structure a likely contemporary of the large rotundas on Level C of the Hiwassee Island mound. Also worth noting is the Nashville negative-painted sherd in Level C. Two more palisades, one a possible rebuilding of Palisade 3 and the other constructed with a trench and bastions (Palisade 5), date well into the Late Mississippian Dallas and/or Mouse Creek phases (Table 7.1). Bastioned palisades are found at many Middle Cumberland sites (Beahm 2013), but are rarer in east Tennessee. One of the few other regional examples is at the Toqua site in the Little Tennessee River valley (Polhemus 1987). Building upon work begun by Cobb and Steadman (Vidoli et al. 2013), the continuing research on biological affiliations of Middle Cumberland and eastern Tennessee populations by Harle and Vidoli (2016) also will help pull together pieces of this unfolding story.

From our current vantage, the process of village formation in southeast Tennessee certainly began by AD 1300 and was relatively rapid. The large, fortified Dallas site, for which the phase is named, burned in the mid-to-late fourteenth century (Sullivan 2007, 2016), but had been occupied long enough for at least four mound stages to be constructed (Lewis et al. 1995:311–313) (Figure 7.5). The fiery ending of this village may be a testament to increasing social pressures and conflict during Meeks and Anderson's (2013) drought event 2, from AD 1385 to 1413, the timing of the most significant abandonment of Middle Cumberland sites. Shortly after the demise of the Dallas site village (Sullivan 2007, 2016), Mouse Creek phase towns were established on the lower Hiwassee River (Sullivan 2016). Towns with community plans that included a large council house fronting a plaza surrounded by household units, such as that at Ledford Island (Sullivan 1987, 1995; Sullivan and Harle 2010), became common in Southern Appalachian during the fifteenth century, although with subregional variations. This town plan continued in use in some areas until the sixteenth century (Eggiman 2010; Hally 2008, Rodning 2015; Sullivan 2016).

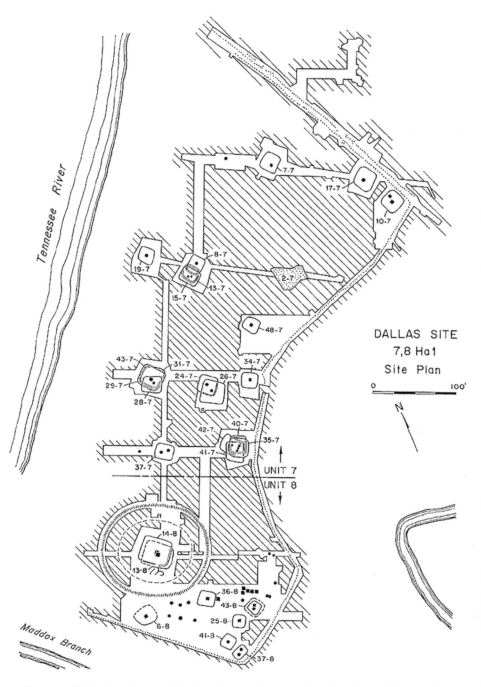

Figure 7.5. Dallas site plan map, Hamilton County, Tennessee (Lewis et al. 1995:Figure 23.3).

Communities in Balance: Councils, Kin, and Power

In-migration and subsequent coalescence with local populations cannot be ignored as possible factors in the transformation to village life in southeast Tennessee. The growing literature on coalescent communities in the Eastern Woodlands, including work by Birch (2012), Ethridge and Hudson (2002), and Kowalewski (2006), documents changes made by human societies to accommodate new groups within communities so as to resolve conflicts and lower tensions. Strategies known to promote coalescence include changes in settlement plans to encourage unification, fostering of concern for collective defense, development of corporate political structures such as councils and confederacies, integration of domestic and kin groups through clans and sodalities, and initiation of new rituals (Birch 2012; Kowalewski 2006).

Many of these processes can be seen in the changes that came about with the establishment of large Mississippian villages during the Dallas phase. As indicated by the building of palisades around the villages, these processes do not presume a peaceful transition or that the local culture was dominant in imposing their traditions upon the migrants. The changes, while relatively rapid in archaeological time, took place over several generations, but can be seen as building upon the region's long history of dispersed, localized groups. The household units and associated burials provide continuity in representation of kinship groups, as did the earlier burial mounds. The large public structures for community meetings or councils recall the rotundas used for communal activities in earlier times. Major changes in the large, nucleated settlements were the new political structures overlaid on these old groupings. The household units and council houses spatially signal the power structures within these villages. The rebuilding of household units as well as council houses in the same place, time and time again at Dallas phase sites, suggests the significance of place-making as part of the identities of the kin groups that occupied the households as well as the significance of the council houses to community government (*sensu* Rodning 2007, 2009). For the first time, there was clear segregation of kinship groups that were associated with the households, in contrast to community leadership that was associated with the council house in each village, and in a context where people had daily face-to-face contact.

As discussed by Sullivan and Rodning (Sullivan 2001, 2006; Sullivan and Rodning 2001, 2011), this segregation also had a basis in gender roles, which is reflected in mortuary practices. The graves of female elders, who would have been likely leaders of matrilineal kin groups, are associated with the household units that were the foci of kinship group life. In contrast, the majority of individuals interred in association with the large public buildings are adult males. These men likely were community leaders responsible for leadership in trade, warfare, or intercommunity relationships, and consequently were interred in a place consistent with these roles rather than in the households of their mothers or sisters.

The village councils run by senior men would have created a cohesive political structure that gave representation to disparate groups, including those of the immigrant kin groups. Male leaders, also representatives of their mothers' and sisters' kin groups and quite possibly chosen for these roles by the matriarchs, met in a context of integration and negotiation. In contrast, the senior women who assumed leadership of the matrilineal kin groups managed agricultural production and also served as tradition keepers, among other roles. Initially, migrants likely would wish to keep some of their own traditions, such as cooking or pottery styles. Cook and Fargher (2008) have shown that Mississippian traditions were kept at some Fort Ancient sites by in-migrants to that region. The senior women, by preserving traditional practices associated with their kin groups, would balance the integrative councils of the men. As time passed, the immigrants were fully integrated and absorbed into the community through exogamy.

Gender duality, with men acting in community leadership roles in councils and women serving as kin group leaders, was a strategy for social integration in a region with a long history of dispersal. An impetus for this power structure may have been the need to integrate refugees from drought-stricken regions to the west. The gendered division of power that was developed for village governance likely helped to manage and to ease inevitable tensions and conflict. Men were placed in long-held traditional roles of community leadership, but in a council format where issues could be discussed and worked out. Senior women presided over households and kin groups where unique traditions could be preserved, and individuals could be integrated into the social fabric of the village through kinship. Council houses, constructed to resemble the winter houses of the individual households, became the new symbol of community throughout the region.

The Power of Coalescence, Cooperation, and Continuity

The rapid changes at the end of the thirteenth century in southeastern Tennessee initially suggest protective actions by resident populations for themselves, their community facilities, and the resting places of their ancestors. These changes included relocation of households from small, scattered settlements to large, nucleated villages within palisades, and a shift in mortuary practices from dispersed burial mounds to graves in and around residences and platform mounds within the palisaded villages. The timing of these changes correlates with the beginning of the documented period of sustained drought and exodus from the Middle Cumberland region, and may relate to an influx of people from this region into East Tennessee at this time. Pottery styles, iconography, and Middle Cumberland–style statuary further denote the origin of these migrants to East Tennessee.

The coalescence of the local and migrant cultures ultimately led to a political structure that emphasized negotiation, compromise, and respect for tradition. Council houses, built to resemble the winter houses of the individual kin group households, represented the larger family of the community or town. The power of these villages emanated from the ability of the kin groups to work together, cooperation that initially may have been facilitated by preservation of customs at the household or kin group level and eventual blending through exogamy.

The towns of the eighteenth-century Overhill Cherokee also are relevant to these regional developments. Council houses (i.e., townhouses) were the focal points of Cherokee towns, but these communities included households dispersed across the surrounding countryside as well as core settlements near the town-houses. Schroedl (2009) notes that at the Overhill town of Chota, "approximately sixty individual domestic households surrounded the plaza and public buildings and extended along the river for nearly a mile." No palisade was found at Chota, a circumstance also in contrast to the tightly nucleated Late Mississippian villages in the region. It is tempting to suggest that changed social circumstances at this time may relate to a return to more dispersed settlement patterns and the lack of palisades.

Continued research is needed to determine the full extent to which the droughts and migrations out of the Middle Cumberland region were factors in the development of large, nucleated villages and Late Mississippian societies in east Tennessee. In this region, the long path to these large villages with council houses led from a deep history of relatively independent, small communities consisting of a few households. The councils in the large villages would have balanced the relative independence of the households by adding an integrative governing structure. By providing forums that facilitated communication and collective action, the councils could have been a vehicle for coalescence among migrants and local cultures.

Note

1. In their Table 19, Lewis and Kneberg (1946) mistakenly identified sherds in Hiwassee Island mound levels A, B, and C as "Overhill Complicated Stamped." These sherds, several of which can be seen in Plate 55A (Lewis and Kneberg 1946), are actually a shell-tempered variety of Savannah Complicated Stamped. This pottery variety dates to AD 1200–1350 and is comparable to some Wilbanks types (Anderson 1994; Caldwell and Waring 1939; Sears 1958).

References Cited

Anderson, David G.

1994 *The Savannah River Chiefdoms: Political Change in the Late Prehistoric Southeast.* University of Alabama Press, Tuscaloosa.

Beahm, Emily Lynne

2013 Mississippian Polities in the Middle Cumberland Region of Tennessee. Ph.D. diss., University of Georgia.

Birch, Jennifer

2012 Coalescent Communities: Settlement Aggregation and Social Integration in Iroquoian Ontario. *American Antiquity* 77(4): 646–670.

Bird, Broxton W., Jeremy J. Wilson, William P. Gilhooly III, Byron A. Steinman, and Lucas Stamps

2017 Midcontinental Native American Population Dynamics and Late Holocene Hydroclimate Extremes. *Nature Scientific Reports* 7:41628.

Bronk Ramsey, C.

2009 Bayesian Analysis of Radiocarbon Dates. *Radiocarbon* 51(1): 337–360.

Cable, John S., and Mary Beth Reed

2000 Archaeological Excavations in Brasstown Valley: Qualla/Lamar Occupations. *Early Georgia* 28(2): 112–143.

Caldwell, Joseph R., and Antonio J. Waring

1939 Pottery Type Descriptions. *Southeastern Archaeological Conference Newsletter* 1(6).

Chapman, Jefferson

1987 The Kittrell Mound and an Assessment of Burial Mound Construction in the Southern Ridge and Valley Province. *Tennessee Anthropologist* 12:51–73.

Cobb, Charles R., and Brian M. Butler

2002 The Vacant Quarter Revisited: Late Mississippian Abandonment of the Lower Ohio Valley. *American Antiquity* 67(4): 625–641.

Cole, Patricia E.

1975 A Synthesis and Interpretation of the Hamilton Mortuary Pattern in East Tennessee. Master's thesis, University of Tennessee.

Cook, Robert A., and Lane F. Fargher

2008 The Incorporation of Mississippian Traditions into Fort Ancient Societies: A Preliminary View of the Shift to Shell-tempered Pottery Use in the Middle Ohio Valley. *Southeastern Archaeology* 27(2): 222–237.

Eggiman, Gretchen Elizabeth

2010 The Reconstruction of Middle Sixteenth Century Architectural Patterns in Chattanooga, Tennessee: The David Davis Farm Site (40HA301). M.S. thesis, University of Georgia.

Ethridge, Robbie F., and Charles Hudson, eds.

2002 *The Transformation of the Southeastern Indians, 1540–1760.* University Press of Mississippi, Jackson.

Faulkner, Charles H.

2002 Woodland Cultures of the Elk and Duck River Valleys, Tennessee. In *The Woodland*

Southeast, edited by David G. Anderson and Robert C. Mainfort Jr., 185–203. University of Alabama Press, Tuscaloosa.

Hally, David J.

2008   *King: The Social Archaeology of a Late Mississippian Town in Northwestern Georgia.* University of Alabama Press, Tuscaloosa.

Harle, Michaelyn S., and Giovanna Vidoli

2016   The Great Divide: Population Structures and Gene Flow in Late Prehistoric Tennessee. Poster presented at the 73rd Annual Meeting of the Southeastern Archaeological Conference, Athens, GA.

Koerner, Shannon D.

2005   Deciphering DeArmond Mound (40RE12): The Ceramic Analysis of an East Tennessee Mississippian Center. M.A. thesis, University of Tennessee.

Kowalewski, Stephen A.

2006   Coalescent Societies. In *Light on the Path: The Anthropology and History of the Southeastern Indians*, edited by Thomas J. Pluckhahn and Robbie F. Ethridge, 94–122. University of Alabama Press, Tuscaloosa.

Lewis, Thomas M. N., and Madeline D. Kneberg

1946   *Hiwassee Island: An Archaeological Account of Four Tennessee Indian Peoples.* University of Tennessee Press, Knoxville.

Lewis, Thomas M. N., Madeline Kneberg Lewis, and Lynne P. Sullivan, comps. and eds.

1995   *The Prehistory of the Chickamauga Basin in Tennessee.* 2 vols. University of Tennessee Press, Knoxville.

Meeks, Scott C.

2009   Understanding Cultural Pattern and Process in the Tennessee River Valley: The Role of Cultural Resource Management Investigations in Archaeological Research. In *TVA Archaeology: Seventy-Five Years of Prehistoric Research*, edited by Erin E. Pritchard, 269–298. University of Tennessee Press, Knoxville.

Meeks, Scott C., and David G. Anderson

2013   Drought, Subsistence Stress, and Population Dynamics: Assessing Mississippian Abandonment of the Vacant Quarter. In *Soils, Climate and Society: Archaeological Investigations in Ancient America*, edited by John D. Wingard and Sue Eileen Hayes, 61–83. University Press of Colorado, Boulder

Patch, Shawn, Sarah Lowry, Lynne Sullivan, David Price, and Lauren Couey

2015   Geophysical Survey of Hiwassee Island 40MG31, Meigs County, Tennessee. New South Associates Technical Report 2515. Report submitted to the Tennessee Valley Authority.

Patch, Shawn, Sarah Lowry, Lynne Sullivan, Stephanie Smith, and David Price

2017   Archaeological Investigations at Hiwassee Island 40MG31, Meigs County, Tennessee. New South Associates Technical Report 2754. Report submitted to the Tennessee Valley Authority.

Polhemus, Richard R.

1987   *The Toqua Site-40MR6, A Late Mississippian, Dallas Phase Town.* Report of Investigations 41. Department of Anthropology, Tennessee Valley Authority Publications in Anthropology, University of Tennessee, Knoxville.

Reimer, P. J., E. Bard, A. Bayliss, J. W. Beck, P. G. Blackwell, C. Bronk Ramsey, P. M. Grootes, T. P. Guilderson, H. Haflidason, I. Hajdas, C. Hatt, T. J. Heaton, D. L. Hoffmann, A. G. Hogg, K. A. Hughen, K. F. Kaiser, B. Kromer, S. W. Manning, M. Niu, R. W. Reimer, D. A. Richards, E. M Scott, J. R. Southon, R. A. Staff, C. S. M. Turney, and J. van der Plicht

2013　IntCal13 and Marine13 Radiocarbon Age Calibration Curves 0–50,000 Years cal BP. *Radiocarbon* 55(4): 1869–1887.

Rodning, Christopher B.

2007　Building and Rebuilding Cherokee Houses and Townhouses in Southwestern North Carolina. In *The Durable House: Architecture, Ancestors, and Origins,* edited by Robin A. Beck Jr., 464–484. Southern Illinois University, Center for Archaeological Investigations Occasional Paper 35, Carbondale.

2009　Mounds, Myths, and Cherokee Townhouses in Southwestern North Carolina. *American Antiquity* 74(4): 627–663.

2015　*Center Places and Cherokee Towns: Archaeological Perspectives on Native American Architecture and Landscape in the Southern Appalachians.* University of Alabama Press, Tuscaloosa.

Schroedl, Gerald F.

2009　Chota. In *The Tennessee Encyclopedia of Culture and History,* Vol. 2.0. Online edition, University of Tennessee Press, Knoxville. http://tennesseeencyclopedia.net/entries/chota/.

Schroedl, Gerald F., C. Clifford Boyd, and R. P. Stephen Davis

1990　Explaining Mississippian Origins in East Tennessee. In *The Mississippian Emergence,* edited by Bruce D. Smith, 175–196. Smithsonian Institution Press, Washington, DC.

Sears, William H.

1958　The Wilbanks Site (9CK-5), Georgia. *Bureau of American Ethnology Bulletin* 169:129–194. Washington, DC.

Smith, Kevin E., and James V. Miller

2009　*Speaking with the Ancestors: Mississippian Stone Statuary of the Tennessee-Cumberland Region.* University of Alabama Press, Tuscaloosa.

Smith, Kevin E., Emily L. Beahm, and Michael K. Hampton

2012　The Castalian Springs Mound Project 2011: Investigations of Mound 3 (Preliminary Interpretations). Paper presented at the 24th Annual Current Research in Tennessee Archaeology Meeting, Nashville.

Sullivan, Lynne P.

1987　The Mouse Creek Phase Household. *Southeastern Archaeology* 6(1): 16–29.

1995　Mississippian Household and Community Organization in Eastern Tennessee. In *Mississippian Communities and Households,* edited by J. Daniel Rogers and Bruce D. Smith, 99–123. University of Alabama Press, Tuscaloosa.

2001　Those Men in Mounds: Gender, Politics, and Mortuary Practices in Late Prehistoric Eastern Tennessee. In *Gender in the Archaeology of the Mid-South,* 101–126. University Press of Florida, Gainesville.

2006　Gendered Contexts of Mississippian Leadership in Southern Appalachia. In *Leadership and Polity in Mississippian Society,* edited by Paul Welch and Brian Butler, 264–285. Southern Illinois University Press, Carbondale.

2007   Shell Gorgets, Time, and the SECC in Southeastern Tennessee. In *Southeastern Ceremonial Complex: Chronology, Content, Context,* edited by Adam King, 88–106. University of Alabama Press, Tuscaloosa.

2009   Archaeological Time Constructs and the Construction of the Hiwassee Island Mound. In *TVA Archaeology: Seventy-Five Years of Prehistoric Site Research,* edited by Erin Pritchard, 181–209. University of Tennessee Press, Knoxville.

2014   The Citico Site (40HA65) in Regional Context. Paper presented in the symposium "Forty Years On: Celebrating the Career of Gerald F. Schroedl," organized by C. Clifford Boyd at the 71st Annual Meeting of the Southeastern Archaeological Conference, Greenville, SC.

2016   Reconfiguring the Chickamauga Basin. In *New Deal Archaeology in the Tennessee Valley,* edited by David Dye, 138–170. University of Alabama Press, Tuscaloosa.

Sullivan, Lynne P., and Michaelyn S. Harle

2010   Mortuary Practices and Cultural Identity at the Turn of the Sixteenth Century in Eastern Tennessee. In *Mississippian Mortuary Practices: Beyond Hierarchy and the Representationist Perspective,* edited by L. P. Sullivan and Robert C. Mainfort Jr., 234–249. University Press of Florida, Gainesville.

Sullivan, Lynne P., and Shannon D. Koerner

2010   New Perspectives on Late Woodland Architecture and Settlement in Eastern Tennessee: Evidence from the DeArmond Site (40RE12). *Tennessee Archaeology* 5(1): 31–50.

Sullivan, Lynne P., and Christopher B. Rodning

2001   Gender, Tradition, and Social Negotiation in Southern Appalachian Chiefdoms. In *The Archaeology of Historical Processes: Agency and Tradition Before and After Columbus,* edited by Timothy R. Pauketat, 107–120. University Press of Florida, Gainesville.

2011   Residential Burial, Gender Roles, and Political Development in Late Prehistoric and Early Cherokee Cultures of the Southern Appalachians. In *Residential Burial: A Multi-Regional Exploration,* edited by Ron Adams and Stacie King, 79–97. AP3A Series, American Anthropological Association. Washington, DC.

Thomas, Cyrus

1894   *Report on Mounds Explorations of the Bureau of Ethnology.* Twelfth Annual Report, Bureau of Ethnology 1890–91, Smithsonian Institution, US Government Printing Office, Washington, DC.

Thompson, Victor D.

2009   The Mississippian Production of Space through Earthen Pyramids and Public Buildings on the Georgia Coast, USA. *World Archaeology* 41(3): 445–470.

Vidoli, Giovanna M., Heather Worne, Dawnie W. Steadman, and Charles R. Cobb

2013   Middle Cumberland Regional Relationships and the Mississippian Geopolitical Landscape. *American Journal of Physical Anthropology* 150:278.

Williamson, Ronald F., and David A. Robinson

1994   Peer Polities Beyond the Periphery: Early and Middle Iroquoian Regional Interaction. *Ontario Archaeology* 58:27–43.

8

The Village Remains the Same

A Fort Ancient Example

ROBERT A. COOK

The present study began for me long ago with two basic questions that I eventually discovered were related to each other: why do Fort Ancient and Mississippian villages look so similar, and how can we connect Fort Ancient villages to historically documented forms? These questions are also generally shared by several other contributors to this volume, such as identifying factors that precipitate village life and what new forms of social relations develop, as well as examining the potential reasons why some villages become larger and more important whether in political or ritual terms (particularly see Thompson and Birch, this volume; Cobb, this volume).

In brief, my findings are as follows. Fort Ancient villages formed as a result of several factors, including a scalar effect that is more nuanced than the common conclusion that villages emerged after population grew as a result of agricultural intensification. While agricultural intensification and population growth are clearly part of the story, they do not explain the specific form villages took. To do this, it is imperative to factor into the equation the migration of Mississippian peoples and where and how they settled. The particular village form that developed is best viewed as a variant of Late Woodland and Mississippian forms. The ultimate function of these villages appears to be that they served to integrate peoples from different cultural backgrounds, perhaps with a fundamental shift in personhood (*sensu* Skousen 2012). The form of personhood that emerged was materially expressed in large posts in the middle of Fort Ancient villages that connected with key solar alignments. This was not only an entity that is generically thought of as an *axis mundi* (Eliade 1957), but also this newly developed person served to integrate multiple social divisions and mitigate dual universal tensions of male/female, earth/sky, dark/light, and so on. A few villages in the region are distinct from the others in terms of size, environmental setting, and number of mounds, among other characteristics (for parallel problems, see Wallis, this volume; West et al., this volume). While there is not a clear case to be made for a marked political hierarchy, evidence does support what I refer to as an ancestral/landscape hierarchy.

While spatial constraints for this volume prohibit a detailed theoretical and methodological discussion, it is important to note that my approach combines general processual and specific historical aspects of human behavior (further elaborated in Cook 2017:40–57), an orientation that best allows us to track the shift to becoming Mississippian, which occurred in various and often unique ways that involved the formation of differing local hybrids with Late Woodland cultures. Methodologically, I integrate environmental, mortuary, biodistance, and chemical analyses, which are crucial in examinations of migration and the multicultural complexity that ensued.

This chapter focuses on one area in the Fort Ancient region (Figure 8.1), which may be different than elsewhere in the larger culture area as it has long been recognized that this culture-historical taxon is not a cohesive unit (Cook 2008, 2017; Graybill 1984). In my region of focus, the Great and Little Miami River valleys, there is a marked continuity of village form from at least AD 1000 to 1675 (Figure 8.2). I further extend this finding into the early historical era as comparisons with village forms of some probable descendants reveal considerable overlap (for some related concerns, see Oland et al. 2012).

Becoming Village People

Fort Ancient origins have long been seen in relation to Mississippian developments, with migration suspected for quite a long time (Griffin 1943:257–60), but not directly examined until my own efforts (Cook and Price 2015). We now know, as Griffin long suspected, that migration occurred, and that he was surprisingly prescient in his arrow drawing from eastern Tennessee and southern Indiana to the Fort Ancient region (see Figure 8.1). A recent strontium analysis found that a large proportion of the total sample, including about one-third of those sampled from the Turpin site, was likely nonlocal to the region (Cook and Price 2015). This is a large proportion, but only captures first-generation migrants; those born locally of migrants would at least double these proportions. The strontium values for nonlocal individuals are consistent with a broad range of geographic regions that contain Mississippian sites, including southern Indiana, the American Bottom, the Central Illinois River Valley, and the Middle Cumberland and eastern portions of Tennessee. To further examine biological linkages

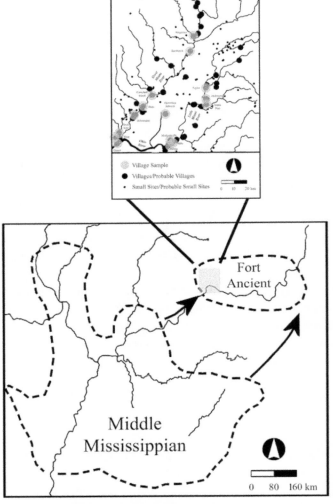

Figure 8.1. The Fort Ancient and Middle Mississippian culture regions showing sources of migrations after Griffin 1967: Figure 5 with inset of study region (after Cook 2017:Figure 4.5).

with several of these potential source areas, biodistance analysis of the cemento-enamel junction of key human teeth was conducted comparing four Fort Ancient sites (Anderson, Guard, SunWatch, Turpin) with three Mississippian ones (Angel, Averbuch, Hiwassee Island). The main consideration was to determine which Fort Ancient sites are most closely related biologically to the Mississippian sites sampled. In line with the strontium analysis, the biodistance results revealed a

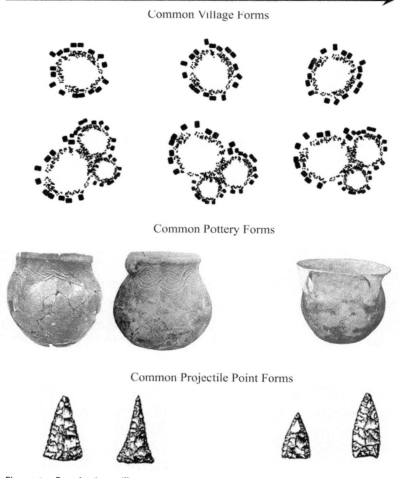

after A.D. 1000   A.D. 1150-1250   after A.D. 1400

Common Village Forms

Common Pottery Forms

Common Projectile Point Forms

Figure 8.2. Fort Ancient village structure over time and corresponding changes in pottery and projectile point forms (after Cook 2017:Figures 2.4, 7.4, 7.5).

close connection between Turpin and Mississippian sites. In particular, there is a closer biological relationship between Turpin and two of the three Mississippian sites (Angel, Hiwassee Island). This finding is important because it adds further support to the strontium results.

I have previously pointed out the similarities in Fort Ancient and Mississippian village form (Cook 2008), a conclusion I believe has only become stronger as we have learned about other Fort Ancient sites, particular those earlier than SunWatch and closer to Mississippians (see Cook et al. 2015). Further comparisons reveal similarities between larger Fort Ancient sites with multiple mounds and some smaller neighboring Mississippian mound centers. If we deepen our perspective, Fort Ancient villages may be viewed as scaled-up versions of local circular Woodland houses and/or post circles and earthen enclosures into which burials were integrated (Figure 8.3). The point is that I certainly recognize that Fort Ancient villagers drew on local pasts and integrated formerly separate mortuary and many small residential units into one village space, along with the nonlocal (Mississippian) contributions to the pattern.

Why were Mississippians interested in moving into the Fort Ancient region? After the so-called big bang at the major Mississippian mound center of Cahokia, there was an outpouring of people voyaging to distant lands (Pauketat et al. 2015; Slater et al. 2014). This is nicely captured by Pauketat's distribution map of wall trench houses throughout a broad region of the Midwest and Southeast United States (Alt and Pauketat 2011:Figure 1). However, my findings indicate an earlier spread of wall trench houses than has previously been depicted in the study region, beginning around AD 1100.

The mouth of the Great Miami River contains some of the largest and earliest Fort Ancient villages with numerous Mississippian-style artifacts. It has been argued that the lower Great Miami River topography created natural routes that facilitated cultural mixing (Reidhead 1976). This area is also located at the intersection of multiple ecozones and in close proximity to large floodplains, oxbows, and other wetlands that are attractive places to settle near from a subsistence standpoint. This is precisely the type of setting that Bruce Smith (1978) described as an optimal Mississippian environmental niche. Moreover, as one moves up the Ohio River, this region is the next such setting from where other Mississippian settlement systems are located (e.g., Angel, Kincaid, Prather).

The Fort Ancient culture developed at the onset of the Medieval Warm Period, during a time of ideal conditions for the intensification of maize agriculture. Large villages developed rather abruptly at the same time as there was a marked increase in maize consumption. There is more, however, to the environmental component of this story. It is not accurate to say that Mississippians and Fort Ancient equally developed in the Medieval Warm Period, as ideal moisture conditions were only present throughout much of the Mississippian and Fort Ancient regions of interest here until about AD 1100. After this time, the Fort Ancient region was the only area that maintained above-average moisture conditions (Comstock and Cook, 2018). This finding provides us with an environmental pull for Mississippians to come into the region. This date is consistent with the Mississippian migrants we have directly dated. This may also be a time when Mississippian communities were being established for other reasons, ranging from spiritual, such as reli-

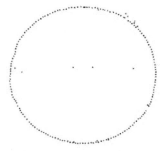

Middle Woodland Post Circle (Stubbs)

Middle Woodland Earthen Enclosure (Newark)

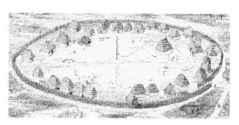

Fort Ancient Village (SunWatch)

Figure 8.3.
Comparison of Fort
Ancient village form
with Woodland
enclosures present
in the culture region.
Newark earthwork
photo by Timothy
Black and SunWatch
drawing by Jeffrey
Dilyard, used with
permission.

gious proselytizing; to social, such as segmenting kin groups or gaining leadership through war exploits; to economic, such as exploiting key raw material locations. Of course, combinations of these and other factors may well have contributed to the development of Fort Ancient culture. Those who spread the word of key aspects of this new way of life were not likely to have been just any individuals, but prehistoric "connectors" of sorts (*sensu* Gladwell 2000). Interestingly, more complex social forms developed in the more mainstream Mississippian regions, which in the more general picture may be best explained in response to the riskier environments.

The Guard site best demonstrates the structure of the earliest Fort Ancient village I have located (Cook et al. 2015). Radiocarbon dates clearly position it at the beginning of the sequence, and we have recently found that it has clear similarities with the subsequently occupied SunWatch site in the presence of a large central post, surrounded by a plaza and a dense zone of trash basins and residential structures. Some structures at both sites are distinct in their placement, as they are located in the western area and are pulled closer to the village center and positioned between solstice alignments with the central pole. In terms of spatial grammar, both sites are similar in overall structure, with the main difference being that the Guard houses are almost exclusively Mississippian-style wall trench forms and there are many more Mississippian artifacts at Guard.

Being Village People

After the initial influx of Mississippians and the formation of Fort Ancient identity, there were fissioning events whereby segments split off from parent communities and moved into upstream locations where there were sizable but scattered Late Woodland groups. It is in these secondary contexts upstream where we really see a truer blend of Late Woodland and Mississippian/Early Fort Ancient cultures. Part of this process is revealed when we consider that SunWatch's strontium values for the majority of the local group are consistent with a wide range of values from areas in the upper Great Miami Valley, strongly suggestive of an aggregation of formerly dispersed Late Woodland descendants into SunWatch village (Cook 2017:157–58). While the bulk of the SunWatch samples were consistent with these values, two individuals better fit the geologic signature of the lower Great Miami Valley where their parent villages were located (Cook and Price 2015).

Mississippian status symbols found in Fort Ancient burials such as large knives, whelk shell pendants, and shell discs appear to be specific references drawing on the mythic corpus associated with the "bird man" and two males locked in combat as later depicted on Hightower/Big Toco–style gorgets buried with individuals at Etowah (Georgia) and at Dallas phase sites in eastern Tennessee (Marceaux and Dye 2007). This style of gorget depicts whelk shell pendants, shell ear discs, and long flint knives as ritual regalia (Figure 8.4). Of course, the comparison with this region of Tennessee was not randomly selected but guided by findings of the strontium and biodistance analyses.

Two sites that formed at this time, SunWatch and Taylor, illustrate similarities and differences regarding the incorporation of Mississippian mythic symbolism and village formation histories. At each site, biodistance study disclosed the presence of a small cluster of two closely related adult males (Cook 2017:Figure 6.19).

Figure 8.4. Mississippian gorget showing items Fort Ancient villagers incorporated into some of their status positions (from Cook 2017:Figure 6.21).

One of the two males at each site was interred with a supralocal status object, a whelk shell pendant at SunWatch and a large chert knife at Taylor. Their outsider status on the basis of biological distance from other males at the site adds an important layer to their story, that being that they were not closely related to the local population, which is typical in many cultures (see Sahlins 2008). More specifically, eighteenth-century Central Algonquian leaders were often outsiders to the multiethnic villages in which they were authorities, as they could better reconcile the frequently quarreling lineages because they were not members of any of them (White 1991:213). Based on the associated prestige goods, I further suggest that such leaders in Fort Ancient villages could have been from "apex families" at other sites around which status differences began to develop in the new one, a process common in cases of similar migrations (Alvarez 1987:133–138; see also Anthony 1990:904). These individuals can be interpreted as "big men" in the cultural sense of possessing a village-level authority position. Interestingly, the SunWatch big man was taller than all other adults in the village, rendering him literally the biggest male in terms of height (Cook 2017:Figure 6.20). Tall individuals in leadership positions are not uncommon either (e.g., Blaker et al. 2013), but this finding at Sun-

Watch adds an important dimension to this individual's status that was originally recognized on the basis of possessing a Mississippian-style whelk shell pendant. Unfortunately in the Taylor case, collection practices in the nineteenth century prohibit us from assessing whether the adult male with the large knife at Taylor was unusually tall.

The two adult male authority figures at SunWatch and Taylor and their close biological male relatives reveal further clues regarding village formation. The SunWatch individual dates to AD 1250–1450 (two-sigma), which is later in the village sequence, after the site grew in size, whereas the Taylor individual dates to AD 1036–1246 (two-sigma), which is very early in that village sequence. The SunWatch case appears to be a good illustration of a scalar threshold dynamic where the outside leader served in part to organize a growing population. In contrast to the SunWatch case, Taylor is a good example of what I consider to be a founding event. In this case, the individual's intrusive interment in what started as a Middle Woodland mound appears to have been an act of constructing social memory. Subsequently, the village was literally formed around him, commemorating and monumentally marking this important event. Similar reuse of such earthen monuments occurred at the Guard, State Line, and Turpin sites.

Within the study region, hybrid village structure is only fully discernible at SunWatch. The overall structure of the village with its central pole is consistent with Mississippian forms, while the housing (primarily single post construction) and pottery manufacture (mostly grit-tempered and cordmarked with lug appendages) are more similar to Late Woodland traditions. There are also hybrid traditions such as a wall trench/post house and grit/shell-tempered pottery that has other mixed characteristics such as negative painting overtop incised guilloche designs (Cook and Fargher 2008). Burial practices also reflect a mixture of Late Woodland (flexed) and new traditions (extended), not to mention the village authority that appears to be of local origin but with a classic item of Mississippian status. This renders the spread of Fort Ancient culture as a process that clearly involved hybrid relationships with local Woodland populations. The overall leadership structure and village form seem most attributable to the Mississippian presence, whereas the Late Woodland contribution appears more visible at the household level. This finding fits well with other forms of cross-cultural interaction (e.g., Lightfoot et al. 1998).

Aggregate/multicomponent villages might represent a degree of settlement hierarchy in the region, suggesting in other words that Fort Ancient might have some "class" after all (contra Griffin 1992). This revives an older idea that a Fort Ancient settlement hierarchy existed (Essenpreis 1978 [but see Essenpreis 1988]; see also Riordan 2000 and Vickery et al. 2000). Here, I further examine this possibility by considering the evidence for multiple components, for it has been argued that if larger sites are shown to be more frequently multicomponent, a case for political hierarchy breaks down (Duffy 2015). In my case, the data do support the conclusion that the largest villages are most likely to have been the result of reuse through time rather than being significantly larger at any one time (*sensu* Drooker 1997).

There is not a case for a strong political hierarchy; however, I do think that it is likely that the Fort Ancient settlement system in the study region was hierarchical, but more of a ritual distinction with key locales being key places through time. These sites are relatively evenly spaced within the study region, predate smaller villages in their respective areas, are usually in defensive locations (bluffs), contain most of the Mississippian objects, and are in excellent environmental locales in terms of access to major food sources, interaction routes, and flood prevention. Moreover, they are most often positioned atop (literally) preceding cultural traditions. Importantly, this is not just a coincidence of using good places at different times, but there were regular interments of their own dead in these earlier monuments. These characteristics may well have been related to mythical connections and are not unusual in cases of similarly small-scale hierarchical settlement patterns. For these reasons, they would have formed centers within their respective settlement systems. I suggest they are most similar to some small-scale Mississippian hierarchies (e.g., Cobb and Butler 2002), in what I suggest is an ancestral and landscape hierarchy. This pattern is possibly more general as it is similar to a very different cultural context in South America whereby villages of higher rank inhabit locations in downriver settings where there are more abundant food sources (specifically fish) and those of lower rank are in upriver settings (Chernela 1993:93).

Full Circle

There were major changes across much of the eastern United States beginning at about AD 1400, near the onset of the Little Ice Age. This time of global cooling and drying appears to have contributed to a significant reduction in maize dependency and considerable population shuffling in the region and more broadly. We know that connections were broadening and pulling Fort Ancient to the west for various reasons, not least of which was the attraction of bison hunting (Drooker 1997). And we now know that Fort Ancient people were eating less maize at this time (Cook and Price 2015) and were increasingly using bison bones to manufacture tools (Drooker 1997). I suggest that some Fort Ancient folks may have left the area at this time to eventually become part of Dhegiha Siouans, and others that stayed might be more related to Central Algonquians. Those that stayed appear to have coalesced into larger sites, but to a much smaller degree than was previously thought. I only have the space here to address aspects in common between Fort Ancient and Dhegiha village structures, but first I provide justification as to the relevance of the comparison.

Anthropologists and historians have long suggested that the Ohio Valley was a Dhegiha Siouan homeland. The Dhegiha move west was recorded by Fletcher and La Flesche (1911) in the names of two of the tribes that formed during their journey, the Omaha and the Quapaw. Omaha means "against the current/upstream," which is in contrast to the Quapaw, which means "with the current/downstream" (i.e., one group turned left and the other right when they reached the Mississippi River). An Osage chief described the members of his parent Dhegihan culture moving in large numbers and mentions passing the Falls of the Ohio (near Louisville, Kentucky). Dorsey (1886) calculates that the split occurred at about AD 1380 or AD 1390. More recently, considering multiple lines of evidence including both linguistic divergence and archaeological data, Henning (1993) suggests that a date range of AD 1289–1513 is most likely for the Dhegiha separations. These estimates for the Dhegiha migration are consistent with each other and should be considered in studies of potential movements out of the Fort Ancient region. This time frame is particularly important concerning the changes in Fort Ancient culture at about the same time with evidence for population reduction in the study region. Henning (1993) offers further insight into the process of Dhegiha Siouans becoming distinct cultures in their new homelands. He suggests that as they split into various tribes, their material culture and diet appear to have changed rapidly, particularly reflecting technological adaptations to varying environments, but their language, legends, religion, and social structure remained more intact. He also specifically suggests that Dhegihan Siouan cultures may have been comprised of Fort Ancient and/or Caborn-Wellborn cultures.

With the preceding justification as to why Dhegiha Siouans are appropriate to consider as a potential Fort Ancient descendant, a comparison of their village structures reveals several striking commonalities (Figure 8.5). Foremost among the findings is the regular structuring of both into a dual division associated with aspects of earth and sky, war and peace, winter and summer, and male and female, and integrated by a central pole (Cook 2017:146–206). As such, I argue that the village in each case is a representation of the whole earth and universe, with the village metaphorically giving birth to the human race. Drawing on my previous research, I stress that in both cases the southern and western parts of the villages are older than the northern segment, and village leadership is associated with these same older areas. There is also evidence in each case for a dog or wolf segment of the village being more recently integrated into the village pattern, and being located in the north in association with evidence for warfare (Cook 2012).

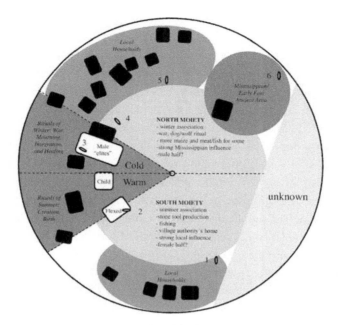

SunWatch Village

Key Ritual/Political Areas
Residential Areas
Plaza (key integrator around symbol [center pole] with both local and non-local roots)
O Red Cedar Central Pole

<u>Key Male Authorities (only burials perpendicular to plaza)</u>

1 Household elder and moiety leader?
2 Only adult in group to be extended and only high maize consumer outside of the wall trench area (see Figure 6.15)
3 Village Authority (whelk pendant, only person with north and south artifacts)
4 Household elder? (no artifacts)
5 Household elder? (no artifacts)
6 Only clear stone box grave, wolf jaw

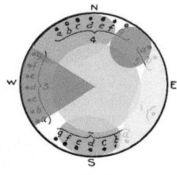

Osage/SunWatch

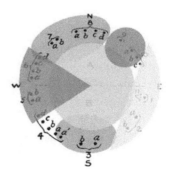

Omaha/SunWatch

Figure 8.5. Comparison of SunWatch village plan with those of select Dhegiha Siouan cultures. Osage and Omaha village maps from Fletcher and LaFlesche 1911 (Figures 9 and 20) and SunWatch map after Cook 2017 (Figure 6.1 and 6.30).

In addition to the clear structural connection in village form between some of the Fort Ancient and Dhegiha Siouans, consideration of diachronic aspects further illuminates the similarities. Oral histories of the Omaha, for example, recount a time when forces were working to disintegrate the culture as it lacked political organization, a situation that was remedied by the development of traditions surrounding the Sacred Pole and the formalization of chiefly offices. The pole symbolized power of chiefs and Thunder, the god of war, and was a symbol of unity. Furthermore, it is said to have begun when the people depended on maize for their food supply and not bison. As nicely put by Fletcher and LaFlesche (1911:251), the ceremony "grew up with the corn." An older Omaha ceremony is particularly interesting as its focal point is a large pole that sometimes stood in the center of the village. This pole served a similar unifying function but is much older than the Sacred Pole and signified a series of dualities (day/night, thunder/death, earth/sky). The pole itself signified a male, and the decorations referenced the cosmic forces that gave and maintained life. As a tree it equaled the entire tribe with the branches referencing all of the people. As was the case with the more recent Sacred Pole, this pole was also associated with village leadership and the southern moiety. Perhaps the original integration ceremonies at the dawn of Fort Ancient served to keep the culture together, commencing at a time of potentially disintegrating cultural complexity.

Multicultural Origins and Descendants

The purpose of this chapter has been to stress the sudden appearance of the Fort Ancient village and its consistent role in serving to integrate peoples from multiple cultural traditions over the course of time. The pole originated as the ultimate person to integrate dualities associated with the locals and newcomers with ties to oral histories of the Dhegiha Siouans. The plaza/pole complex is the common thread from beginning times, as exemplified at Guard, to middle times, as exemplified by SunWatch, to some descendant times, as exemplified by the Dhegiha case. This thread of continuity occurred despite marked changes in diet, material culture, and climate. I am not declaring that Fort Ancient is related only to the Dhegiha cultures, simply that they are one of many likely descendants. This is meant to imply, however, that we need to open up our static models to allow for variability in the composition of Fort Ancient villages to include Mississippian connections through space and time and to allow for multiple connections with living descendants.

Acknowledgments

Thanks go first to Victor Thompson and Jennifer Birch for inviting me to participate in this stimulating symposium. It was a pleasure to learn so much about villages from so many other researchers. Much of this chapter is derived from a larger work recently published by Cambridge University Press (Cook 2017). Financial support for much of the study was provided by the National Science Foundation (NSF-1122499 and 1545138) and the National Geographic Society (9104-12).

References Cited

Alt, Susan M., and Timothy R. Pauketat
2011   Why Wall Trenches? *Southeastern Archaeology* 30:108–122.
Alvarez, Robert R., Jr.
1987   *Familia: Migration and Adaptation in Baja and Alta California, 1800–1975*. University of California Press, Berkeley.
Anthony, David
1990   Migration in Archeology: The Baby and the Bathwater. *American Anthropologist* 92:895–914.
Aubry, B. Scott, and Robert A. Cook
2017   Multiple Measures of Migration. *American Journal of Physical Anthropology*, under review.
Blaker, Nancy M., Irene Rompa, Inge H. Dessing, Anne F. Vriend, Channah Herschberg, and Mark van Vugt
2013   The Height Leadership Advantage in Men and Women: Testing Evolutionary Psychology Predictions about the Perceptions of Tall Leaders. *Group Processes and Intergroup Relations* 16:17–27.
Chernela, Janet M.
1993   *The Wanano Indians of the Brazilian Amazon: A Sense of Space*. University of Texas Press, Austin.
Cobb, Charles R., and Brian M. Butler
2002   The Vacant Quarter Revisited: Late Mississippian Abandonment of the Lower Ohio Valley. *American Antiquity* 67:625–641.
Comstock, Aaron R., and Robert A. Cook
2018   Climate Change along the Mississippian Periphery: A Fort Ancient Example. *American Antiquity* 83(1):93–108.
Cook, Robert A.
2008   *SunWatch: Fort Ancient Development in the Mississippian World*. University of Alabama Press, Tuscaloosa.
2017   *Continuity and Change in the Native American Village: Multicultural Origins and Descendants of the Fort Ancient Culture*. Cambridge University Press, Cambridge.
Cook, Robert A., and Lane F. Fargher
2008   The Incorporation of Mississippian Traditions into Fort Ancient Societies: A Preliminary View of the Shift to Shell-Tempered Pottery Use in the Middle Ohio Valley. *Southeastern Archaeology* 27:222–237.
Cook, Robert A., and T. Douglas Price
2015   Maize, Mounds, and the Movement of People: Isotope Analysis of a Mississippian/Fort Ancient Region. *Journal of Archaeological Science* 61:112–128.

Cook, Robert A., Aaron R. Comstock, Kristie R. Martin, Jarrod Burks, Wendy Church, and Melissa French

2015   Early Village Life in Southeastern Indiana: Recent Field Investigations at the Guard Site (12D29). *Southeastern Archaeology* 34:95–115.

Dorsey, James Owen

1886   Migrations of Siouan Tribes. *American Naturalist* 20:210–222.

Drooker, Penelope B.

1997   *The View from Madisonville: Protohistoric Western Fort Ancient Interaction Patterns.* Memoirs of the Museum of Anthropology No. 31, University of Michigan, Ann Arbor.

Duffy, Paul R.

2015   Site Size Hierarchy in Middle-Range Societies. *Journal of Anthropological Archaeology* 37:85–99.

Eliade, Mircea

1957   *The Sacred and the Profane.* Harvest Books, New York.

Essenpreis, Patricia S.

1978   Fort Ancient Settlement: Differential Response at a Mississippian–Late Woodland Interface. In *Mississippian Settlement Patterns*, edited by Bruce D. Smith, 143–167. Academic Press, New York.

1988   An Introduction to the Fort Ancient Cultural Complexes of the Middle Ohio Valley. In *A History of 17 Years of Excavation and Reconstruction: A Chronicle of 12th Century Human Values and the Built Environment*, edited by James M. Heilman, Malinda C. Lileas, and Christopher A. Turnbow, 1–22. Dayton Society of Natural History, Dayton, OH.

Fletcher, Alice C., and Francis La Flesche

1911   *The Omaha Tribe.* Twenty-Seventh Annual Report of the Bureau of American Ethnology. Government Printing Office, Washington, DC.

Gladwell, Malcolm

2000   *The Tipping Point: How Little Things Can Make a Big Difference.* Little, Brown, New York.

Graybill, Jeffrey R.

1984   The Eastern Periphery of Fort Ancient. *Pennsylvania Archaeologist* 54:40–50.

Griffin, James B.

1943   *The Fort Ancient Aspect: Its Cultural and Chronological Position in Mississippi Valley Archaeology.* Museum of Anthropology Anthropological Papers No. 28, University of Michigan, Ann Arbor.

1967   Eastern North American Archaeology: A Summary. *Science* 156:175–191.

Henning, Dale R.

1993   The Adaptive Patterning of the Dhegiha Sioux. *Plains Anthropologist* 38:253–264.

Lightfoot, Kent G., Antoinette Martinez, and A. M. Schiff

1998   Daily Practice and Material Culture in Pluralistic Social Settings: An Archaeological Study of Culture Change and Persistence from Fort Ross, California. *American Antiquity* 63:199–222.

Marceaux, Shawn, and David H. Dye

2007   Hightower Anthropomorphic Marine Shell Gorgets and Duck River Sword-Form Flint Bifaces: Middle Mississippian Ritual Regalia in the Southern Appalachians.

In *Southeastern Ceremonial Complex: Chronology, Content, Context,* edited by Adam King, 165–184. University of Alabama Press, Tuscaloosa.

Oland, Maxine, Siobhan M. Hart, and Liam Frink

2012   *Decolonizing Indigenous Histories: Exploring Prehistoric/Colonial Transitions in Archaeology.* University of Arizona Press, Tucson.

Pauketat, Timothy R., Robert F. Boszhardt, and Danielle M. Benden

2015   Trempealeau Entanglements: An Ancient Colony's Causes and Effects. *American Antiquity* 80:260–289.

Reidhead, Van

1976   Optimization and Food Procurement at the Prehistoric Leonard Haag Site, Southeastern Indiana: A Linear Programming Approach. Ph.D. diss., Indiana University.

Riordan, Robert

2000   Peas in a Pod? Diversity at Small Late Prehistoric Components in Southwest Ohio. In *Cultures Before Contact: The Late Prehistory of Ohio and Surrounding Regions,* edited by Robert A. Genheimer, 404–424. Ohio Archaeological Council, Columbus.

Sahlins, Marshall D.

2008   The Stranger-King or, Elementary Forms of the Politics of Life. *Indonesia and the Malay World* 36:177–199.

Skousen, B. Jacob

2012   Posts, Places, Ancestors, and Worlds: Dividual Personhood in the American Bottom Region. *Southeastern Archaeology* 31:57–69.

Slater, Phillip A., Kristin M. Hedman, and Thomas E. Emerson

2014   Immigrants at the Mississippian Polity of Cahokia: Strontium Isotope Evidence for Population Movement. *Journal of Archaeological Science* 44:117–127.

Smith, Bruce D.

1978   Variation in Mississippian Settlement Patterns. In *Mississippian Settlement Patterns,* edited by Bruce D. Smith, 479–503. Academic Press, New York.

Vickery, Kent D., Theodore S. Sunderhaus, and Robert A. Genheimer

2000   Preliminary Report on Excavations at the Fort Ancient State Line Site, 33Ha58, in the Central Ohio Valley. In *Cultures Before Contact: The Late Prehistory of Ohio and Surrounding Regions,* edited by Robert A. Genheimer, 272–328. Ohio Archaeological Council, Columbus.

White, Richard

1991   *The Middle Ground: Indians, Empires, and Republics in the Great Lakes Region, 1650–1815.* Cambridge University Press, Cambridge.

9

Population Aggregation and the Emergence of Circular Villages in Southwest Virginia

RICHARD W. JEFFERIES

The study of settlement structure and organization has been an integral part of anthropological research for more than a century (Mindeleff 1900; Morgan 1881; Phillips et al. 1951; Steward 1937, 1938; Willey 1953). Many of these studies have focused on the origins of village life and assessing how changes in village location, plan, and architecture can reflect regional-scale perturbations of the cultural landscape on which these communities were situated (Chang 1968; Deetz 1968; Kent 1990; Means 2007; Yeager and Canuto 2000).

In some parts of the Americas, the emergence of village life was marked by the appearance of compact, ring-shaped communities, much like the one shown in John White's 1585 illustration of the "Indian Village of Pomeiooc" located in what is now eastern North Carolina (Hulton 1984:62, 177–178). Circular site plans have a long history in eastern North America, with some of the first examples represented by the Watson Brake mound complex in Louisiana and the Late Archaic shell rings along the Georgia and South Carolina coasts (Reichel-Dolmatoff 1965, 1971, 1985; Saunders et al. 2007; Saunders and Russo 2002; Thompson 2007, 2010; Thompson et al. 2004).

Farther south, some agricultural groups that inhabited central Brazil were constructing ringed villages by AD 1000, characterized by a central plaza, a surrounding ring of houses, and an outlying midden ring (Heckenberger 1996:322; Heckenberger et al. 1999:364). Wüst and Baretto (1999:18–19) have proposed that the appearance of these Amazonian ringed villages coincided with more intensive intergroup feuding, population increase, and other internal and external pressures. Substantial defensive ditches surrounding many of these villages support the case for a turbulent social landscape (Heckenberger et al. 1999:364, Figures 9 and 10).

In the central Appalachian region of eastern North America, the period extending from ca. AD 900 to 1650, known as the *Late Woodland* in regional archaeological terminology (Means 2014), is also characterized by an ever-increasing number of large, circular, often palisaded villages (Means 2007; Milner et al. 2013). These communities were populated by the former residents of small, dispersed farmsteads and hamlets that were typical of the regional settlement pattern prior to ca. AD 1200. Gallivan's (2003:84) research to the east in the James River watershed revealed a similar pattern in that part of Virginia, with settlements being "uniformly small prior to A.D. 1200, while after that date community sizes were larger and more variable."

Clearly, the physical and cultural landscapes of Brazil and the central Appalachians are quite distinct. However, descriptions of Amazonian circular communities, as well as many of the social and economic factors contributing to their origin, are remarkably similar to those found in the central Appalachians and other parts of eastern North America just prior to European contact (Hatch and Bondar 2001:151; Heckenberger 1996).

This chapter synthesizes data collected by Virginia archaeologists from a series of Late Woodland ring-shaped villages in southwestern Virginia and assesses factors associated with the appearance of these complex communities on a socially dynamic landscape. The availability of multiple radiocarbon dates from numerous village sites affords the opportunity to explore diachronic trends in community organization and strategies behind village placement on the landscape.

The aggregation and increased cooperation of community members in these highly visible and formally defined spaces resulted in stronger connections to place and to each other. More frequent and intensive social relations among village residents contributed to a stronger cultural identity. The power of this more highly integrated community was communicated to each other and to outsiders by the placement, design, and architecture of the symbol of that new identity—the formidable palisaded village. An assertion of their power is reflected in the construction of villages near communication and transportation routes where residents (or some residents) could potentially influence the interregional flow of goods and information.

The Emergence of Village Life in Late Woodland Eastern North America

In the central Appalachians, the Late Woodland period was a time of dramatic culture change characterized by population growth and aggregation; the movement of people into less desirable habitats; increasing reliance on cultivated plants, particularly maize; changing patterns of exchange and interaction; and regional climate deterioration (Egloff 1992; MacCord 1989; Means 2007; Milner et al. 2013). Starting shortly before AD 1200, these dynamic changes are reflected in the archaeological record by a demographic shift that resulted in the inhabitants of at least some dispersed farmsteads and hamlets relocating, reorganizing, and establishing large, ring-shaped, often palisaded villages (Hart and Means 2002:353; Hatch and Bondar 2001:151, Maps 10.3 and 10.4; Means 2007; Milner et al. 2013:Figure 2). Although some villages may date to as early as AD 900 (MacCord 1979; Means 2007:1), their number and distribution dramatically increased after AD 1200, reaching a peak between AD 1400 and 1600 (Means 2007:149; Milner et al. 2013:101).

Hatch and Bondar suggest that much of this area was "occupied by local tribes undergoing generally similar experiences during the Late Woodland period, with documented increases in both their reliance on maize agriculture and the intensity of warfare" (2001:151). The increased likelihood of intercommunity conflict may have contributed to the aggregation of some closely affiliated hamlets, resulting in increased community size and the establishment of new communities in more easily defended positions (Hatch and Bondar 2001:166; Milner 1999:125). Unlike Mississippian chiefdoms in which defensive works were constructed only around the largest civic/ceremonial towns, central Appalachian groups constructed palisades around their villages regardless of size, suggesting that each one had to provide for its own protection (Milner 1999:125; Milner et al. 2013:98).

Palisaded villages continued to be constructed throughout the northern Eastern Woodlands well into the seventeenth century, reflecting the cultural landscape's volatile nature. The region's hostile environment is supported by an account from the 1671 Batts and Fallam expedition to Virginia's New River valley stating that they terminated their explorations because their Indian guides were afraid of the native groups that lived in this region (Cox 2010).

Palisaded Villages of Southwestern Virginia

In the 1980s, longtime Virginia state archaeologist Howard A. MacCord applied the name *Intermontane Culture* to a cluster of Late Woodland ring-shaped communities centered in and around Tazewell County, Virginia, that shared a number of architectural, ceramic, and mortuary traits (1989:89) (Figure 9.1). The topography of this area is characterized by southwest-to-northeast-trending ridges that rise up to 900 m in elevation. Dense stands of oak-hickory forests provided an abundant and diverse food source and, where present, the rich bottomlands were suitable for cultivating native and tropical cultigens (Egloff 1992:212).

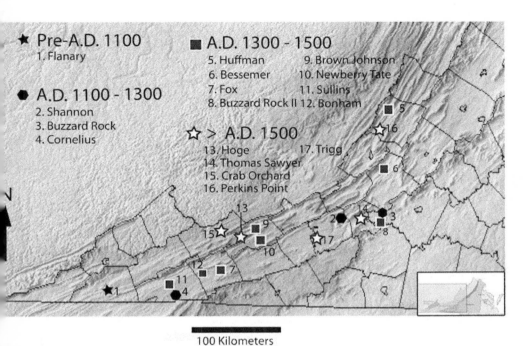

Pre-A.D. 1100
1. Flanary

A.D. 1100 - 1300
2. Shannon
3. Buzzard Rock
4. Cornelius

A.D. 1300 - 1500
5. Huffman   9. Brown Johnson
6. Bessemer   10. Newberry Tate
7. Fox   11. Sullins
8. Buzzard Rock II 12. Bonham

> A.D. 1500
13. Hoge   17. Trigg
14. Thomas Sawyer
15. Crab Orchard
16. Perkins Point

100 Kilometers

Figure 9.1. Chronological placement of southwestern Virginia Late Woodland villages.

This part of Virginia is situated near the headwaters of several major rivers, including the New and Big Sandy, which flow to the Ohio River; the Powell, Clinch, and Holston, which merge to form the Tennessee River; and the Roanoke and James, which flow east to the Atlantic Ocean. These rivers connected a variety of culturally diverse societies such as Dallas phase Mississippian chiefdoms in extreme southwestern Virginia and northeastern Tennessee (Jefferies 2001; Meyers 2002, 2011), Fort Ancient villages in southern West Virginia (Graybill 1981; Pollack and Henderson 2015; Pollack et al. 2002), Monongahela groups in southwestern Pennsylvania (Means 2007), and Dan River groups in central Virginia (MacCord 1989:98, 2001:18–25).

These strategically situated rivers served as conduits for the movement of people, materials, and ideologies among contemporary groups that lived throughout much of eastern North America during the Late Woodland period, just as they had for the preceding millennia. Late Woodland groups that occupied their headwaters could facilitate or hinder those interregional interactions, as well as experience the negative impacts of neighboring groups that wanted to play a bigger role in the goings-on in this part of the world. Numerous overland trails also traversed this

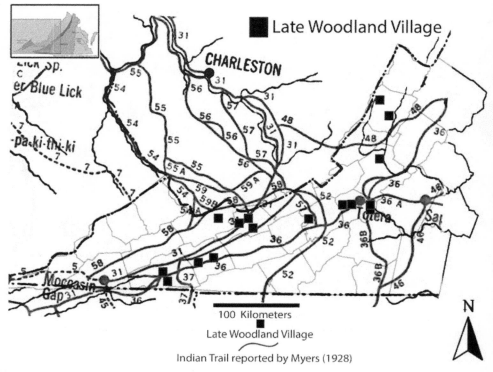

Figure 9.2. Southwestern Virginia Late Woodland villages and historic trails documented by Myers (1928).

part of Virginia, providing other avenues for interactions (Myers 1928:Plate 15) (Figure 9.2). As suggested by Gallivan (2003:42), southwestern Virginia's ridge and valley region was a veritable "societal crossroads" during the last 500 years of prehistory.

The first recorded European presence in the region occurred during the late seventeenth century when fur-trading parties explored the upper reaches of the Roanoke River. In 1671, one of these groups, headed by Thomas Batts and Robert Fallam, visited several towns occupied by Siouan-speaking people, such as Tetera Town, located near present-day Salem, Virginia. The expedition eventually made its way northwest along the New River to Peters' Mountain near what is now the Virginia–West Virginia border. Along the way, they encountered a recently abandoned "Moketan" village overgrown with "weeds and small prickly Locust and Thistles to a very great height that it was almost impossible to pass" and fields having "corn stalks in the ground" near an abandoned "Mohecan" Indian village (Summers 1929). Unfortunately, no descriptions of these towns are known to exist.

Little is known about southwestern Virginia Late Woodland settlement strate-

gies prior to the appearance of the first ringed villages; however, limited archaeological data suggest that prior to AD 1200, most people lived in small, scattered
settlements having the same house forms, ceramics attributes, and mortuary
practices as found on the later ringed-villages (MacCord 1989:89, 104). Bernard
Mean's (2007:1) investigation of Monongahela tradition settlement in southwestern Pennsylvania indicates a similar pattern with a landscape dotted with small
hamlets, limited procurement camps, and rockshelters (Means 2007:20). These
kinds of sites continued to be integral parts of the regional settlement system following the appearance of villages around AD 1100 (Means 2007:20, 26).

Since the 1960s, Virginia archaeologists have documented nearly 20 Late
Woodland ringed villages in far southwestern Virginia. In some cases, complete
village plans were exposed, providing details on community structure, organization, and architecture. Most villages were situated on fertile bottomlands or on
terraces along major rivers or their tributaries (MacCord 1989:100). Some upland
sites are thought to have been strategically placed relative to regional trade and
communications routes (Bott 1981:38–45, cited in Egloff 1992:212).

Like their Amazonian counterparts, activities in most central Appalachian Late
Woodland villages were organized according to a concentric geometric plan characterized by a central plaza surrounded by several concentric bands dedicated to specific
purposes such as domestic tasks, mortuary activities, or storage (Means 2007:19).
Diachronic changes in community layout appear to reflect attempts to mitigate the
impacts of unifying formerly dispersed, socially distinct groups that were now living
in a relatively constricted space (Hart and Means 2002:347; Means 2007:34).

In southwestern Virginia, most Late Woodland villages were circular to oval
in outline; however, some, like the Shannon site (44My8), were less symmetrical
(Benthall 1969:Figure 10). The irregular shape of the Brown Johnson site (44Bd1)
palisade (MacCord 1971:Figure 3) suggests that the structures were built first, with
the surrounding palisade constructed later (MacCord 1971:238) (Figure 9.3).

Villages ranged from ca. 37 m to nearly 125 m in diameter (MacCord 1989:Table
3), approximating the dimensions of Monongahela villages to the north (Means
2005:Figure 3). Diachronic trends in community size remain unclear, but Means
(2007:147) noted that later Monongahela villages were not necessarily larger than
earlier ones, but that there was greater diversity in size through time.

Palisades were constructed by placing small (12–15 cm diameter) posts in individual holes spaced ca. 30 cm apart (MacCord 1989:100) (Figure 9.4). Spacing between post holes suggests that additional materials (vines, brush, branches, etc.)
were woven between the posts to make entry more difficult (MacCord 1971:236;
Milner 2000:54–59). No evidence of daub has been found, so the dry material
forming the palisade would have been very susceptible to burning. In general,

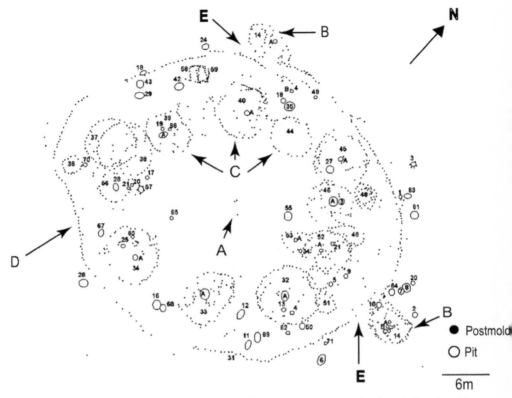

Figure 9.3. Plan of the Brown Johnson Late Woodland village (MacCord 1971) showing: (*A*) central posts; (*B*) gate house; (*C*) circular structures; (*D*) palisade; and (*E*) entrances.

these palisades were not very substantial and reflected less planning than those built by Mississippian groups (Milner 1999:125).

Some villages, such as Trigg (44My3) and Crab Orchard (44Tz1), had multiple palisade lines (Buchanan 1986:316; MacCord and Buchanan 1980:Figure 3), indicating that the wall was rebuilt several times as village size changed (MacCord 1989:101) or that multiple palisade lines were used simultaneously (Milner 2000:55). MacCord (1989:101) proposed that villages lacking evidence for palisade repair or replacement were occupied for as few as 10 to 15 years based on local "life expectancy" for wall posts. Villages exhibiting no evidence for palisade repair, little midden accumulation, and few burials or storage pits may have been occupied for even less time (MacCord 1989:101).

As with many Monongahela villages (Means 2007), access to the interior of most southwestern Virginia villages was through long, narrow passageways formed by an overlap in the palisade wall. At least five villages had rectangular structures

Figure 9.4. Shannon site palisade line. Image courtesy of the Virginia Department of Historic Resources.

interpreted as "gate houses" positioned near the entrance (MacCord 1971:Figure 4). Large, deeply set posts near a gate house at the Brown Johnson site may be associated with a watchtower (MacCord 1971:242, 1989:100–101) (Figure 9.3).

The central feature of the village was an open circular plaza. Some plazas lacked interior features (MacCord 1971:Figure 2), while others, such as Trigg, contained numerous burials, pits, and post molds (Buchanan 1986). At the Sullins (44Wg12) and Brown Johnson (44Bd1) villages (Figure 9.3), large posts (22–30 cm in diameter) once stood in the plaza's center (MacCord 1981:98), perhaps serving as the community's *axis mundi*. Similar features are known for some Monongahela (Means 2007:126), Fort Ancient (Cook 2007; Pollack and Henderson 2015), Late Woodland Patrick phase (AD 600–800), and Emergent Mississippian villages (Kelly, Finney, et al. 1984:Figure 51; Kelly, Ozuk, et al. 1984:Figure 47). Proposed functions for these "sacred poles" include a focal point for ceremonies (Pollack and Henderson 2015:316) or a symbol of community existence or identity (Hally 2008:158).

Residential structures were arranged in a circular pattern between the edge of the central plaza and the palisade wall (MacCord 1971:Figure 2, 1981:Figure 2). Few of the circular villages have been completely excavated, but available data suggest that many had at least 12 structures; the Trigg site (44My3) had nearly 30 (Mac-Cord 1989:Table 3).

Domestic structures were circular to oval in outline, usually 4 to 8 m in diameter, and constructed using small saplings (less than 12.5 cm diameter) set in individual post holes (MacCord 1989:Table 3) (Figure 9.3). Internal posts marking the location of partitions, benches, or sleeping platforms were evident in larger structures. Clusters of nearby burials and pits are associated with many structures (MacCord 1989:99–100). In several villages, square or rectangular buildings constructed within or just outside the palisade may be communal structures used for sacred or secular activities (Buchanan 1986:316; MacCord and Buchanan 1980:Figure 5; Egloff and Reed 1980:132, cited in Egloff 1992:209; MacCord 1981:96, Figure 2). Pollack and Henderson (2015:298) report similar kinds of structures in some Middle Fort Ancient communities.

Small circular-to-oval patterns of posts located adjacent or connected to some residential structures may represent the remains of storage "huts." Similar structures, also interpreted as storage facilities, are often associated with Monongahela structures in southwestern Pennsylvania (MacCord 1989:100; Means 2007:19).

The architecture and arrangement of most residential structures suggest that there were no major social distinctions among village households. Virtually all structures were placed around the central plaza, offering equal access to all community events performed there. Minor variations in house size and shape may simply indicate that some household groups were larger than others.

Subsistence remains reflect a combination of wild and cultivated plants, combined with local mammals, birds, and fishes. The Late Woodland plant assemblage from the Buzzard Rock II site on the Roanoke River was dominated by hickory nut and maize, along with weedy plant seeds and fruits, suggesting a mixed farming/foraging strategy (VanDerwarker and Idol 2008:72). Maize was introduced about AD 1000, but widespread cultivation did not occur until after AD 1200 (Means 2014). Although maize is sometimes given as the factor responsible for the initiation of village life (for examples, see Wymer 1993:143), the 200- to 300-year gap between its introduction to the central Appalachian region and the peak of village construction suggests that it was not just maize cultivation, but its becoming a major dietary staple was the catalyst for the transition to Late Woodland village life (Gallivan 2003:87; Means 2007:21).

The Late Woodland burial program included interments placed within, adjacent to, or between houses; between houses and the palisade; or in the plaza itself (Boyd and Boyd 1992:256; Buchanan 1986:316; MacCord 1981:12). Nearby caves probably also had a role in the mortuary program (Boyd and Boyd 1992:257). The variety of burial methods used and the presence of exotic burial goods suggest a fairly elaborate mortuary complex (Egloff 1992:214), contrasting with the lack of evidence for social distinction in other components of the material culture.

Analyses of human skeletal remains have yielded limited evidence for conflict-induced trauma, but occasional decapitation victims (MacCord 1971:248) and human bones with embedded projectile points (Benthall 1969:48) have been reported. However, as Milner (2005) has cautioned, the skeletal evidence for warfare probably underestimates the actual number of casualties. At the regional scale, casualties attributable to warfare "appear to increase in the early centuries of the second millennium AD, along with more palisades" (Milner et al. 2013:101).

Discussion

When MacCord first introduced his Intermontane Culture in the 1980s, little information existed with which to investigate the temporal variability or occupation history of its palisaded villages (1989:103). Diachronic consistency in ceramic traits, mortuary practices, house forms, and other cultural attributes suggested that population aggregation and the formation of circular villages was an in situ process and that earlier Late Woodland groups were cultural and biological antecedents of these village dwellers (MacCord 1989:104). Dating of components was based on a combination of temporally diagnostic artifacts, largely ceramics and European items, and barely a dozen radiocarbon dates from six villages (MacCord 1989:103).

Over the past 25 years, the number of radiocarbon dates from Late Woodland villages has dramatically increased, from 13 to more than 80 from at least 17 southwestern Virginia palisaded village sites (Virginia Division of State Archaeology 2016) (Figure 9.5). The number of dates from each site range from 1 to more than 10, producing occupation histories of varying chronological detail. As a way of approximating the time of construction and occupation for each of the 17 villages used in this chapter, I calculated the pooled mean radiocarbon age for each site having multiple radiocarbon dates using the CALIB Radiocarbon Calibration Program. The occupation range for each site is based on the two-sigma range having the highest statistical probability as determined by the CALIB SumProb option (Stuiver and Reimer 1993; Stuiver et al. 2017).

The pooled means of the calibrated dates for the 17 villages ranged from AD 1021 to 1629; however, they are not uniformly distributed over this roughly 600-year interval. As Figure 9.5 illustrates, the pooled means for 6 percent of the sites (n=1) is pre–AD 1100, and another 18 percent (n=3) fall between AD 1100 and 1300. Palisaded village construction/occupation appears to have reached its peak in southwestern Virginia between AD 1300 and 1500, with 47 percent (n=8) of the

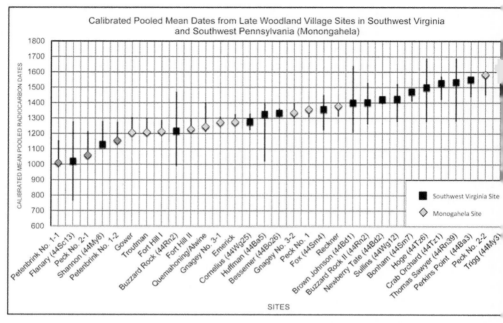

Figure 9.5. Pooled mean radiocarbon dates from southwestern Virginia and southwestern Pennsylvania (from Means 2005:Table 4) Late Woodland villages.

sites having pooled mean dates falling in this range. Twenty-nine percent (n=5) had a pooled mean later than AD 1500. The latest date (AD 1629) was recorded for the Trigg site in Montgomery County. Glass beads and other European items found at the Trigg, Crab Orchard, Thomas Sawyer, and other "Intermontane Culture" sites indicate that palisaded villages were occupied well into the seventeenth century (Egloff 1992:195; MacCord 1989:103).

Comparison of Late Woodland settlement data from surrounding regions reveals that population aggregation in compact circular villages was an ongoing process throughout much of the northern Eastern Woodlands (Hatch and Bondar 2001:151; Milner 1999, 2000:67; Milner et al. 2013), particularly among neighboring Fort Ancient and Monongahela groups (Drooker and Cowan 2001:83–106; Graybill 1984:44; Means 2007). For example, Figure 9.5 shows the distribution of the pooled mean dates from 17 southwest Virginia villages and 14 Monongahela villages in southwest Pennsylvania as reported by Means (2005:Table 4). Comparison of the distributions indicates that Monongahela village construction began and ended at about the same time, but that it reached its peak between AD 1300 and 1500, roughly 100 years earlier than in southwest Virginia. This suggests that the cultural and/or environmental factors that contributed to the initiation of circular village construction did not develop simultaneously throughout the central Appalachians and that the aggregation of people in compact, palisaded, circular villages was influenced by different local cultural and/or environmental factors. Another factor may be that the Monongahela dates were all AMS dates; the southwestern Virginia chronology was primarily based on traditional radiocarbon dates.

Nevertheless, the chronological trends in both southwestern Virginia and southwestern Pennsylvania generally conform to that reported by Milner et al. (2013:Figure 1), showing that the frequency of palisaded villages increased throughout the northern Eastern Woodlands during the Late Prehistoric period, peaking about AD 1550. They attributed this to ongoing intergroup conflict possibly related to deteriorating climatic conditions at the onset of the Little Ice Age (Milner et al. 2013:98).

Egloff's (1992:212) study of the spatial distribution of southwest Virginia Late Woodland villages revealed that they occurred throughout the Ridge and Valley province, but primarily along the well-drained higher terraces adjacent to the Holston, New, Roanoke, James, and Tennessee Rivers. Some of these sites, particularly in the Tennessee drainage, were strategically positioned near saddles, near gaps, or along ridgetops near the numerous trails (Myers 1928:Plate 15) that traversed this area (Egloff 1992:211) (Figure 9.2). Conceivably, villages placed near these trails had some degree of control over the flow of people and materials over those trails (Bott 1981).

A closer examination of site location and radiocarbon dates suggests that there was a diachronic shift in favored village location. Prior to ca. AD 1400, villages tended to be constructed along the bottomlands of major streams and rivers—approximately 75 percent of the pre–AD 1400 sites included in this study occurred there (Figure 9.1). In contrast, nearly 60 percent of the post–ca. AD 1500 villages were situated in more remote upland areas (600–1300 m asl), often near the headwaters of several watersheds. This trend is illustrated by a cluster of four late villages (sites 9, 10, 13, and 15) dating from ca. AD 1400 to 1600 that are clustered at the headwaters of the New, Big Sandy, Clinch, Powell, and Holston Rivers (Figure 9.1). The movement of people, goods, and information between the Ohio Valley, Tennessee Valley, and eastern Virginia could have been influenced by the placement of these communities.

Conclusion

Starting around AD 1200, the relatively sudden appearance of compact, circular, palisaded villages in southwestern Virginia suggests the emergence of more complex forms of sociopolitical organization and the centralization of political power. Similar occurrences are seen at about the same time throughout many other parts of northeastern North America, although the specific timing of village development appears to have been influenced by local cultural and environmental events. This date also corresponds to the widespread appearance of palisaded and bastioned Mississippian towns in parts of the southern Midwest and Southeast, the construction of which has been interpreted as a display of defensive military power on a landscape marked by dramatic social changes (Krus 2016:381).

Explanations for the establishment of circular villages in the Eastern Woodlands center on increased sedentism, the growing importance of intensive agriculture, population growth, and a greater threat of intergroup violence (Hatch and Bondar 2001:166; Milner 1999:125). These factors may have been amplified by the onset of the colder conditions and increased variability of growing conditions as the impacts of the Little Ice Age took hold ca. AD 1300 (Milner et al. 2013:98). Similar kinds of environmental uncertainty documented in other parts of North America also have contributed to significant cultural changes, including a major increase in large village settlements, occupation of fortified positions, and projectile point trauma (Chatters 2004, cited in Prentiss et al. 2007).

Milner (1999:123) suggests that increased energy expenditure associated with clearing fields, tending crops, and storing food made the option of building defensive palisades more attractive than running away from danger. In southwestern Virginia, this danger could have come from any one of the many groups that inhabited the surrounding regions, from transitory groups that traversed the region's many trails or rivers, or perhaps even from neighboring villages.

Surprisingly, the archaeological record of southwestern Virginia offers little evidence for actual intensive intergroup conflict or feuding despite the presence of apparently defensive fortifications. Aside from accidental fires, there is little evidence to suggest that any of the villages were intentionally burned (MacCord 1989:100). The relatively flimsy construction and wide spacing of wall posts characteristic of many palisades also raises doubts about their defensive value. Evidence for conflict-induced trauma in human skeletons is also rare, but possibly underrepresented (Milner 2005).

The architectural and organizational characteristics of circular villages also appear to have been a response to internal factors, such as helping to mitigate increased levels of internal social stress created by more intense contact and interaction among formerly dispersed village residents. In particular, the arrangement of household units around the central plaza could have served as a leveling mechanism by providing village residents with equal access to integrative plaza activities and the ritual features (central posts and pits) that symbolized this new social arrangement.

One reason behind the placement of southwestern Virginia villages was their strategic position with respect to the rivers and trails that connected groups living throughout much of eastern North America (Figure 9.2). Mississippian artifacts found at some sites serve as evidence for that interaction (Barber and Barfield 2000:Table 2; Holland 1970; MacCord 1979:20, 27). The discovery of similar kinds of Mississippian items at Ohio Valley Fort Ancient sites indicates that exchange relationships also extended far to the north and west (Pollack et al. 2002).

What impact did the desire to maintain the complex web of cultural connections, as reflected by the interregional flow of marine shell, salt, and other goods, have on these culturally diverse groups? Was the desire to maintain access to the coveted materials and social connection that came with them strong enough to keep the causes of intergroup conflict and violence under control? Were the circular, palisaded communities the "insurance policies" that would protect Late Woodland groups in case interregional relations took a turn for the worse? At least in this part of the Eastern Woodlands, the threat of conflict, more than actual violence, may have helped to shape the Late Woodland cultural landscape. In reality, the palisades that enclosed villages like Crab Orchard, Brown Johnson, and Trigg may have been sort of a Late Woodland version of Cold War fallout shelters—never used, but available in case the need arose.

In her recent study of circular villages in Amazonia and the eastern United States, Rautman (2016) has emphasized the importance of the surrounding cultural landscape on village formation. She proposes that "this form of village organization may not be tied so closely to internal social organization as to regional context. The circular village layout may have been important in creating an uneasy but workable group identity vis-à-vis outsiders within a specific social context: that of regional demographic change, social uncertainty and violent inter-village conflict" (Rautman 2016:125).

Rautman's (2016) ideas seem particularly relevant to Late Woodland southwestern Virginia, given the potentially volatile nature of the cultural landscape. The consistent architectural footprint of Late Woodland villages (palisade, circular plan, central plaza and associated ritual features, activity zones, etc.) may reflect their residents' efforts to express their cultural identity, much in the way the architecture and organization of Mississippian town and mound centers was an outward expression of their inhabitants' social, political, and ideological principles.

The palisaded village represented a large investment of time and labor by its inhabitants, which reflected their place on the landscape and their willingness to defend it. Krus (2011:238) estimated that 17.0 person-hours were required to erect a palisade post at Cahokia, with the greatest part of that time associated with procuring the logs (Milner 1998:147). Clearly, the ring-village palisades were not as extensive or substantial as Cahokia's, but their construction still drew heavily on the community's labor pool.

The most important thing about the palisade may have been what it communicated about the people who lived there, not merely its defensive function. To the outsider, the village, much like its Mississippian counterparts, was symbolic of its inhabitants' power and prestige. It provided its residents with a sense of place and reinforced their cultural identity.

Clearly, much more research is needed before we can fully understand the complex processes that led to these major changes in Late Woodland settlement in southwestern Virginia and the surrounding central Appalachian province. Primary among these is investigating the various scenarios proposed for the rapid spread of palisaded villages during the post–AD 1000 era. Was it for protection from external threats associated with the increasing importance of maize agriculture and all of the social, political, ideological trappings, particularly intervillage warfare? Or perhaps it was the increased level of social integration and cooperation required to maintain a productive agricultural economy. Identification of the archaeological correlates associated with these various scenarios will be the key to understanding these complex issues.

References Cited

Barber, Michael B., and Eugene B. Barfield
2000   The Late Woodland Period in the Environs of Saltville: A Case for Petty Chiefdom Development. *Journal of Middle Atlantic Archaeology* 16:117–132.

Benthall, Joseph L.
1969   *Archaeological Investigations at the Shannon Site, Montgomery County, Virginia.* Virginia State Library, Richmond.

Bott, Keith E.
1981   *44RU7: Archaeological Test Excavations at a Late Woodland Village in the Lower Uplands of Southwest Virginia.* Research Report Series 2, Division of Historic Landmarks, Richmond, VA.

Boyd, C. Clifford, and Donna C. Boyd
1992   *Late Woodland Mortuary Variability in Virginia.* In *Middle and Late Woodland Research in Virginia*, edited by Theodore Reinhart and Mary Ellen Hodges, 249–276. Archaeological Society of Virginia Special Publication 29. Dietz Press, Richmond, VA.

Buchanan, William T.
1986   *The Trigg Site, City of Radford, Virginia.* Special Publication 14, Archaeological Society of Virginia, Richmond.

Chang, Kwang-Chih
1968   *Settlement Archaeology.* National Press Books, Palo Alto, CA.

Chatters, James. C.
2004   Safety in Numbers: Conflict and Village Settlement on the Plateau. In *Complex Hunter-Gatherers: Evolution and Organization of Prehistoric Communities on the Plateau of Northwestern North America*, edited by W. C. Prentiss and I. Kuijt, 67–83. University of Utah Press, Salt Lake City.

Cook, Robert A.

2007 *SunWatch: Fort Ancient Development in the Mississippian World*. University of Alabama Press, Tuscaloosa.

Cox, W. Eugene

2010 Batts and Fallam Expedition. Electronic resource. e-WV: *West Virginia Encyclopedia*, December 21, 2010.

Deetz, James F.

1968 The Inference of Residence and Descent Rules from Archaeological Data. In *New Perspectives in Archaeology*, edited by S. R. Binford and L. R. Binford, 41–49. Aldine, Chicago.

Drooker, Penelope B., and C. Wesley Cowan

2001 Transformation of the Fort Ancient Cultures of the Central Ohio Valley. In *Societies in Eclipse: Archaeology of the Eastern Woodlands Indians, A.D. 1400–1700*, edited by David S. Brose, C. Wesley Cowan, and Robert C. Mainfort, 83–106. Smithsonian Institution Press, Washington, DC.

Egloff, Keith T.

1992 The Late Woodland Period in Southwestern Virginia. In *Middle and Late Woodland Research in Virginia*, edited by Theodore Reinhart and Mary Ellen Hodges, 187–223. Archaeological Society of Virginia Special Publication 29. Dietz Press, Richmond, VA.

Egloff, Keith T., and Celia Reed

1980 Crab Orchard Site: A Late Woodland Palisaded Village. *Quarterly Bulletin of the Archaeological Society of Virginia* 42:1–15.

Gallivan, Martin D.

2003 *James River Chiefdoms: The Rise of Social Inequality in the Chesapeake*. University of Nebraska Press, Lincoln.

Graybill, Jeffrey R.

1981 The Eastern Periphery of Fort Ancient (A.D. 1050–1650): A Diachronic Approach to Settlement Variability. Ph.D. diss., University of Washington.

1984 The Eastern Periphery of Fort Ancient. *Pennsylvania Archaeologist* 54:40–50.

Hally, David J.

2008 *King: The Social Archaeology of a Late Mississippian Town in Northwest Georgia*. University of Alabama Press, Tuscaloosa.

Hart, John P., and Bernard K. Means

2002 Maize and Villages: A Summary and Critical Assessment of Current Northeast Early Late Prehistoric Evidence. In *Northeast Subsistence-Settlement Change: A.D. 700–1300*, edited by John p. Hart and Christina B. Rieth, 345–358. University of New York, Albany.

Hatch, James W., and Gregory H. Bondar

2001 Late Woodland Palisaded Villages from Ontario to the Carolinas. In *Archaeology of the Appalachian Highlands*, edited by L. P. Sullivan and S. C. Prezzano, 149–167. University of Tennessee Press, Knoxville.

Heckenberger, Michael J.

1996 War and Peace in the Shadow of Empire: Sociopolitical Change in the Upper Xingu of Southeastern Amazonia, A.D. 1400–2000. Ph.D. diss., University of Pittsburgh.

Heckenberger, Michael J., James B. Peterson, and Eduardo Goes Neves

1999 Village Size and Permanence in Amazonia: Two Archaeological Examples from Brazil. *Latin American Antiquity* 10:353–376.

Holland, C. G.

1970 *An Archaeological Survey of Southwest Virginia.* Smithsonian Contributions to Anthropology 12. Smithsonian Institution, Washington, DC.

Hulton, Paul

1984 *America 1585: The Complete Drawings of John White.* University of North Carolina Press and the British Museum Publications, Chapel Hill and London.

Jefferies, Richard W.

2001 Living on the Edge: Mississippian Settlement in the Cumberland Gap Vicinity. *Archaeology of the Appalachian Highlands,* edited by Lynne P. Sullivan and Susan C. Prezzano, 198–221. University of Tennessee Press, Knoxville.

Kelly, John E., Fred A. Finney, Dale L. McElrath, and Steven J. Ozuk

1984 Late Woodland Period. In *American Bottom Archaeology: A Summary of the FAI-270 Project Contribution to the Culture History of the Mississippi River Valley,* edited by Charles J. Bareis and James W. Porter, 104–127. Illinois Department of Transportation, Urbana.

Kelly, John E., Steven Ozuk, Douglas K. Jackson, Dale L. McElrath, Fred A. Finney, and Duane Esarey

1984 Emergent Mississippian Period. In *American Bottom Archaeology: A Summary of the FAI-270 Project Contribution to the Culture History of the Mississippi River Valley,* edited by Charles J. Bareis and James W. Porter, 128–157. Illinois Department of Transportation, Urbana.

Kent, Susan

1990 Activity Areas and Architecture: An Interdisciplinary View of the Relationship between Use of Space and Domestic Built Environments. In *Domestic Architecture and the Use of Space: An Interdisciplinary Cross-Cultural Study,* edited by Susan Kent, 1–8. Cambridge University Press, Cambridge.

Krus, Anthony M.

2011 Refortifying Cahokia: More Efficient Palisade Construction through Redesigned Bastions. *Midcontinental Journal of Archaeology* 36:3227–3244.

2016 The Timing of Precolumbian Militarization in the U.S. Midwest and Southeast. *American Antiquity* 81(2): 375–388.

MacCord, Howard A.

1971 The Brown Johnson Site, Bland County, Virginia. *Quarterly Bulletin of the Archaeological Society of Virginia* 25:230–270.

1979 The Flanary Site, Scott County, Virginia. *Quarterly Bulletin of the Archaeological Society of Virginia* 34:1–32.

1981 The Sullins Site, Washington County, Virginia. *Quarterly Bulletin of the Archaeological Society of Virginia* 36:94–121.

1989 The Intermontane Culture: A Middle Appalachian Late Woodland Manifestation. *Archaeology of Eastern North America* 17:89–108.

2001 Dan River Culture and Its Expansion West of the Blue Ridge. *Quarterly Bulletin of the Archaeological Society of Virginia* 56:18–25.

MacCord, Howard A., and William T. Buchanan

1980 *The Crab Orchard Site, Tazewell County, Virginia.* Archaeological Society of Virginia, Richmond.

Means, Bernard

2005   Late Woodland Villages in the Allegheny Mountains Region of Southwestern Pennsylvania: Temporal and Social Implications of New Accelerator Mass Spectrometry Dates. In *Uplands Archaeology in the East: Symposia VIII & IX*, edited by Carole L. Nash and Michael B. Barber, 13–25. Special Publication 38-7, Archaeological Society of Virginia.

2007   *Circular Villages of the Monongahela Tradition*. University of Alabama Press, Tuscaloosa.

2014   Late Woodland Period (AD 900–1650). *Encyclopedia Virginia. Virginia Foundation for the Humanities*, May 30, 2014.

Meyers, Maureen

2002   The Mississippian Frontier in Southwestern Virginia. *Southeastern Archaeology* 21:178–191.

2011   Political Economy of Exotic Trade on the Mississippian Frontier: A Case Study of a Fourteenth Century Chiefdom in Southwestern Virginia. Ph.D. diss., University of Kentucky.

Milner, George R.

1998   *The Cahokia Chiefdom: The Archaeology of a Mississippian Society*. Smithsonian Institution Press, Washington, DC.

1999   Warfare in Prehistoric and Early Historic Eastern North America. *Journal of Archaeological Research* 7:105–151.

2000   Palisaded Settlements in Prehistoric Eastern North America. In *City Walls*, edited by J. D. Tracy, 46–70. Cambridge University Press, Cambridge.

2005   Nineteenth-Century Arrow Wounds and Perceptions of Prehistoric Warfare. *American Antiquity* 70(1): 144–156.

Milner George R., G. Chaplin, and E. Zavodny

2013   Conflict and Societal Change in Late Prehistoric Eastern North America. *Evolutionary Anthropology* 22:96–102.

Mindeleff, Cosmos

1900   Localization of Tusayan Clans. In *Nineteenth Annual Report of the Bureau of American Ethnology* 19:639–653. Smithsonian Institution, Washington, DC.

Morgan, Lewis H.

1881   Houses and House-Life of the American Aborigines. In *Contributions to North American Ethnology, Volume IV*. United States Geological Survey, Washington, DC.

Myers, William E.

1928   Indian Trails of the Southeast. In *Forty-Second Annual Report of the Bureau of American Ethnology, 1924–25*. Smithsonian Institution, Washington, DC.

Phillips, Philip, James A. Ford, and James B. Griffin

1951   *Archaeological Survey in the Lower Mississippi Alluvial Valley, 1940–1947*. Papers of the Peabody Museum of Archaeology and Ethnology 25, Harvard University, Cambridge, MA.

Pollack, David, and A. Gwynn Henderson

2015   Fort Ancient Public Structures. In *Building the Past: Prehistoric Wooden Post Architecture in the Ohio Valley–Great Lakes*, edited by Brian Redmond and Robert Gehheimer, 295–320. University Press of Florida, Gainesville.

Pollack, David, A. Gwynn Henderson, and Christopher T. Begley

2002   Fort Ancient/Mississippian Interaction on the Northeastern Periphery. *Southeastern Archaeology* 21:206–220.

Prentiss, Anna Marie, Natasha Lyons, Lucille E. Harris, Melisse R. P. Burns, and Terrence M. Godin

2007   The Emergence of Status Inequity in Intermediate Scale Societies: A Demographic and Socio-economic History of the Keatley Creek Site, British Columbia. *Journal of Anthropological Archaeology* 26:299–327.

Rautman, Alison E.

2016   "Circling the Wagons" and Community Formation: Interpreting Circular Villages in the Archaeological Record. *World Archaeology* 48:125–143.

Reichel-Dolmatoff, G.

1965   *Excavaciones Arqueologicas en Puerto Hormiga (Departamento de Bolivar).* Universidad de los Andes, Bogota.

1971   Early Pottery from Colombia. *Archaeology* 24:338–345.

1985   *Monsu: Un Sitio Arqueologico.* Banco Popular, Bogota.

Saunders, Joe W., Rolfe D. Mandel, C. Garth Sampson, Charles M. Allen, E. Thurman Allen, Daniel A. Bush, James K. Feathers, Kristen J. Gremillion, C. T. Hallmark, H. Edwin Jackson, Jay K. Johnson, Reca Jones, Roger T. Saucier, Gary L. Stringer, and Malcolm F. Vidrine

2007   Watson Brake: A Middle Archaic mound complex in Northeast Louisiana. *American Antiquity* 70(4): 631–668.

Saunders, Rebecca, and Mike Russo, eds.

2002   *The Fig Island Complex (38CH42): Coastal Adaptation and the Question of Ring Function in the Late Archaic.* South Carolina Department of Archives and History, Columbia.

Steward, J. H.

1937   Ecological Aspects of Southwestern Society. *Anthropos* 32:87–104.

1938   Basin-Plateau Aboriginal Socio-political Groups. *Bureau of American Ethnology Bulletin* 120.

Stuiver M., and P. J. Reimer

1993   Extended 14C Data Base and Revised CALIB 3.0 14C Age Calibration Program. *Radiocarbon* 35(1): 215–230.

Stuiver, M., P. J. Reimer, and R. W. Reimer

2017   CALIB 7.1 [WWW program], http://calib.org.

Summers, Lewis P.

1929   *The Expedition of Batts and Fallam: A Journey from Virginia to beyond the Appalachian Mountains, September, 1621.* Electronic version by Donald Chestnut, 2000. http://donchesnut.com/genealogy/pages/battsandfallamjournal.pdf.

Thompson, Victor D.

2007   Articulating Activity Areas and Formation Processes at the Sapelo Island Shell Ring Complex. *Southeastern Archaeology* 26:91–107.

2010   The Rhythms of Space-Time and the Making of Monuments and Places during the Archaic. In *Trend, Tradition, and Turmoil: What Happened to the Southeastern Archaic?* edited by David Hurst Thomas and Matthew Sanger, 217–227. Anthropological Papers No. 93, American Museum of Natural History, New York.

Thompson, Victor, Matthew Reynolds, Brian Haley, Richard Jefferies, Jay Johnson, and
Catherine Humphries

2004   The Sapelo Shell Rings Site: Remote Sensing on a Georgia Sea Island. *Southeastern Archaeology* 23:192–201.

VanDerwarker, Amber, and Bruce Idol

2008   Rotten Food and Ritual Behavior: Late Woodland Plant Foodways and Special Purpose Features at Buzzard Rock II, Virginia (44RN2/70). *Southeastern Archaeology* 27(1): 61–77.

Virginia Division of State Archaeology

2016   http://dhr.virginia.gov/arch_DHR/archaeo_index.htm.

Willey, G. R.

1953   *Prehistoric Settlement Patterns in the Virù Valley, Peru*. Bureau of American Ethnology Bulletin 155. Smithsonian Institution, Washington, DC.

Wüst, Irmhild, and Cristiana Barreto

1999   The Ring Villages of Central Brazil: A Challenge for Amazon Archaeology. *Latin American Antiquity* 10:3–23.

Wymer, Dee Anne

1993   Culture Change and Subsistence: The Middle Woodland and Late Woodland Transition in the Mid-Ohio Valley. In *Foraging and Farming in the Eastern Woodlands*, edited by C. Margaret Scarry, 138–156. University Press of Florida. Gainesville.

Yeager, Jason, and Marcello Canuto

2000   Introducing an Archaeology of Communities. In *The Archaeology of Communities: A New World Perspective*, edited by M. Canuto and J. Yeager, 1–15. Routledge, London.

10

The Power of Powhatan Towns

Socializing Manitou in the Algonquian Chesapeake

MARTIN D. GALLIVAN, CHRISTOPHER J. SHEPHARD,
AND JESSICA A. JENKINS

In 1608, the residents of Quiyoughcohanock (KWEE-aw-kuh-HAAN-awk), a Powhatan settlement on the James River, hosted a Huskanaw—a rite of passage that transformed boys into men (Smith 1986b:171–172; Strachey 1953:98–100; White 1998). Virginia Algonquian communities staged Huskanaw rites periodically within different communities throughout the lower Chesapeake. The Huskanaw at Quiyoughcohanock offers a glimpse at key cultural categories and social dynamics behind the power of villages in the Powhatan core, an area that includes the tidal portions of the James and York Rivers (Figure 10.1). In this chapter we briefly summarize the Huskanaw and two other colonial-era events relevant to the power of Powhatan places, before turning to the archaeological record of villages in the Algonquian Chesapeake. Powhatan villages during the seventeenth century were centers of considerable authority, raising questions relevant to this volume: How was power structured and practiced in these settings? How did Powhatan settlements initially become powerful? With a substantial colonial-era archive and an archaeological record spanning the colonial/precolonial divide, the Powhatan past presents the opportunity to pursue a "deep historical anthropology" attentive to place-making, power, and politics at the village scale (Cobb 2005).

Our goal here is to further understanding of a *Powhatan* theory of power and to identify links between this ideology and the deep history of villages in the lower Chesapeake. During the early colonial era, riverside settlements in the Chesapeake were centers of social life from the spring planting through fall harvest feasts. Larger villages—referred to as "towns" by English colonists—housed 100 to 200 residents, while other smaller farmsteads dotted the area's riverfront terraces (Turner and Opperman 1993; Smith 1986b:162). Towns typically spread across 5 to

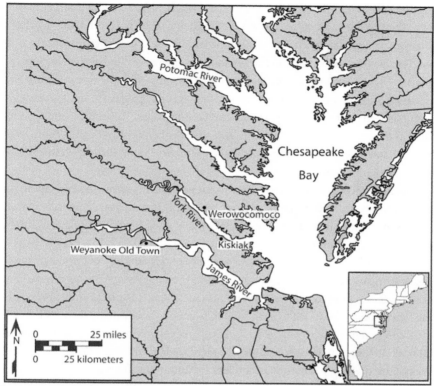

Figure 10.1. Lower Chesapeake region and sites in the study.

10 ha of river floodplains and overlooking bluffs, and some included palisades and ditch enclosures with more concentrated areas of settlement. *Weroances*—men and women described by colonists as "commanders" or "war captains"—resided in towns labeled by colonists as "Kings' Houses" (Smith 1986b:174). The Powhatan chiefdom consisted of over 30 Kings' Houses in Tidewater Virginia that fell under the sway of Wahunsenacawh, also known as Powhatan, in the years before Jamestown's settlement in 1607. A King's House was not, in fact, a single elite structure but was instead a dispersed riverfront community.

Kings' Houses and other Powhatan towns offer another context in which to consider the nature of power dynamics in Native North American village societies. As places where communities of Algonquians resided and interacted regularly, Powhatan towns often had continuous occupational histories stretching back to the thirteenth century AD when large, permanent communities first appeared across the Coastal Plain and Piedmont regions (Gallivan 2003; Rountree and Turner 2002). Powhatan towns do, however, diverge in one important sense from the conception of villages offered by Thompson and Birch in the introduction to this volume. During the early colonial era, most residents departed from their riverfront towns to forage in upland areas during the summer while their crops were maturing. Families dispersed again in the late fall after the harvest to hunt in the forested interior (Rountree 1989:45). In fact, the Powhatan appear in the documentary and archaeological records as both highly mobile—traveling regularly along waterways and upland to hunt—and deeply rooted to riverine places. This combination of mobility and emplacement heightens the importance of understanding the role played by Powhatan towns as nodal sites for the reproduction and transformation of social structures in the region.

Previous efforts to characterize Powhatan political life have relied on chiefdom models emphasizing weroances' control over staple production (especially maize) and wealth items (including copper gorgets and shell beads) that financed their elite status (e.g., Binford 1964; Potter 1993; Turner 1976). While probably correct in their broad outlines, these models offer little regarding the cultural categories and historical processes specific to the Algonquian Chesapeake, as others have noted (Hantman 1990). Drawing from other scholars' historical anthropology of the Powhatan world (Gleach 1997; Williamson 2003), we pursue the idea that the early colonial history highlights a recurring process whereby dangerously powerful outside forces, materials, and people were socialized within Powhatan towns. We suggest that a key Algonquian concept for understanding this process is "manitou"—the vital spiritual force manifest in powerful people, animals, objects, and places (Bragdon 1996:184; Jones 1905; Shephard 2017:74–79). Weroances and priests of the early seventeenth-century Chesapeake orchestrated the process of socializing manitou in different ways, and their ability to do so appears to have been central to the power of Kings' Houses. As detailed in the following pages, archaeological evidence of ditches, palisades, feasting, and ceremony within three Kings' Houses in the James and York River drainages points toward similar power dynamics with a deep history in the lower Chesapeake, extending back to at least the thirteenth century AD.

The Huskanaw Ceremony

The Huskanaw ceremony at Quiyoughcohanock commenced with feasting at the edge of the town during which initiates were painted white and instructed by sacred practitioners who were painted black and adorned with antlers (White 1998:138). For several days the boys danced around a circuit measuring a quarter-mile, led by a weroance and encouraged by repeated beatings. The initiates were subsequently painted black, given hallucinogens, and brought deep into the forest. There they were confined, living nearly naked in all types of weather, in a pen fashioned from a bentwood framework. After nine months, the surviving boys were reborn into village life, where they reportedly remembered nothing of their former lives (Beverley 1947:209).

The Huskanaw transformed boys into *quioccosuks*, men who embodied a divine status through spiritual contact orchestrated by antler-wearing men and signaled by black, a color associated with danger and death (Gerard 1907; White 1998:140–141). Powhatan priests were reportedly "able to make a truer judgment of things" due to their considered instruction in the region's history and their considerable knowledge of the natural world (Beverley 1947:213). At the same time, they alone were able to communicate with otherworldly actors whose voices were inaccessible to the unqualified ear. Manipulating manitou, or spiritual potencies that flowed through particular places, persons, and objects, priests wielded transformative capacities that guided the making and remaking of the Powhatan sociopolitical world (Crosby 1988; Haefeli 2007). Manifested in the marvelous, the beautiful, and the dangerous, manitou hints at a Virginia Algonquian understanding of the world without the same distinctions between culture and nature, the animate and inanimate, the powerful and passive drawn by the English colonists like Smith (Shephard 2017:74–79). Boys became quioccosuks through a ritual process closely linked to places imbued with manitou— note the shared Algonquian root in the terms "quioccosuks" and "Quiyoughcohanock." The Huskanaw ceremony at Quiyoughcohanock illustrates the role that select towns played as sites for the production of ideology and the reproduction of society. Spatial components of this process appear to have been important. The initial stage of the Huskanaw ritual occurred at the town's boundary with the forest edge and was centered on a large circular track that enclosed a series of dances, feasts, and other rites.

Werowocomoco and the Tributary Economy

During the same year that the Quiyoughcohanock hosted the Huskanaw, paramount chief Powhatan invited John Smith and other English colonists to visit him at Werowocomoco (WAYR-uh-wah-KOH-muh-koh). Werowocomoco was Powhatan's primary residence and the political center of his polity (Smith 1986a:63–79, 1986c:215–217). Virginia Algonquians referred to Powhatan as the *Mamanatowick* (muh-mahn-uh-TOH-wihk), the very embodiment of manitou (Strachey 1953:56). Smith reported that Virginia Algonquians viewed Powhatan not only as a king, but as half a god (Smith 1986b:174). Powhatan acted as a mediator of material and immaterial worlds, his power stemming not only from his ability to socialize dangerous objects but also to socialize strangers, remaking them into vessels through which manitou flowed. Manitou allowed quioccosuks and weroances to engage with powerful places and objects that would otherwise cause harm.

When John Smith arrived at Werowocomoco, Powhatan reminded the colonist that he was now a Powhatan weroance (Smith 1986a:63–79, 1986c:215–217). The colonists were no longer to be considered strangers, but *Powhatans*. As Powhatan's people, the colonists would be provided gifts of corn, women, and land. "The next day," wrote Smith, "the King conducted mee to the River, shewwe me his Canowes, and described unto me how hee sent them over the Baye, for tribute: and also what Countries paid him Beads, Copper, or Skins" (Smith 1986a:69).

In Powhatan's representation of this political landscape, the movement of canoes across the estuary traced flows of gifts from the edges of the world to Werowocomoco at its center and outward again to communities subsumed within the Powhatan orbit, including Jamestown for a time. A similar flow of valued objects occurred within other Kings' Houses in the Powhatan world, if on a more modest scale. Powhatan used his canoe fleet at Werowocomoco to index linkages in the political economy. The most highly valued objects traveling through these estuarine pathways—shell beads and copper—moved from the edges of the Chesapeake to its center at Werowocomoco. Shell bead production was concentrated in locations on the Eastern Shore and along the Atlantic fringes of Powhatan's influence. While shell flowed from the east, red copper moved in the opposite direction, coming from western outcrops near the Blue Ridge Mountains or from the northwest and more distant sources along the Great Lakes (Hantman 1993). These materials flowed into chiefs' storehouses and, from there, on to Werowocomoco through tributary networks, then again outward through the politics of gift giving. Quite distinct from a labor theory of value, these objects were desired, in large part, because of their uncanny origins. Shell and copper came from other worlds that were difficult to access and located underwater or high in the mountains. Where in other chiefly societies the value of wealth objects stemmed from control over specialized craft production, imported shell and copper ornamentation transcended physical labor and other demands associated with production for the Powhatan.

Palisades and Enclosures

A third reference from the colonial era that helps us understand the power of Powhatan towns comes from English colonist Robert Beverley. Beverley (1947:177) wrote that some towns in the Chesapeake were surrounded by a palisade measuring 10 to 12 feet in height:

Martin D. Gallivan, Christopher J. Shephard & Jessica A. Jenkins

They often encompass their whole town; but for the most part only their king's houses, and as many others as they judge sufficient to harbor all their people when an enemy comes against them. They never fail to secure within their palisade all their religious relics, and the remains of their princes. Within this inclosure, they likewise take care to have a supply of water, and to make a place for a fire, which they frequently dance round with great solemnity.

In this description, palisaded enclosures kept outside forces at bay and contained materials, ancestors, and events integral to the social order. The circular villages that proliferated in southwest Virginia between AD 1300 and 1500 included a similar configuration of village spaces (see Jefferies, this volume). At times, a concentric series of stockade walls and ditches surrounded the sacred icons, ancestors, and fire within. Tributary networks brought powerful objects, including copper and shell beads, across these boundaries and into these spaces from the outside world. Infused with manitou, the improper handling of these objects could render them antisocial and dangerous. Weroances socialized these outside materials before moving them outward through gift pathways to the Powhatan world.

Powhatan did much the same to colonist John Smith—a dangerous outsider (Smith 1986a:53, 1986c:213–214, 1986d:150–151). Powhatan, the Mamanatowick, first threatened to execute Smith at Werowocomoco, then declared that the colonist would be allowed to live as one of his weroances. The Huskanaw also reincorporated dangerous forces into Kings' Houses through a rite of passage. Initiates were first separated from their old status at the edge of the town, painted black, and held in a liminal status in the woods, and then brought back into the world with a new status. In this process of socializing forces from outside, antler-wearing priests—quioccosuks—played a central role.

Rather than simply being powerful individuals in their own right, the abilities of weroances and priests to socialize dangerous forces, objects, and people evidently drew from the social and spatial *contexts* in which people and objects exhibited their transformative capacities. Such "instrumentalities through which individuals or groups direct or circumscribe the actions of others within determinate settings" are what Eric Wolf (1999:5) termed "organizational" or "tactical" power. One of four power modalities in his typology, organizational power differs from the authority vested in a religious practitioner, the power of a political official to impose his will on another, and the structural force of values, ethics, and ideology. Powhatan towns—large, permanent, horticultural communities along the rivers of the Chesapeake estuary—represented not only the *settings* where these processes played out. They also played a role as social agents in Powhatan power dynamics involving the incorporation of dangerous outside forces. Within Kings' Houses, Powhatan weroances and priests practiced a tactical power largely dependent on the existence of towns with long histories of settlement.

The Archaeology of Riverine Towns in the Chesapeake

Some of the historical processes behind Powhatan power may be seen in the archaeology of large, complex settlements that began to appear one to two centuries after the adoption of horticulture in AD 1100 (Potter 1993:81–87). Research at the Werowocomoco site has focused on tracing the site's deep history and on its changing place within Virginia Algonquian landscapes of the past and present (Gallivan 2003, 2007, 2016). Circa AD 1200, residents cleared forests in the area, planted gardens, erected houses along the riverfront, and constructed a small ditch enclosure in the interior of the site (Figure 10.2). During the fourteenth century AD, residents excavated a much larger earthwork enclosure with two parallel trenches surrounding the earlier one. Separated from residential spaces along Purtan Bay by a considerable distance of 400 m, these concentric ditches surrounded an area containing nonlocal ceramics, smoking pipe fragments, and several architectural structures. The largest of these structures dates to the early seventeenth century and contained pieces of copper traded from James Fort. The location, layout, and materials associated with this building suggest that it was in all likelihood Powhatan's residence.

This archaeological sequence indicates that the settlement represented a prominent Native town with a history of large landscape features from the thirteenth century through the early seventeenth century. Well before Powhatan established a regional chiefdom centered on Werowocomoco, the town contained extensive ditch features marking an area where Powhatan eventually lived. Like Quiyough-cohanock, Werowocomoco emerges from the early colonial narratives as a place of ceremony, with events that featured antler-wearers and men painted black. In fact, the town's name translates as "place of the antler-wearers" (Strachey 1953:189). Werowocomoco's spaces included curving trenches that measured roughly a quarter-mile in diameter situated along the boundaries of the settlement at the forest edge, landscape features that resemble the ritual circuits around which Huskanaw initiates traveled. At Quiyoughcohanock, such areas, located at the edges of settled space, held the first stage of a rite of passage performed by antler-wearing men painted black. A similar association with quioccosuks and the Huskanaw appears likely for Werowocomoco.

Excavated by an avocational archaeologist during the 1970s and 1980s, the Weyanoke Old Town site has only begun to see attention from professional archaeologists (Blick 2010; Gregory 1980; Gregory 1986). Weyanoke was part of the

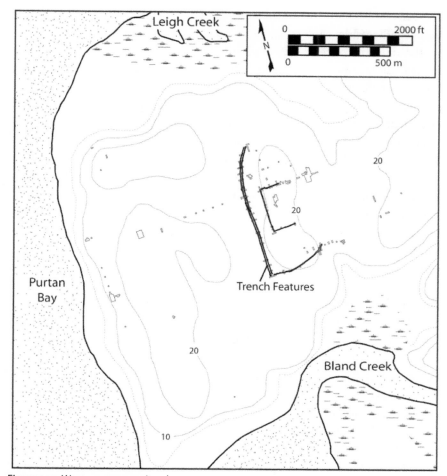

Figure 10.2. Werowocomoco site plan.

Powhatan chiefdom and figured prominently in early colonial encounters with the English. The Weyanoke resided on both sides of the James upstream from James Fort. John Smith's *Map of Virginia* depicted a Weanock "King's House" on the *north* side of the James, though other sources indicate that the town was actually on the *south* shore in the vicinity of the Weyanoke Old Town site (Mook 1943).

Our preliminary assessment of the site records indicates that the site contained 123 dog burials as well as a series of large (3–4 m diameter) pit features containing dense concentrations of deer bone, fish scales, charcoal, and highly decorated ceramics (Figure 10.3). These features are concentrated on one side of two parallel ditches with dimensions similar to those of the ditches identified at the Werowocomoco site. We have only begun to interpret the site's chronology and its spaces, though radiocarbon dating suggests occupations between AD 1000 and 1300.

The unusual concentration of dog burials, some with indications of head trauma, call to mind the range of ritualized practices involving dog sacrifices and canid symbolism by Native groups in the postcontact Eastern Woodlands. For example, the Midewiwin ceremony celebrated by a range of Algonquian groups began with a dog sacrifice to placate dangerously powerful spirit beings—Manitos (Cook 2012:504). Another ethnographic parallel may be seen in the White Dog Sacrifice practiced by some Iroquoian groups during the historic period (Becker and Lainey 2013; Kerber 1997; Tooker 1965). The White Dog Sacrifice was part of the Midwinter Feast in the Five Nations Iroquois. The sacrifice involved the killing by strangulation of pure white dogs. Dog burials (usually in much smaller numbers than we see at the Weyanoke Old Town site) appear within Algonquian and Iroquoian sites across the Northeast (Fitzgerald 2009). Eyewitness accounts and historical ethnography indicate that Algonquian, Iroquoian, and Siouan groups sacrificed dogs in a range of circumstances during the historic era. Running through many of these references, though, is a similar underlying purpose of propitiation (Oberholtzer 2002:8).

It is too early in our analysis to make any sweeping conclusions about Weyanoke Old Town, though it is striking that portions of the site are bounded by parallel ditch features remarkably similar to those identified at Werowocomoco. The ditches at Weyanoke Old Town are alongside features suggesting feasting and the ritualized sacrifice of dogs.

Another King's House and part of the Powhatan chiefdom, Kiskiak is located 12 miles downstream from Werowocomoco on the York River (Gallivan 2016:79–93). Spread across the bluffs overlooking Indian Field Creek, Kiskiak contains several shell middens and adjacent residential structures. While most of the Kiskiak site consists of light artifact densities spread across riverine bluffs, one area of the site contains Late Woodland deposits in much higher concentrations. Our testing in this area of the site has uncovered two parallel ditch features adjacent to a palisade line. Radiocarbon dates indicate that the features were constructed early in the thirteenth century AD.

An analysis of the oysters recovered from Kiskiak's ditches indicates that they were all harvested from subtidal reefs offshore (Jenkins and Gallivan 2016). Most of the oysters deposited in Kiskiak's shell midden, by contrast, were harvested from intertidal reefs found in the shallow waters of Indian Field Creek. The subtidal oysters recovered from the ditches are substantially larger and more deeply cupped than the intertidal oysters recovered from shell middens, and their source reefs are more difficult to access than the intertidal sources near shore. There are

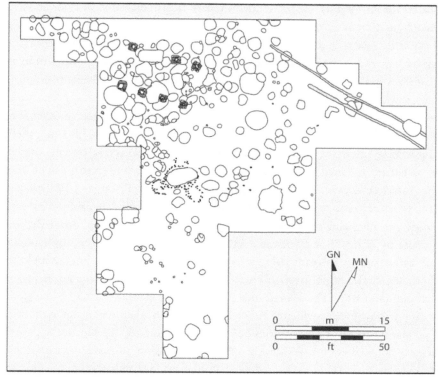

Figure 10.3. Weyanoke Old Town site plan.

clear indications that the Kiskiak made use of the subtidal reefs offshore more selectively than other parts of the oyster fishery. The archaeological evidence indicates that a part of the Kiskiak site was marked by parallel ditch features and a palisade line constructed circa AD 1200. The dense concentration of oyster shells recovered from one of the ditches suggests evidence of a large-scale feasting event.

Conclusion

Taken together, the archaeological evidence from the three Kings' Houses summarized above points toward important developments that played out on a regional scale in Tidewater Virginia. Circa AD 1200, large horticultural towns appeared along the Coastal Plain portions of the James and York Rivers for the first time (Gallivan 2003). While perhaps not as dramatic as the monumental architecture of a Mississippian center or the shell mounds of the Archaic and Woodland Southeast (see Wallis, this volume; Thompson, this volume), the ditch features that appeared within Virginia Tidewater towns record the mobilization of labor and the reconfiguration of space on an impressive scale. Something new was happening in these settlements—a historical process of place-making that differed in important ways from what came before. Ditch boundaries and enclosures appear within at least three settlements that, by the early seventeenth century, had become political centers within the Powhatan chiefdom.

Similar concentric boundaries and circular arrangements appear in other Virginia Algonquian settings before and after European contact, highlighting their importance for these communities. They appear in collective burials known as ossuaries, in dance circles used in public ceremonies, and in maps depicting the Native landscape. In fact, circles appear so often that Margaret Williamson (2003:226–228) has suggested that they provided a basis for Powhatan social categories, emphasizing relationships between center and periphery. Similarly, the dichotomy of inside and outside evidently served as an organizing principle in Powhatan society. The early colonial-era effort to incorporate the English into the Powhatan circle, ethnohistorian Fred Gleach (1997:113–115) has argued, required that the colonists first be refined and civilized.

The archaeological evidence indicates that Virginia Algonquians set in motion a pivotal transformation centuries before colonial contact relevant to the power of early colonial-era towns. Modest shifts in population, subsistence, and ritualized spaces circa AD 1200 opened new affordances for kinship, feasting, and the ceremonial cycle. The resulting towns generated new modalities of power, which were eventually leveraged by the weroances and priests of the Powhatan chiefdom during the 1500s and early 1600s.

Connecting the power dynamics of early colonial towns in the Powhatan region to the cultural significance of ditches and enclosures constructed centuries earlier is neither simple nor direct. There are, however, indications that during the early colonial era, the power of towns may be linked to the socialization of objects, people, and forces coming from outside the community by weroances and priests. By harnessing manitou, a dangerous spiritual force in the Algonquian world, Powhatan religious practitioners and political leaders exercised a tactical power grounded within Kings' Houses. During the early colonial era, the Powhatan theory of power centered on the capacity of weroances and priests to socialize people and objects within riverine towns. Constructed 400 years prior to this, the ditch features associated with feasting and ceremony suggest physical and semiotic boundaries that defined inside and outside. If the power of towns in the Algonquian Chesapeake may indeed be linked to the movement of outside objects and people across these boundaries, then this process began centuries before the colonial era in towns that included Werowocomoco, Kiskiak, and Weyanoke.

References Cited

Becker, Marshall J., and Jonathan C. Lainey
2013   *The White Dog Sacrifice: A Post-1800 Rite with an Ornamental Use for Wampum*. Transactions of the American Philosophical Society 103. American Philosophical Society, Philadelphia.

Beverley, Robert
1947 [1705]   *The History and Present State of Virginia*. University of North Carolina Press, Chapel Hill.

Binford, Lewis R.
1964   Archaeological and Ethnohistorical Investigation of Cultural Diversity and Progressive Development among Aboriginal Cultures of Coastal Virginia and North Carolina. Ph.D. diss., University of Michigan.

Blick, Jeffrey P.
2010   New Radiometric Dates and Canine-Human Burial Ceremonialism at Weyanoke Old Town, (44PG51), Virginia. *Quarterly Bulletin of the Archeological Society of Virginia* 68(3): 103–132.

Bragdon, Kathleen Joan
1996   *Native People of Southern New England, 1500–1650*. University of Oklahoma Press, Norman.

Cobb, Charles R.
2005   Archaeology and the "Savage Slot": Displacement and Emplacement in the Premodern World. *American Anthropologist* 107(4): 563–574.

Cook, Robert A.
2012   Dogs of War: Potential Social Institutions of Conflict, Healing, and Death in a Fort Ancient Village. *American Antiquity* 77(3): 498–523.

Crosby, Constance A.
1988   From Myth to History, or Why King Phillip's Ghost Walks Abroad. In *The Recovery of Meaning: Historical Archaeology in the Eastern United States*, edited by Mark P. Leone and Parker B. Potter, 183–210. Smithsonian Institution Press, Washington, DC.

Fitzgerald, Jennifer A.
2009   Late Woodland Dog Ceremonialism on the Chickahominy and Beyond. *Journal of Middle Atlantic Archaeology* 25:105–110.

Gallivan, Martin D.
2003   *James River Chiefdoms: The Rise of Social Inequality in the Chesapeake*. University of Nebraska Press, Lincoln.
2007   Powhatan's Werowocomoco: Constructing Place, Polity, and Personhood in the Chesapeake, C.E. 1200–C.E. 1609. *American Anthropologist* 109(1): 85–100.
2016   *The Powhatan Landscape: An Archaeological History of the Algonquian Chesapeake*. University Press of Florida, Gainesville.

Gerard, William R.
1907   Virginia Indian's Contribution to English. *American Anthropologist, n.s.* 9:87–112.

Gleach, Frederic W.
1997   *Powhatan's World and Colonial Virginia: A Conflict of Cultures*. Studies in the Anthropology of North American Indians. University of Nebraska Press, Lincoln.

Gregory, Eve S.

1986 Weyanoke Old Town. *Quarterly Bulletin of the Archeological Society of Virginia* 41(2): 49–71.

Gregory, Leverette B.

1980 The Hatch Site: A Preliminary Report (Prince George County, Virginia). *Quarterly Bulletin of the Archeological Society of Virginia* 34(4): 239–248.

Haefeli, Evan

2007 On First Contact and Apotheosis: Manitou and Men in North America. *Ethnohistory* 54(3): 407–443.

Hantman, Jeffrey L.

1990 Between Powhatan and Quirank: Reconstructing Monacan Culture and History in the Context of Jamestown. *American Anthropologist* 92(3): 676–690.

1993 Powhatan's Relations with the Piedmont Monacans. In *Powhatan Foreign Relations, 1500–1722*, edited by Helen C. Rountree, 94–111. University Press of Virginia, Charlottesville.

Jenkins, Jessica, and Martin Gallivan

2016 Shell on Earth: An Archeomalacological Approach to Precolonial Powhatan Social Life. Paper presented at the Southeastern Archaeological Conference, Athens, GA.

Jones, William

1905 The Algonkin Manitou. *Journal of American Folklore* 18(70): 183–190.

Kerber, Jordan E.

1997 Native American Treatment of Dogs in Northeastern North America: Archaeological and Ethnohistorical Perspectives. *Archaeology of Eastern North America* 25:81–95.

Mook, Maurice A.

1943 Virginia Ethnology from an Early Relation. *William and Mary College Quarterly Historical Magazine* 23(2): 101–129.

Oberholtzer, Cath

2002 Fleshing Out the Evidence: From Archaic Dog Burials to Historic Dog Feasts. *Ontario Archaeology* 73:3–14.

Potter, Stephen R.

1993 *Commoners, Tribute, and Chiefs: The Development of Algonquian Culture in the Potomac Valley.* University Press of Virginia, Charlottesville.

Rountree, Helen C.

1989 *The Powhatan Indians of Virginia: Their Traditional Culture.* University of Oklahoma Press, Norman.

Rountree, Helen C., and E. Randolph Turner

2002 *Before and after Jamestown: Virginia's Powhatans and Their Predecessors.* University Press of Florida, Gainesville.

Shephard, Christopher J.

2017 The Materiality of Authority: Ornamental Objects and Negotiations of Sovereignty in the Algonquian Middle Atlantic (A.D. 900–1680). Ph.D. diss., College of William and Mary.

Smith, John

1986a [1608] A True Relation. In *The Complete Works of Captain John Smith (1580–1631)*, edited by Philip L. Barbour, 1:5–117. 3 vols. University of North Carolina Press, Chapel Hill.

1986b [1608]   A Map of Virginia. In *The Complete Works of Captain John Smith (1580–1631)*, edited by Philip L. Barbour, 1:119–189. 3 vols. University of North Carolina Press, Chapel Hill.

1986c [1612]   The Proceedings. In *The Complete Works of Captain John Smith (1580–1631)*, edited by Philip L. Barbour, 2:191–279. 3 vols. University of North Carolina Press, Chapel Hill.

1986d [1623]   Generall Historie of Virginia. *In The Complete Works of Captain John Smith (1580–1631)*, edited by Philip L. Barbour, 2:5–475. 3 vols. University of North Carolina Press, Chapel Hill.

Strachey, William

1953 [1612]   *The Historie of Travell into Virginia Britania Expressing the Cosmographie and Commodities of the Country Togither with the Manners and Customes of the People.* Printed for the Hakluyt Society, London.

Tooker, Elisabeth

1965   The Iroquois White Dog Sacrifice in the Latter Part of the Eighteenth Century. *Ethnohistory* 12(2): 129–140.

Turner, E. Randolph, III

1976   An Archaeological and Ethnohistorical Study of the Evolution of Rank Societies in the Virginia Coastal Plain. Ph.D. diss., Pennsylvania State University.

Turner, E. Randolph, III, and Anthony F. Opperman

1993   Archaeological Manifestations of the Virginia Company Period: A Summary of Surviving Powhatan and English Settlements in Tidewater Virginia, circa 1607–1624. In *The Archaeology of 17th-Century Virginia*, edited by Theodore R. Reinhart and Dennis J. Pogue, 67–104. Dietz Press, Richmond, VA.

White, William

1998 [1613]   The Black Boys Ceremony. In *Jamestown Narratives: Eyewitness Accounts of the Virginia Colony, the First Decade, 1607–1617*, edited by Edward W. Haile, 138–141. RoundHouse, Champlain, VA.

Williamson, Margaret H.

2003   *Powhatan Lords of Life and Death: Command and Consent in Seventeenth-Century Virginia.* University of Nebraska Press, Lincoln.

Wolf, Eric

1999   *Envisioning Power: Ideologies of Dominance and Crisis.* University of California Press, Berkeley.

11

From Nucleated Villages to Dispersed Networks

Transformations in Seneca Haudenosaunee (Iroquois)
Community Structure, circa AD 1669–1779

KURT A. JORDAN

This chapter discusses a series of sequentially constructed villages[1] occupied by
members of the Seneca Nation, *Onöndowa'ga:'* in their own language, who were
part of the *Hodinöhsö:ni'* (Haudenosaunee), or Iroquois, Confederacy in what is
today western New York State.[2] I examine fields of power that affected Seneca
communities in the seventeenth and eighteenth centuries, a period when archaeological data can be supplemented with textual and cartographic records penned
by Europeans and Americans. Documents greatly aid interpretation because they
include eyewitness descriptions of sites and can shed light on occupation spans,
inhabitants, alliances and antagonisms, and regional conditions. These sources,
of course, have their drawbacks (Galloway 2006:33–42), and details on Seneca
settlements are infrequent and inevitably are framed by the biases of the observer.
Nonetheless, the combination of textual and archaeological evidence permits
detailed and tightly dated reconstruction of Seneca settlement choices and their
relationship to internal and external power relations. The ability to precisely determine political-economic contexts for Seneca decisions about village placement,
defensibility, and internal arrangement may prove instructive to archaeologists
working in settings that lack associated documentary or oral-historical records.

The Senecas discussed in this chapter were long-standing farmers and villagers; their ancestors had adopted year-round, semipermanent villages of a
few hundred residents provisioned by staple agriculture, hunting, fishing, and
gathering by circa AD 1100 (Birch and Williamson, this volume). By the early
1600s, Senecas had adopted a settlement pattern of two large principal villages
housing 1,000–3,000 people each, surrounded by smaller satellite settlements of
a few hundred residents. The Senecas discussed in this chapter thus were aided

in dealing with the social complications of village life by an array of institutions that had helped large numbers of people to live in close quarters for centuries. As I show, the on-the-ground outcomes produced by these institutions exhibited a surprising degree of flexibility. Seneca settlements during 1669–1779 used a variety of forms, employing both nucleated and dispersed settlement plans, and only some sites were fortified.

By design, Haudenosaunee communities periodically relocated. The need for relocation was built into the settlement system, prompted by ecological conditions such as increasing distance to firewood sources and heightened levels of pest infestation (Engelbrecht 2003). Some scholars have retreated from the earlier view that soil depletion was the principal reason for relocation due to recent studies by agricultural scientists (e.g., Mt. Pleasant 2015). Communities also relocated for sociopolitical reasons, either as direct responses to invasion or due to shifts in regional political-economic conditions.

Wesley Bernardini describes similar relocation in the American Southwest as *serial migration,* noting that "the identity of a particular migrating group at any one point in time can be understood only as the cumulative product of a long and unique history of movements that preceded it" (2005:8). It is also useful to distinguish between the enduring *community* and the various *village sites* it occupied over time: the community continued even as particular sites were abandoned as active residential spaces (O'Gorman 2010). Given that many Haudenosaunee village moves were done over short distances—frequently only 2–8 km (Vandrei 1987:Table 3)—they cumulatively resulted in a mosaic of active, revisited, and abandoned sites. Ecologically, relocation over time produced regional-level anthropogenic landscapes (Gerard-Little 2017); culturally, the moves resulted in "villagescapes" (Fowles 2009) laden with the significant places, the stories, and the remains of the ancestors that accumulated as the community moved (Birch and Williamson 2015). It is also important to recognize that Haudenosaunee communities were not homogenous, as they included multiple kin groups that had the ability to attach and detach themselves from particular settlements (Wright 2006), as well as (on occasion) large numbers of incorporated outside individuals and groups (Jordan 2013, 2018; Lynch 1985).

Earlier scholars overvalued nucleated, palisaded hilltop settlements comprised of bark-covered longhouses, viewing them as the "climax" form of Northern Iroquoian culture, and saw any departure from this norm as evidence for social and cultural decline (see review in Jordan 2008). More recent study has critiqued this fixed model of "timeless, traditional" Iroquoian culture, and treats settlement reconfigurations as flexible, pragmatic responses to changes in ecological conditions and the regional balance of power (Jones 2008, 2010; Jones and Wood 2012; Jordan 2008, 2010; Ryan 2017). Newer work also emphasizes Haudenosaunee communities' ability to keep European settlers and installations to the margins of their territories (Jordan 2010, 2013; Parmenter 2010). Senecas, in particular, allowed substantial European installations no closer than Niagara and Oswego—each 75 km or more from a Seneca principal village—during the period examined here.

Thus, my discussion of power does not focus on indigenous responses to European colonialism; despite periodic setbacks, the Senecas in question during 1669–1779 were for the most part politically, economically, and culturally autonomous. The chapter instead draws attention to regional fields of power involving Senecas, Europeans, and indigenous allies and adversaries, and to Seneca internal dynamics, in particular to the community relocation process. While my earlier thinking viewed Seneca settlement transformation as an incredibly sensitive "barometer" for regional conditions—and it is—that position accorded little agency to the Senecas engaged in the hard labor of clearing land, building houses, erecting palisades, moving from site to site, and starting new agricultural fields. Here, I focus on the *lived experience* of settlement relocation as an arena for contentious decision making and the exercise of power (see Creese 2013; Silliman 2009).

Seneca Settlement Choices, circa 1669–1779

I review the sequence of Seneca settlement choices by presenting a series of "snapshots" set in a single calendar year. Some are based on primary-source descriptions of Seneca territory; others are keyed to the approximate dates of significant reconfigurations known through archaeological evidence. Pioneering avocational archaeologists Frederick Houghton, Charles Wray, and Harry Schoff formulated the general settlement pattern model and provided a preliminary sequence for Seneca sites (Houghton 1912; Wray 1973, 1983; Wray and Schoff 1953); subsequent work (e.g., Sempowski and Saunders 2001) has refined and tested their assumptions. I emphasize principal villages and smaller local satellites in the Seneca homelands; due to space constraints, I will not discuss what I have termed "extra-regional satellites" (Jordan 2010, 2013), those Seneca settlements located at some distance from the homeland. Extra-regional satellites illustrate another layer of the complexity of Seneca social lives but do not alter the model presented here. While site population estimates are contentious, as a rule of thumb nucleated sites from this era housed about 500 persons per hectare of residential space; it is difficult to estimate the population of residentially dispersed communities (see Jordan 2008:163–197).

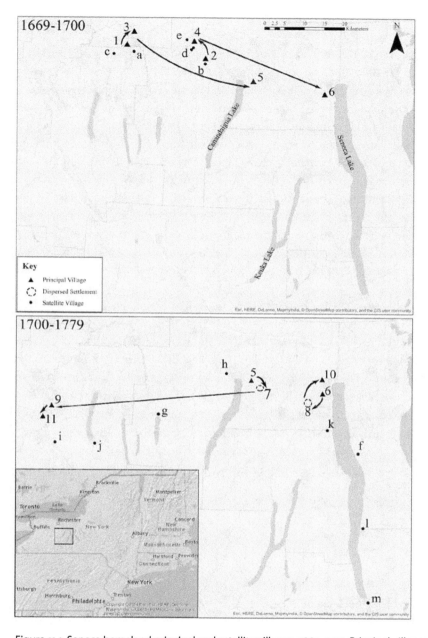

Figure 11.1. Seneca homeland principal and satellite villages, 1669–1779. Principal villages: 1, Dann; 2, Marsh; 3, Rochester Junction; 4, Ganondagan; 5, Snyder-McClure; 6, White Springs; 7, Huntoon; 8, New Ganechstage; 9, Fall Brook; 10, Kanadesaga; 11, Genesee Castle. Satellite villages: a, Menzis; b, Wheeler Station; c, Kirkwood; d, Cherry Street and Beal; e, Fort Hill; f, Kendaia; g, Honeoye; h, Canandaigua; i, Gathtsegwarohare; j, Conesus; k, Kashong; l, Condawhaw; m, Catherine's Town. Map prepared by Peregrine Gerard-Little.

1669

In 1669, the Sulpician priest René de Bréhant de Galinée documented a visit to Seneca territory and later made a map of his travels (Coyne 1903). The text and map do not agree on all details (Hamell 1980), but Galinée describes four or five Seneca settlements, consisting of two principal villages and at least two smaller local satellites. He normatively describes these communities as "nothing but a lot of cabins" surrounded by square wooden palisades of "poles 12 or 13 feet high" (Coyne 1903:23). Due to their lack of flanking bastions, Galinée thought the settlements were "not defensible" (1903:23). The principal sites Galinée observed presumably were the Dann and Marsh sites, while the satellites may have been at Menzis and Wheeler Station (Figure 11.1:Sites 1, 2, a, b).[3] These sites likely were founded in in the 1650s, one of them perhaps after its predecessor was destroyed by an invading force of Eries in 1654 (Thwaites 1959:41:81). At least three of these sites contained small Jesuit chapels, which had been established in 1668 (Hamell 1980:96–97).

Eric Jones describes the settings of Dann and Marsh as "unrestricted," on a broad hill and flat area, respectively (2008:Table 3.10). Vandrei (1987:Table 1) estimates the size of these sites at 5.1 ha and 6.1 ha, respectively, although these estimates likely encompass nonresidential spaces; his size estimate for the satellite at Menzis is 0.6 ha (1987:Table 1). Various excavations at the Dann site have confirmed the existence of a palisade, although most of the information contained in Charles Wray's map of the site (Ryan and Dewbury 2010:Figure 1), including the predominantly ovoid shape of the palisade, is extrapolated. The fortifications at Dann and Marsh may have made up for the sites' lack of natural defensibility; both are near watercourses and ample farmland. The Haudenosaunee at this time were engaged in active conflicts with indigenous neighbors, particularly the Susquehannocks living in what is now southern Pennsylvania, and had warred with the French as recently as 1667 (Parmenter 2010:130).

1677

In 1677, New York agent Wentworth Greenhalgh visited and documented two principal villages and two satellites in Seneca territory (Snow et al. 1996:191). In contrast to Galinée's account, Greenhalgh asserted that "none of their towns are stockadoed" (Snow et al. 1996:191). The principal villages likely were the Rochester Junction and Ganondagan[4] sites; the satellites are likely to have been at the Kirkwood and Beal sites (Figure 1:Sites 3, 4, c, d). Shovel-test survey across the entire Ganondagan site revealed its domestic precinct to be 3.7 ha in size (Hayes et al. 1978); Vandrei's (1987:Table 1) less precise estimates are 6.1 ha for Rochester Junction and 1.0 ha for Kirkwood. Jones describes Ganondagan's setting as a large ridgetop and Rochester Junction's as a large plateau; Beal and Kirkwood are described as being on a low hill and broad hill, respectively (Jones 2008:Table 3.10). Extensive excavations at Ganondagan through the years have not found traces of a palisade (Dean 1984).

These villages likely were established in the early-to-mid-1670s; Greenhalgh noted that Rochester Junction "has nott much cleared ground" (Snow et al. 1996:191), implying a more recent founding than for the other sites. Beal appears to have replaced another small eastern satellite that burned accidentally in 1671 (Thwaites 1959:55:79); this may have been at the close-by Cherry Street site (Figure 11.1:Site d). Chapels run by French Jesuits likely were present in at least three of these sites (Hamell 1980; Thwaites 1959:55:79). The lack of attention to fortification during the early 1670s founding of these sites may have been related to the pending defeat of the Susquehannocks, which took place in 1675 (Richter 1992:136).

1684

In 1680, the Haudenosaunee began a series of attacks on French-allied western Indian groups that initiated what historian Richard Aquila (1983) terms the "Twenty Years' War." In response to these assaults on their allies, a French force of almost 1,300 men led by Governor Joseph-Antoine le Fèbvre de La Barre left New France in July 1684, destined for Seneca territory (Parmenter 2010:175). Upon hearing rumors of the invasion, Jesuits fled the Seneca villages (O'Callaghan 1969:9:229), and the Senecas themselves constructed a fortified enclosure (O'Callaghan 1969:9:254, 261) on a steep-sided hilltop near Ganondagan called "Fort Hill" (Figure 11.1:Site e). Noted antiquarian Ephraim G. Squier mapped the fortification in 1848 (Figure 11.2), based on "the nature of the ground and the recollection of persons familiar with the site before it was disturbed by the plough" (Squier 1850:64, Plate XIV). Although the text on Squier's map indicates that the Fort Hill palisaded area enclosed 20 acres (8.1 ha), overlaying his map on a modern one shows that the palisade could not have been more than 3.2–4.0 ha in size.[5] Local historian Irving Coates found burned palisade posts eroding out of the side of Fort Hill in 1890 (Coates 1893). While other scholars have identified Fort Hill (somewhat implausibly) as a granary or pigpen, it is more likely that it was intended to be a fortified settlement for the consolidated eastern Seneca population (Jordan 2008:170). La Barre's force never made it, stalled by illness and Haudenosaunee opposition more than 120 km from the Seneca villages (Parmenter 2010:176–179), and Fort Hill never housed a substantial Seneca population.

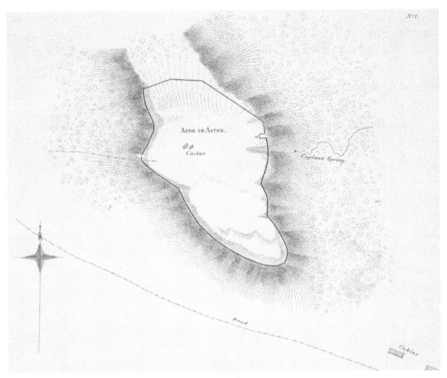

Figure 11.2. Ephraim G. Squier's 1848 map of the Fort Hill site (detail from Squier 1850:Plate XIV, No. 1). The cabins and road are nineteenth-century landmarks. Squier's 20 acre (8.1 ha) figure for the palisaded area is in error (see text). Image courtesy of Rare and Manuscript Collections, Cornell University Library.

1687

A second French invasion force of 2,100-plus men led by the Marquis de Denonville *did* make it to Seneca territory in 1687, with disastrous consequences (Parmenter 2010:190–195). Senecas burned their own villages in advance of French arrival, and Denonville's troops then destroyed what remained. Four Seneca settlements—two principals at the Rochester Junction and Ganondagan sites, and two satellites at Kirkwood and likely at Beal—and Fort Hill were obliterated, along with stored food and crops growing in fields (Figure 11.1:Sites 3, 4, c, d, e). Although Senecas and other Haudenosaunee had been at war with western groups since 1680, and the conflict was not going well for the Five Nations, three of the four Seneca communities destroyed in 1687 were not palisaded. The only fortification aside from Fort Hill described in the Denonville accounts was at the western satellite at Kirkwood (O'Callaghan 1969:9:367), which presumably had been erected since Greenhalgh's 1677 visit. Further, Senecas had not built any more than a few scattered structures at Fort Hill by the time Denonville's army arrived. Notably, Denonville's forces quickly left Seneca territory; their token effort to establish a fort at Niagara failed one year later (Parmenter 2010:202).

1688

The Denonville destruction generated major changes in Seneca settlements. Senecas lost their houses, growing and stored crops, material possessions, and seed stock. To protect their settlements, Senecas moved about 35 km southeast, away from Lake Ontario and toward their Cayuga allies. In doing so, they abandoned a region where they and their ancestors had modified surrounding environments since 1550, and moved to an area of unimproved land where no village-size populations had lived since the 1400s. During the move, the four homeland villages occupied in 1687 appear to have consolidated into just two principal settlements at Snyder-McClure and White Springs (Figure 11.1:Sites 5, 6).

A Cornell University excavation team under my direction has worked at the eastern White Springs principal village site since 2007 (Gerard-Little et al. 2012; Gerard-Little et al. 2016; Jordan and Gerard-Little 2019). Based on current evidence derived from shovel-testing, surface collection, and test unit and trench excavations across portions of the site, White Springs appears to have been a palisaded village of approximately 3.4 ha, somewhat smaller than its predecessor at Ganondagan. Given that satellite community populations may have coalesced with principal village residents at White Springs, the site likely was more crowded than Ganondagan had been. One excavation trench yielded what Cornell researchers interpret to be a possible palisade segment; the posts used there are smaller than those from earlier Seneca fortifications, suggesting that White Springs residents used new construction techniques with more substantial cross-pieces. Based on this segment and the distribution of domestic artifacts, the best fit for at least part of the palisade shape at White Springs is ovoid. This contrasts with what Galinée described as square or rectangular palisades at Dann and Marsh, and also with the European-style square palisades and bastions featured at other Haudenosaunee villages erected in the last quarter of the 1600s (Snow 1995:431–443; Sohrweide 2001).

The defensive topography of the western principal at the Snyder-McClure site suggests it may have been palisaded as well; the domestic precinct at Snyder-McClure tentatively is estimated to be 2.0 ha (Follett 1930, Site 163). Although the construction of Seneca fortifications at White Springs and (possibly) Snyder-McClure was prompted by European-led invasion, the Senecas' primary adversaries during these sites' occupations were other indigenous groups. Indigenous foes never besieged these villages, but documents note fatal skirmishes in close proximity to them (O'Callaghan 1969:4:597; Parmenter 2010:200). French Jesuits and smiths were present in Seneca territory during a period of Haudenosaunee-French peace during 1702–1709, but their activities are poorly documented (Jordan 2008:60–61). Use of satellite communities does not appear to have resumed until Kendaia (Figure 11.1:Site f) was founded on the eastern shore of Seneca Lake in about 1704 (Jordan 2008:182).

1715

In about 1715, Senecas again dramatically altered their settlements. In place of nucleated villages, Senecas segmented and dispersed their settlements (Figure 11.1:Sites 7, 8). The eastern community, termed the New Ganechstage Site Complex, is the better known of the two (see detailed treatment in Jordan 2008). It consisted of at least six discrete neighborhoods (Figure 11.3); the 1996–2000 archaeological investigations I directed concentrated on one of them, the Townley-Read site. Houses at Townley-Read were built in a line along a watercourse, spaced 60–80 m apart. The neighborhoods were in low terrain poorly situated for defense, not even having good views of the surrounding territory. Field notes indicating that archaeological deposits at the western Huntoon site were found 1,500 feet (457 m) apart (Follett 1930, Site 452) suggest that Huntoon also was composed of dispersed neighborhoods.

This novel community form—unprecedented in the Seneca archaeological record—coincided with a sustained period of regional peace that had its start in a set of peace treaties negotiated in 1700 and 1701 and solidified after 1713. My interpretation suggests that dispersal was advantageous in a number of ways, lessening labor demands, especially required daily foot travel, for both women and men compared with what was needed in a nucleated village. Archaeological and textual evidence suggests that two-family "short longhouse" dwellings were the modal residential form at this time (Jordan 2008:261–271).

Small parties of Europeans, including diplomats, traders, and smiths from both New France and New York, visited Seneca territory with much greater regularity after 1713 (Jordan 2008:66–88). The French erected a trading outpost (and later fort) at Niagara in 1719, and New Yorkers put up a similar establishment at Oswego in 1724. As noted previously, these outposts were over 75 km from the Seneca principal villages; they also had relatively small garrisons and did not attract large numbers of settlers. Senecas likely found these posts advantageous because they lessened the travel required for trade, and also because their business could be directed to whichever post offered the best prices and range of merchandise.

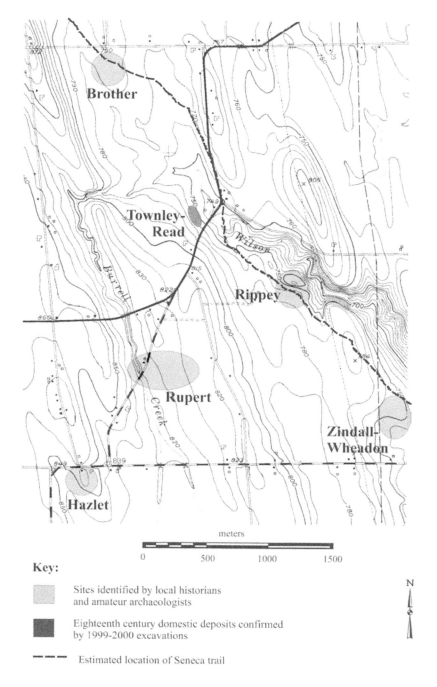

Key:

Sites identified by local historians
and amateur archaeologists

Eighteenth century domestic deposits confirmed
by 1999-2000 excavations

Estimated location of Seneca trail

N

Figure 11.3. The New Ganechstage Site Complex, ca. 1715–1754, showing segmented
neighborhoods (adapted from Jordan 2008:Figure 6.6).

1750

By the time of Moravian missionary Johann Cammerhoff's 10-day tour of Seneca territory in 1750 (Beauchamp 1916), the Seneca settlement system had further diversified (Figure 11.1:Sites 8, 9, f, g, h). During the early 1740s, the western principal community moved from Huntoon to Fall Brook in the Genesee Valley, putting the principal communities 70 km apart as opposed to the 15–20 km distances seen previously. This move may have been motivated by the western community's desire to be closer to the French at Niagara and also to routes to the Ohio River drainage; the eastern principal community at New Ganechstage continued to spatially privilege the colony of New York, eastern Haudenosaunee Nations, and the British trading post at Oswego. By 1750, settlements at Canandaigua and Honeoye (Figure 11.1:Sites g, h) had been built intermediate between the two principals, and others may have existed off Cammerhoff's route. New Ganechstage, Canandaigua, Honeoye, and Fall Brook each were no more than 25 km apart, a distance easily traversed in a day over the well-maintained Seneca trail system.[6] Thus, by 1750 Senecas appear to have used a *network* of smaller villages extended over space, rather than using principals and satellites in a more concentrated area.

1754

In about 1754, New Ganechstage Site Complex residents relocated about 6 km north to Kanadesaga (Figure 11.1:Site 10). Interestingly, with tensions building toward the start of the Seven Years' War, eastern Senecas abandoned low-lying, nondefensible terrain and moved back to a hilltop. They also nucleated, although not as tightly as at earlier settlements, and no fortifications were constructed at the time. Based on documentary accounts, Kanadesaga appears to have been a "semi-dispersed" community of about 5.0 ha in size composed of a roughly circular array of houses each surrounded by agricultural fields and work areas (Jordan 2008:190–191). This layout appears to have been a compromise between hilltop defensibility and the labor-saving advantages of dispersed dwellings. In 1756, imperial official Sir William Johnson ordered British construction of a small fort at Kanadesaga, but (presumably at Seneca request) it was built in a *downhill*, nondefensible location and was never garrisoned (Squier 1850:Plate XIII, No. 1).

1779

In 1779, a second settler military force invaded Seneca territory (Jordan 2008:187–192). The American Sullivan and Brodhead expeditions destroyed the vast majority of existing Seneca settlements in the homeland and others on the Chemung and Allegheny Rivers (selected Seneca sites occupied in 1779 are shown in Figure 11.1:Sites 10, 11, f–m). There were few battlefield casualties, but the American invaders destroyed Seneca houses, crops, and orchards in a manner reminiscent of the Denonville expedition. Also like Denonville, the Americans departed Seneca territory after completing their devastation. The American soldiers' journals (Conover 1887; Division of Archives and History 1929) reveal that the Senecas had a more complex network of settlements than had been the case in 1750. The network was centered on the principal villages at Genesee Castle and Kanadesaga (Figure 11.1:Sites 10, 11), but a large number of satellites (many established since 1750) afforded many more routes and access points (Figure 11.1:Sites f–m).

The Senecas lost considerably from the 1779 invasions. Initially sheltering at Fort Niagara under inadequate British protection during the harsh winter of 1779–1780, Senecas then both reoccupied old settlement zones and relocated to new areas, starting the process of clearance, house construction, and anthropogenic modification afresh (Ryan 2017). This process was constrained after 1784 by gradual Seneca confinement to reservations, land cessions, and large-scale American settlement that followed from a series of state and federal treaties, many of which were coerced or patently illegal under U.S. federal law. These developments resulted in the full force of Euroamerican settler colonialism being applied to Senecas for the first time.

Conclusion

This review of 110 years of Seneca settlement choices reveals consistent change and recalibration. Each set of Seneca villages is quite distinct from the others, and one would be hard-pressed to find a normative settlement pattern during this time. This has important implications for considering power dynamics within the Seneca Nation.

When viewed from the perspective of lived experience, the accumulated physical and textual evidence represents a series of decisions made by individuals, families, clans, communities, and the Seneca nation as a whole. The fact of Haudenosaunee relocation systemically required periodic discussion as to how to proceed. The years and months prior to a major settlement move were a dynamic time for negotiation, reimagination, assessment of political-economic conditions, and the exercise of power (Birch and Williamson 2015:141; Creese 2013:187). Resettlements often, but not always, unfolded over a matter of years, so even initial plans were mutable. Further, significant tinkering with settlement forms also took place within village occupation spans, such as the construction of Fort Hill in 1684 and the budding off of the Kendaia satellite around 1704.

Did Senecas come to consensus, or was a certain amount of internal coercion involved? This is difficult to determine based on the accumulated evidence. We can look for evidence for *dissent* in the material and textual records—people erecting different village forms than their contemporaries, staying behind at old locations, or "voting with their feet" and joining non-Seneca settlements elsewhere. However, these forms of dissent may be quite difficult to capture archaeologically. Deposits from a small group who stayed behind at an otherwise abandoned site, for example, would be hard to distinguish from the original occupation, and after 1687 there is little domestic pottery to provide clues to group movements and affiliations.

Texts suggest that decision-making was broad-based, and often seemingly designed to prevent quick and decisive action. When New York officials advised then-dispersed Senecas to nucleate in 1741, Seneca negotiators said they could not reply until they had consulted with the women, who have "so much to say in that affair" (Albany Commissioners for Indian Affairs 1722–1748:1820:218a). In 1744, a New York official had to demand that French agents be expelled from Seneca territory in front of a set of French-inclined Senecas, as all of the leaders "in the English interest" allegedly were out hunting at the time (Albany Commissioners for Indian Affairs 1722–1748:1820:309). While small segments of the population—particularly newly incorporated war captives—were subject to surveillance and discipline, there is little evidence for coercion among the general population.

The synchronic diversity of Seneca settlement forms implies that provision for differences of opinion was built into the system. The presence of large and small Seneca communities, seen in most of the sequence presented here, may have spatially reflected different political judgments. Segmented and dispersed communities—like the New Ganechstage Site Complex—presumably allowed even more fine-grained divergence. Similarly, the networked communities of the 1740s through the 1770s may have permitted smaller groups of like-minded people to settle wherever they felt they could make the best lives for themselves, while simultaneously remaining a part of the larger Seneca system of political cooperation.

We also can compare the record of the eastern and western Seneca communities. The two principal communities made similar decisions from the 1650s through about 1740. Spacing between the principals remained consistent; both eastern and western groups employed and abandoned palisades and satellites at close to the same time; both moved southeast after Denonville; and both communities dispersed circa 1715. The relative decoupling of the principal communities—initiated when the western principal left for the Genesee Valley in the 1740s—appears to have been a physical manifestation of diverging opinions.

It is notable that the Haudenosaunee settlement and subsistence system ensured that opportunities to voice and decide on these sorts of concerns were raised again and again, often two or three times in a person's lifetime. It is quite clear that Senecas made decisions—about whether to nucleate or disperse, to palisade or not to palisade, to concentrate settlement around principals or to construct a network of villages, to move nearby or far away, and the like—based on careful consideration of current events. But they did not only think about the present, they also—critically—made predictions for the future. Some of these decisions, such as the never-occupied palisade at Fort Hill, did not work out as planned, but for the most part Senecas seem to have attentively assessed the regional balance of power and responded in pragmatic ways. Senecas not only looked back at tradition, and synchronically at bundles of resources on the landscape, but also forward to the future—sometimes with confidence and sometimes, no doubt, with trepidation. Archaeologists will do well to pay attention to all of these perspectives when trying to understand the social dynamics behind Seneca choices.

Acknowledgments

My great thanks to the editors for organizing the SEAC session this volume grew out of, and for seeing the volume through to publication. Two anonymous reviewers provided useful comments that improved the text. I also thank Andrew Crocker and Perri Gerard-Little for their assistance in the production of this chapter. Research design and field methods for the Townley-Read and White Springs sites were developed in consultation with members of the Seneca Nation of Indians. Townley-Read fieldwork was supported by Columbia University, Hobart and William Smith Colleges, the National Science Foundation, and the Early American Industries Association. Cornell University has supported field and lab work, analysis, and scholarships for indigenous participants for the White Springs project.

Notes

1. Indigenous scholars have questioned the use of the term "village" to describe the very large Haudenosaunee communities that housed 1,000–3,000 people, suggesting that "town" better describes the scale of these communities (G. Peter Jemison, personal communication 2008). I employ "village" here in keeping with usage in the rest of the volume. That said, the social dynamics of these large Seneca communities may have differed from the smaller communities discussed in this volume because it was not possible to have regular face-to-face interactions with a thousand or more people.

2. The five original members of the *Hodinöhsö:ni'* Confederacy were (from west to east) the Seneca, Cayuga, Onondaga, Oneida, and Mohawk Nations; Tuscaroras joined

as the sixth nation in the 1720s. *Haudenosaunee* is the most commonly deployed variant of *Hodinöhsö:ni'* in academic writing and will be used in this chapter. The orthography for Seneca-language terms is from the website of the Seneca-Iroquois National Museum (www.senecamuseum.org).

3. While many scholars place the Menzis site at an earlier date (Jones 2008:359; Sempowski and Saunders 2001:Figure Intro-3), it and Wheeler Station appear to be the best candidates for the two substantial 30-house satellite villages observed by Galinée (Coyne 1903:25; see Parmenter 2010:367 n.6).

4. The Ganondagan site also has been known as Gannagaro, which is reflected in some of the entries in the bibliography.

5. I am grateful to Cornell University graduate student Andrew Crocker for determining the likely area of the Fort Hill palisade. Note that Houghton (1912:429) erroneously assumes that Squier mapped the Ganondagan site and incorrectly oriented a republished version of Squier's map; Squier's text refers quite clearly to Fort Hill (1850:63–64).

6. The Kendaia satellite (Figure 11.1:Site f) appears to have been occupied in 1750 as well; it likely could have been accessed from New Ganechstage in less than a day's travel by canoe.

References Cited

Albany Commissioners for Indian Affairs
1722–1748   Minutes of the Albany Commissioners for Indian Affairs, Microfilm, Reels C-1220 and C-1221, Vols. 1819–1821, Record Group 10, National Archives of Canada, Ottawa.

Aquila, Richard
1983   *The Iroquois Restoration.* Wayne State University Press, Detroit.

Beauchamp, William M., ed.
1916   *Moravian Journals Relating to Central New York, 1745–66.* Dehler Press, Syracuse, NY.

Bernardini, Wesley
2005   *Hopi Oral Tradition and the Archaeology of Identity.* University of Arizona Press, Tucson.

Birch, Jennifer, and Ronald F. Williamson
2015   Navigating Ancestral Landscapes in the Northern Iroquoian World. *Journal of Anthropological Archaeology* 39:139–150.

Coates, Irving W.
1893   *In the Footprints of Denonville.* Ontario County Times Printing House, Canandaigua, NY.

Conover, George S., ed.
1887   *Journals of the Military Expeditions of Major General John Sullivan against the Six Nations of Indians in 1779.* Knapp, Peck, and Thompson, Auburn, NY.

Coyne, James H., ed.
1903   *Galinée's Narrative and Map.* Translated by James H. Coyne. Ontario Historical Society Papers and Records 4, Toronto.

Creese, John L.

2013   Rethinking Early Village Development in Southern Ontario: Toward a History of Place-Making. *Canadian Journal of Archaeology* 37:185–218.

Dean, Robert L.

1984   *Archaeological Investigations at Gannagaro State Historic Site: Victor, Ontario County, New York 1983–1984.* Prepared for New York State Office of Parks, Recreation, and Historic Preservation. Dean and Barbour Associates, Buffalo, NY.

Division of Archives and History

1929   *The Sullivan-Clinton Campaign in 1779.* University of the State of New York, Albany.

Engelbrecht, William

2003   *Iroquoia: The Development of a Native World.* Syracuse University Press, Syracuse, NY.

Follett, Harrison C.

1930   Archaeology of the Counties of Monroe, Livingston, Ontario, and Genesee, New York. Manuscript on file, Research Division, Rochester Museum and Science Center, Rochester, NY.

Fowles, Severin M.

2009   The Enshrined Pueblo: Villagescape and Cosmos in the Northern Rio Grande. *American Antiquity* 74(3): 448–466.

Galloway, Patricia

2006   *Practicing Ethnohistory: Mining Archives, Hearing Testimony, Constructing Narrative.* University of Nebraska Press, Lincoln.

Gerard-Little, Peregrine A.

2017   "A Pleasure Garden in the Desert, to Which I Know No Comparison in This Country": Seneca Iroquois Landscape Stewardship in the 17th and 18th Centuries. Ph.D. diss., Cornell University.

Gerard-Little, Peregrine A., Amanda K. Moutner, Kurt A. Jordan, and Michael B. Rogers

2016   The Production of Affluence in Central New York: The Archaeology and History of Geneva's White Springs Manor, 1806–1951. *Historical Archaeology* 50(4): 36–64.

Gerard-Little, Peregrine A., Michael B. Rogers, and Kurt A. Jordan

2012   Understanding the Built Environment at the Seneca Iroquois White Springs Site Using Large-scale, Multi-instrument Archaeogeophysical Surveys. *Journal of Archaeological Science* 39(7): 2042–2048.

Hamell, George R.

1980   Gannagaro State Historic Site: A Current Perspective. In *Studies on Iroquoian Culture,* edited by Nancy Bonvillain, 91–108. Occasional Publications in Northeastern Anthropology 6, Peterborough, NH.

Hayes, Charles F., III, Daniel M. Barber, and George R. Hamell

1978   *An Archaeological Survey of Gannagaro State Historic Site, Ontario County, New York.* Archaeological Site Report. Prepared for New York State Parks and Recreation Division for Historic Preservation. Research Division, Rochester Museum and Science Center, Rochester, NY.

Houghton, Frederick

1912   The Seneca Nation from 1655 to 1687. *Bulletin of the Buffalo Society of Natural Sciences* 10(2): 363–464.

Jones, Eric E.

2008   *Iroquois Population History and Settlement Ecology, AD 1500–1700.* Ph.D. diss., Pennsylvania State University, College Park. ProQuest Dissertations Publishing, Ann Arbor, MI.

2010   Sixteenth- and Seventeenth-Century Haudenosaunee (Iroquois) Population Trends in Northeastern North America. *Journal of Field Archaeology* 35(1): 5–18.

Jones, Eric E., and James W. Wood

2012   Using Event-History Analysis to Examine the Causes of Semi-Sedentism among Shifting Cultivators: A Case Study of the Haudenosaunee, AD 1500–1700. *Journal of Archaeological Science* 39(8):2593–2603.

Jordan, Kurt A.

2008   *The Seneca Restoration, 1715–1754: An Iroquois Local Political Economy*. University Press of Florida and Society for Historical Archaeology, Gainesville.

2010   Not Just "One Site Against the World": Seneca Iroquois Intercommunity Connections and Autonomy, 1550–1779. In *Across a Great Divide: Continuity and Change in Native North American Societies, 1400–1900*, edited by Laura L. Scheiber and Mark D. Mitchell, 79–106. Amerind Studies in Archaeology Vol. 4. University of Arizona Press, Tucson.

2013   Incorporation and Colonization: Postcolumbian Iroquois Satellite Communities and Processes of Indigenous Autonomy. *American Anthropologist* 115(1): 29–43.

2018   Markers of Difference or Makers of Difference?: Atypical Practices at Haudenosaunee (Iroquois) Satellite Sites, ca. 1650–1700. *Historical Archaeology* 52(1):12–29.

Jordan, Kurt A., and Peregrine A. Gerard-Little

2019   Neither Contact nor Colonial: Seneca Iroquois Local Political Economies, 1670–1754. In *Indigenous Persistence in the Colonized Americas: Material and Documentary Perspectives on Entanglement*, edited by Heather Law Pezzarossi and Russell Sheptak. University of New Mexico Press, Albuquerque, in press.

Lynch, James

1985   The Iroquois Confederacy and the Adoption and Administration of Non-Iroquoian Individuals and Groups Prior to 1756. *Man in the Northeast* 30:83–99.

Mt. Pleasant, Jane

2015   A New Paradigm for Pre-Columbian Agriculture in North America. *Early American Studies* 13(2): 374–412.

O'Callaghan, E. B., ed.

1969 [1853–1887] *Documents Relative to the Colonial History of the State of New York*. 15 vols. Facsimile ed. A.M.S. Press, New York.

O'Gorman, Jodie A.

2010   Exploring the Longhouse and Community in Tribal Society. *American Antiquity* 75(3): 571–597.

Parmenter, Jon

2010   *The Edge of the Woods: Iroquoia, 1534–1701*. Michigan State University Press, East Lansing.

Richter, Daniel K.

1992   *The Ordeal of the Longhouse*. University of North Carolina Press, Chapel Hill.

Ryan, Beth

2017   Crowding the Banks: The Historical Archaeology of Ohagi and the Post-Revolutionary Haudenosaunee Confederacy, ca. 1780–1826. Ph.D. diss., Cornell University.

Ryan, Beth, and Adam G. Dewbury

2010   *The Eugene Frost Collection: Artifacts from the Seneca Iroquois Dann Site, circa 1655–1675.*
        Cornell University Archaeological Collections Documentation Project Report No. 1.
        Manuscript on file, Division of Rare and Manuscript Collections, Cornell University
        Library, Ithaca, NY.

Sempowski, Martha L., and Lorraine P. Saunders

2001   *Dutch Hollow and Factory Hollow: The Advent of Dutch Trade among the Seneca.* Rochester Museum and Science Center Research Records No. 24, Rochester, NY.

Silliman, Stephen W.

2009   Change and Continuity, Practice and Memory: Native American Persistence in Colonial New England. *American Antiquity* 74(2): 211–230.

Snow, Dean R.

1995   *Mohawk Valley Archaeology: The Sites.* Institute for Archaeological Studies, University
        at Albany, SUNY, Albany, NY.

Snow, Dean R., Charles T. Gehring, and William A. Starna, eds.

1996   *In Mohawk Country: Early Narratives About a Native People.* Syracuse University
        Press, Syracuse, NY.

Sohrweide, Gregory A.

2001   Onondaga Longhouses in the Late Seventeenth Century on the Weston Site. *The
        Bulletin: Journal of the New York State Archaeological Association* 117:1–24.

Squier, Ephraim G.

1850   *Aboriginal Monuments of the State of New York.* Smithsonian Contributions to Knowledge 2. Smithsonian Institution, Washington, DC.

Thwaites, Reuben Gold, ed.

1959 [1896–1901] *The Jesuit Relations and Allied Documents.* 73 vols. Facsimile ed. Pageant
        Book, New York.

Vandrei, Charles E.

1987   Observations on Seneca Settlement in the Early Historic Period. *The Bulletin: Journal
        of the New York State Archaeological Association* 95:8–17.

Wray, Charles F.

1973   *A Manual for Seneca Iroquois Archeology.* Cultures Primitive, Honeoye Falls, NY.

1983   Seneca Glass Trade Beads c. A.D. 1550–1820. In *Proceedings of the 1982 Glass Trade
        Bead Conference,* edited by Charles F. Hayes III, 41–49. Rochester Museum and Science Center Research Records No. 16, Rochester, NY.

Wray, Charles F., and Harry L. Schoff

1953   A Preliminary Report on the Seneca Sequence in Western New York, 1550–1687.
        Pennsylvania Archaeologist 23:53–63.

Wright, Joyce V.

2006   Ceramic Vessels of the Wendat Confederacy: Indicators of Tribal Affiliation or Mobile Clans? *Canadian Journal of Archaeology* 30:40–72.

12

It Took a Childe to Raze the Village

CHARLES R. COBB

For an entity that seems to have such unpretentious connotations, the village looms large in archaeological thought. A village seems to imply, for all its modesty, a significant break in the history of human collective life. There seems to be a tacit agreement among archaeologists that the eventual demise of the practice of living in mobile bands effectively heralded a qualitatively different way of living and interacting with other humans. Sedentism, higher population densities, more intensive and sustained interactions with neighbors, significant investments in infrastructure—all of the accouterments of village life—seemingly represent a new parcel of social organization and even worldview. The ongoing question, however, is what exactly does this bundle contain beyond these general traits?

This is the central issue addressed by the contributions to this volume. Although geographically limited to eastern North America, the case studies illustrate immense variability in what constitutes a village both synchronically and diachronically. Given this diversity, we are faced with an even broader question: why is the village a useful concept for anchoring our research? There is no one best response to this concern. As I attempt to show, the answer to "why study villages?" is to respond somewhat paradoxically with a number of fundamental subqueries, which I will take in turn: What is a village? What precipitates a village? What does the village mean experientially? What are the consequences of village life?

What Is a Village?

At one time villages were based almost purely on demographic criteria. A defining characteristic of the Near Eastern Bronze Age village was a semipermanent cluster of 20 some odd houses. Then, as the story went, through the course of time these grew into towns; and then, before you knew it, priestly kings had urbanized your backyard and were taxing you for their own improvements. Even in the heyday of the cultural-historical paradigm this trajectory had evolutionary connotations that would neatly fit into later theoretical trends. In Gordon Willey's (1953) classic Virú Valley survey, an important study in "proto-processualism," he defined several village types that seemed to have an evolutionary cast to them, beginning with the "Scattered Small-House Village" that seemed to segue into various forms of the "Agglutinated Village." But he also noted that there was some apparent overlap, so these types did not necessarily represent a clearly linear trajectory.

In the aftermath of this study, the rise of the importance of settlement system studies in Americanist archaeology seemed to place the concept of the village into a dual category. First, the lifeways leading to and surrounding the village represented an important move up in the neo-evolutionary scale of complexity. Second, as societies grew ever more complex, the village became overshadowed by towns and cities as an unassuming peg in a regional settlement pattern—certainly worthy of study but more representative of a rural way of life. The latter view became normalized in the Southeast in publications focusing on the late prehistoric era, notably *Mississippian Settlement Patterns* (Smith 1978), where villages were eclipsed by mound centers with advances in social complexity.

Nevertheless, the first perspective, centering on villages and their emergence and early growth, and which is the primary focus of this volume, has continually drawn interest as well. Only a few years before Bruce Smith's edited volume came out, Kent Flannery's (1976) *The Early Mesoamerican Village* set forth rigorous multiscalar methodological and theoretical approaches for the study of households, communities, and villages. Interestingly, though, the significance of the village in that compilation is more of a taken-for-granted, as there is no real critical evaluation of the concept or its importance.

Nevertheless, with the development of the Formative concept as the New World version of the Old World Neolithic, the idea that sedentism, agriculture, and pottery were intertwined gained a strong foothold that led to a widespread acceptance of the importance of village life and its basic attributes. So much so that even major processual works like *The Early Mesoamerican Village* could leave the concept relatively unexamined. In his grand synthesis of American Formative cultures, James Ford (1969:5) laid out the basic precepts of the village that made it such an important unit of comparative analysis, even for archaeologists of differing theoretical views:

> Willey and Phillips (1958, p. 144) have defined the Formative stage "by the presence of maize and/or manioc agriculture and by the successful socio-economic integration of such an agriculture into well-established sedentary village life." This is parallel to Childe's definition for the beginning of the Old World Neolithic as the point at which man became a food producer rather than a predator.

The interesting thing is that this really is not parallel to V. Gordon Childe's model for the Neolithic, because Childe took some pains to underscore the variability of what constituted a village—and in his view the presence of agriculture was not a unifying trait.

In his landmark publication *Man Makes Himself*, Childe (1951:63) provided a critical evaluation of what constitutes the village that is clearly at odds with Ford's characterization of his work:

> The adoption of cultivation must not be confused with the adoption of a sedentary life. It has been customary to contrast the settled life of the cultivator with the nomadic existence of the "homeless hunter." The contrast is quite fictitious. Last century the hunting and fishing tribes of the Pacific coasts of Canada possessed permanent villages of substantial, ornate, and almost luxurious wooden houses.

As with so many issues, Childe was a bit ahead of his time in his critical perspective of where the village should be, or should not be, situated in our taxonomic thinking. His prescient appreciation of the diversity of forms and contexts of villages set the perfect stage for recent studies in archaeology that have led us to completely reevaluate the conditions under which sedentary life emerged and what the ensuing communities actually looked like. For example, the various studies in Bandy and Fox's (2010) edited volume *Becoming Villagers* echo Childe's appreciation of the incredible variety of forms of village life, none of which is necessarily closely linked to "Formative" attributes such as agriculture or even social complexity.

Given this history, the diversity of villages described in the preceding chapters in this compilation is impressive, but perhaps not unanticipated. Jordan (chapter 11) documents cycling between dispersed and nucleated villages among the Senecas; Jones (chapter 5) describes nucleated Piedmont villages in drainages just over the hill from streams where small clusters of structures continued to thrive, while people upriver might live in dispersed villages; meanwhile Wallis (chapter 3), Thompson (chapter 2), and West and his colleagues (chapter 4) have nonagricultural Woodland settlements that are defined more by aggregations around either productive loci or else sacred points in the landscape.

Thankfully, no one here has suggested a unified theory of villages because there does not seem to be one. Instead, there seems to be a medley of variables and processes that led people to live together under certain conditions and in certain ways. For the chapters in this book, Jordan (chapter 11) sees local political-economic dynamics as important determinants in the nature of the village; for Wallis (chapter 3) as well as West et al. (chapter 4), it seems to be cosmology and ritual; Jones (chapter 5) and Thompson (chapter 2) see ecological factors as critical; and Jones (chapter 5), in addition to Jefferies (chapter 9) and Sullivan (chapter 7), emphasizes the role of conflict in the long-term aggregation of peoples. Cook (chapter 8) traces a process of secondary village formation based on ecological variables, but where the notion of a village is imported from elsewhere.

So, maybe we can agree that a village is a generic clustering of people brought together for a variety of reasons, and sustained in a certain kind of arrangement, also for a variety of reasons. However, much of our existence as humans precedes village life, as do all of the variables that I just enumerated. We have evidence for ritual life among Neanderthals and even earlier; sadly, we keep pushing the dates for organized conflict farther and farther back in time; and there are always abundant places on the landscape that could lend themselves to village life, but often do not.

Given this, we have to ask ourselves:

What Precipitates Village Life?

In the year 2000, Malcolm Gladwell did what a lot of popular writers do. That is, he wrote a best seller based on a simple and pervasive idea embedded in anthropology and related fields—a book any one of us archaeologists potentially could have written but did not because we are usually not so handy at translating our provocative ideas for a larger audience. In *The Tipping Point: How Little Things Can Make a Big Difference*, Gladwell pointed out how organizations, structures, and systems reach points in their history where it takes only the additional proverbial straw to provoke significant transformations. This idea, which is fundamental to complexity science (West 2017), clearly has its adherents in archaeology. As just one example, Vandkilde has remarked that the Bronze Age in Europe was characterized by "historical sequences with intervals [that] were terminated by tipping points which were brief and dramatic phases which transpired through radical material change and signs of crisis" (2016:116).

A provocative aspect of this compilation is that it embodies so much organizational and temporal variation. As a result, the path to village life seems to be composed of a variety of smooth(ish) or undulating trajectories, as well as a considerable diversity of tipping points. Birch and Williamson (chapter 6) document somewhat of a gradual movement to village life for some Iroquoian villages. A similar pattern seems to be exhibited in some sections of the Carolina Piedmont described by Jones (chapter 5). Notably, however, even in the close confines of the Piedmont there are adjoining drainages that witnessed significantly different trajectories.

Some of the most abrupt tipping points can be seen in the studies at the Garden

Patch site (chapter 3) and at Kolomoki (chapter 4), where there seems to be a rapid and saltational emergence and growth of villages. What is difficult to fathom is the degree of predetermination in these histories—as if the idea of a village preceded the formation of a village, a notion that completely inverts traditional logic. Thompson's (chapter 2) research on shell midden villages suggests that even if the idea of a village may exist, though, the reality of enacting a village to some degree relies on a stable food supply, what he refers to as "anticipated surplus." Although he does not find this kind of surplus equating with clear evidence for hierarchy in his region, I have to believe there is a fine line—and another tipping point—between anticipated surplus and planned surplus, where individuals or interested groups may deliberately intensify production toward their own ends as they learn to manipulate the anticipated elements of the economy.

Some of the studies describe tipping points even after the formation of village life, where one village type may transform into another. Both Sullivan (chapter 7) and Jefferies (chapter 9) see new tipping points after the formation of village life in the larger Appalachian region that may be related both to an upsurge of violence and to climate change. The emergence of the distinctive Dallas phase villages in eastern Tennessee is associated with in-migration and conflict, and may have been prompted ultimately by a series of significant droughts. Likewise the intermontane region circular villages that Jefferies (chapter 9) discusses adopted a defensive characteristic that correlates with the Little Ice Age.

As these studies emphasize, tipping points seem to be manifested as historical and local manifestations of large-scale processes. In addition to climate change and regional violence, demography clearly is another broad variable contributing to the coalescence of a village. Perhaps the best archaeological portrait we have of the impacts of the complex interplay of these kinds of factors on the history of village life is provided by the Village Ecodynamics Project in the American Southwest. Although not all of the conclusions from that work can necessarily be extrapolated to eastern North America, some of the aspects of the population dynamics in that region are provocative. As examples, for the Mesa Verde study area, aggregation occurred during cycles of regional population decline, the rise and fall of settlements was greatly impacted by migration as well as local demographic factors, and population centers (villages and towns) seemed to have constraints on their size imposed by ecological and sociopolitical variables (Varien et al. 2007). We can only hope that someone from the Eastern Woodlands takes on a project of similar scope and ambition to address the historical ecology of village life in a very different environmental setting.

Aside from materialist factors, even the sweep of belief systems and ideologies may stir rapid changes in the organization of communities. For the Fort Ancient region, Cook (chapter 8) sees the importation of Mississippian notions of the village as spurring an Ohio Valley hybrid of Mississippian and Woodland cultures. Yet in other places, it seems merely the gravitational effects of sacred places and emplacement can foster the sudden appearance of sedentary communities, whereby village life itself seems to be preceded by scattered, somewhat mobile communities who occasionally get together at nodal points on the landscape. Sullivan, for example (chapter 7), posits that Woodland previllage "burial mounds and . . . rotundas are best interpreted as communal facilities used by dispersed populations." Such off-and-on-again gathering places also seem to be present at hunter-gatherer-fisher sites in Georgia and Florida.

These kinds of observations lead to a number of puzzling and intriguing questions. Where did the people come from, why did they leave, and what brought them together? Was there an advance guard from elsewhere scoping out the landscape? Even given the innate sacred characteristics of the predestined landscape of a place like Garden Patch, what events or processes triggered a new kind of lifestyle based on recurrent gathering?

I wonder if these kinds of periodic gatherings are proving grounds for the kinds of communal social relations that will be necessary to live in villages? As Wallis points out with regard to Garden Patch (chapter 3), perhaps these are novel social experiments in aggregation. Similarly, Birch and Williamson (chapter 6) propose that the power dynamics in the first villages differed little from earlier base camps. Do hunter-gatherer-fishers organize by one set of social relations in a small group setting, then have the flexibility to adopt new sets of norms when they convene at these ritual settings? And do these communal norms provide the basis for more inscribed rules of group living as a village comes together? Further, can we detect this kind of organizational variation within hunter-gatherer-fisher groups, as well as the transition from mobile to sedentary lifestyles?

I also wonder whether the institutions that are borne from a history of close-knit village living eventually allow for the ability for groups to maintain community in a dispersed setting in a way that would not have been possible before those lessons had been learned. Stephen Kowalewski and James Hatch (1991) documented a spread of farmsteads and hamlets throughout the Oconee drainage following a period of chiefly cycling in north-central Georgia—small settlements that still seem to have been in regular contact following their dispersal. Likewise, as Mississippian mound centers were abandoned on the Tombigbee drainage in Mississippi, we seem to see the formation of dispersed settlement systems in the Blackland Prairie around the 1500s that persists up through the historic era (Cegielski and Lieb 2011). Many of these clusters do not look like villages in the classic archaeological sense. But they could be loose village communities whose cohesion was made possible by a tradition of communal interactions that had a deep history going back to clustered villages.

What Does the Village Mean Experientially?

Village life seems to usher in a new way of conceiving the world. I think that three works help us to triangulate around thinking about these changes. These are Ian Hodder's *The Domestication of Europe* (1990), Severin Fowles's "The Enshrined Pueblo" (2009), and Timothy Pauketat's "Politicization and Community in the Pre-Columbian River Valley" (2000). No single one of these covers the entire range of how to think about the lifeways and phenomenology of villages, but together I think they encompass many of perspectives in these chapters concerning the experiential dimensions of settled life.

When Hodder introduced *The Domestication of Europe* over a quarter of a century ago, it somewhat took archaeology by storm—at least for those who were interested in the birth of the Neolithic and village life. In his view, the formation of the village lifestyle initiated a completely different worldview and a way of conducting and performing culture experientially as well as functionally. The study did have a structural cast to it that was somewhat off-putting to some; but these structures perhaps can be appreciated as empirical generalizations if not universals. As Hodder put it, we often see village life fostering the segregation of gender roles, where females often assume greater responsibilities for the so-called *domus*. In contrast, males venture into the dangerous outside world. As a result, village life often promotes a notion of inside and outside, as well as a corresponding duality of safe and dangerous, those who belong and those who are outsiders.

Fowles's Southwestern study has adopted a softer structural stance that asks us to think about villagescapes. He is particularly interested in how these communities situated themselves in a larger cosmological and ritual landscape that transcended village boundaries. His study parts ways somewhat with Hodder in his critique that "even though most now acknowledge that landscapes are constructed no less than villages, there remains a tendency to contrast village and landscape as one would culture and nature" (Fowles 2009:449). In other words, we must move past a dichotomy that views villages as somehow detached from their natural surroundings. Shrines, orchards, rock art, dispersed agricultural fields, fishing weirs—all of these kinds of features and more are part of the everyday lives of villages, enfolded into a cultural landscape where the living quarters may be a central node, but hardly a circumscribed world.

Pauketat's (2000) study applied a somewhat similar larger-scale perspective to the habitations of the Mississippian Southeast, but it relied more on the concept of community rather than village. A community could be a village, but it could also transcend a village; a community in his perspective is not an entity, but a set of relations—it is an identity formation process that takes place at multiple scales.

In part, Pauketat was arguing against Jon Muller's (1997) idea that Mississippian villages were modular accumulations of farmsteads; instead, he maintained they were a qualitatively different kind of entity and experience, not merely a stepping stone between the household and the town.

None of these studies denies that villages become manifest as some kind of physical thing. But they emphasize that villages embody community relations that involve a sense of belonging and identity that transcends the household; further, villages do have a sense of boundaries that imply outside(r) and inside(r), yet at the same time may draw on a large spatial scale to inscribe solidarity at a local scale; finally, they seem to involve a reorientation of interaction related specifically to a higher density of face-to-face relations.

The notion that village settings and their landscapes are intertwined with various aspects of identity and personhood is commonplace in this volume. Jefferies (chapter 9) views the circular village of the Intermontane Culture as a repetitive design that is an expression of identity. According to West et al. (chapter 4), the marked spatial duality of Kolomoki is a "bold declaration of identity." Wallis (chapter 3) and Gallivan et al. (chapter 10) also emphasize the mediating role of the built environment. To both, villages seem to constitute sociograms that structure power and social relations; further, they seem to see the built environment as instrumental for socializing the body, a perspective now widely held in archaeological landscape studies (e.g., Thomas 2001; Tilley 2008). In a similar vein, for Birch and Williamson (chapter 6), as well as Sullivan (chapter 7), the arrangement of gender relations is pivotal to understanding the organization and transformation of village life. The way in which the latter two studies remark upon the flexible nature of personhood is reminiscent of Lynn Meskell's (1998) work on gender and Egyptian villages, where she has argued that studies of identity must be about fluidity and difference, not just the entrenchment of categories.

The idea that villages were as much about evolving relations as evolving places is also emphasized in Jordan's research (chapter 11), where Seneca villages always seemed to be in a state of flux and experienced a lot of "tinkering." This is good evidence that, while demography and surplus may be preconditions for villages, the emergence and continued coherence of villages were not an inherently natural process; they were something that had to be worked at and were never static entities. Thompson's (chapter 2) study of shell ring villages emphasizes this point, one that has also been made for the Southwest, where Alison Rautman (2014) argues that the active construction and maintenance of villages and village life were critical to their coherence and unity.

In several of the contributions, village communities are involved in a dialectical interplay with boundaries and borders that incorporated relatively long-distance interactions into the realm of the everyday: Birch and Williamson (chapter 6) argue that territoriality was very important to Iroquois villages, yet they also exhibited broad-scale patterns of ceramic homogeneity that speak to the importance of extensive social networks. When we consider water as well as terrestrial distance, as does Thompson (chapter 2), it may not have been uncommon for villages to consider their normal zone of interaction to encompass distances in the tens to scores of kilometers. In the Powhatan communities that Gallivan and his colleagues describe (chapter 10), external long-distance trade was crucially important; nonetheless, the architecture and social relations of villages were shaped so as to sharply define semiotic boundaries of inside and outside. I like their idea that villages or towns may in fact be important for socializing dangerous forces, materials, and powers that are outsiders. Could this be what we are seeing at Kolomoki, where West et al. (chapter 4) describe two distinct subgroups, one of which seems to consist of more permanent residents in one part of the village, and transient outsiders in another part? Are there portions of the built landscape that in effect launder the existential dimensions of external threats?

Finally, I think it important that several authors focused on longer spans of village life. These studies were important reminders that villages have a temporality that involves both secular time and an experiential sense of building on the past. Some archaeologists have observed that temporality is embedded in the landscape (Cobb and King 2005; Hicks 2016; Ingold 1993), and certainly the same is true for the built environment and the villagescape. In the Fort Ancient settlements that Cook describes, it was common for villagers to build on and integrate earthen monuments from earlier, Woodland times. Here we seem to see a sense of laying claim to the past and a cultural insistence on continuity. Jordan's chapter is provocative because it shows that the maintenance of cultural tradition through the built environment did not have to occur in the same location. Seneca villagers had become quite adept at adopting a punctuated village life, where communities uprooted on a regular basis. These communities were not always re-created in the same way, though, and one wonders what were the key building blocks—the longhouse?—that sustained tradition through repeated migration and reorganization episodes.

What Are the Consequences of Various Forms of Village Life?

It seems clear from this compilation that a commitment to village life has both positive and negative implications—and it is not always easy to tell which is which in the short term. As with so many of the benchmarks that we associate with social complexity, the transition to the village lifestyle is replete with unintended consequences.

Some of the authors, notably Birch and Williamson (chapter 6) as well as Wallis (chapter 3), touch on the idea that density of people and emplacement likely were accompanied by considerable social stress that had to be relieved through various social mechanisms. In this sense, villages not only result from tipping points, they may generate their own forms of scalar stress. Napoleon Chagnon (1968) argued that when Yanomamo villages reached a size of about 60 people, the political dimensions of kinship were not sufficiently robust to dampen disputes. Community fissioning thus was a frequent response to intravillage conflict. Although I have raised some skepticism about a grand theory of villages, one is reminded that Gregory Johnson (e.g., Johnson 1982) at one time did considerable research on scalar stress and on how groups with increasing "face-to-face" interaction required the development of institutions to mediate the flow of information and to foster social cohesion. So perhaps the empirical data provided from some regions in the Southeast supports these earlier systemic arguments that some conditions will consistently lead to a need for a resolution, even if one cannot exactly predict what that resolution will be.

Interestingly, these same authors (Birch and Williamson, chapter 6; Wallis, chapter 3), as well as Jefferies (chapter 9), view the spatiality of villages as potentially mitigating the tensions of denser living conditions. Indeed, there is a pervasive notion throughout all of the chapters that the built environment creates dialectical space both for hierarchy and for the egalitarian alleviation of tension. This is in my mind an important and timely addition to the older arguments about scalar stress, which is that materiality itself is an important constituent of how the consequences of stress may be played out.

As a gross generalization, village life seems to be accompanied by territoriality and forms of me and mine behaviors that prompt intercommunity conflict, in turn giving rise to the palisaded villages we see described by Jefferies (chapter 9), Birch and Williamson (chapter 6), and Jordan (chapter 11). This kind of cloistered living, while perhaps serving important defensive purposes, had its own negative outcomes. VanDerwarker and Wilson (2016) are doing innovative work on the structural violence that is prompted by nucleated village life associated with the threat of external violence, including, but not limited to, significant decreases in dietary breadth and adverse health outcomes. Similar arguments have been made for the Neolithic Near East with regard to how poor sanitation in crowded villages may instigate illness and infectious disease (Goring-Morris and Belfer-Cohen 2010). Village life may have represented some kind of resolution—ritual, defensive, or otherwise—but these resolutions generated their own sets of problems.

Conclusion

It seems only fitting to close with another taxonomic critique by Childe, one that conforms nicely with the tenor of this volume: "there was . . . no 'neolithic' civilization, only a multitude of different concrete applications of a few very general principles and notions" (1951:82). It follows, as the chapters herein suggest, that there is no single kind of village or universal rules for the rise of villages. I have never been that adverse to empirical generalizations, however. It may be that there are a few very general principles that structure the rise of hunter-gatherer-fisher villages based on ritual places on the landscape, or the emergence of circular nucleated villages under the right ecological conditions. To believe otherwise is to close the door on the value of comparative research.

For this reason, as one modest overarching critique of this collection, I would observe that there is not much recourse to the ethnographic literature on villages. Like most archaeologists, I do not believe in the tyranny of the ethnographic record. But if we do believe in comparative research, then surely there is more to be gained from our colleagues' research in sociocultural anthropology and ethnohistory. Beyond Chagnon's work cited previously, Robert Netting's (1963) work on the dispersal and clustering of Kofyar villages in Africa provides potentially interesting analogies for us, and there is a wealth of ethnohistoric information on California hunter-gatherer-fishers who display patterns of aggregation, dispersal, and ranking that evoke some of the studies dealing with sedentary hunter-gatherer-fishers in Georgia and in Florida (Bean and Blackburn 1976). Despite the relatively scarcity of these kinds of data in the assembled chapters, these southeastern studies still open up vistas on the diversity of village life that might surprise ethnographers, as in fact I was often surprised.

References Cited

Bandy, Matthew S., and Jake R. Fox, eds.
2010   *Becoming Villagers: Comparing Early Village Societies.* University of Arizona Press, Tucson.
Bean, Lowell J., and Thomas C. Blackburn, eds.
1976   *Native Californians: A Theoretical Perspective.* Ballena Press, Ramona, CA.
Cegielski, Wendy, and Brad R. Lieb
2011   *Hina' Falaa,* The Long Path: An Analysis of Chickasaw Settlement Patterns Using GIS in Northeast Mississippi, 1650–1840. *Native South* 4:24–54.
Chagnon, Napoleon
1968   *Yąnomamö: The Fierce People.* Holt, Rinehart and Winston, New York.
Childe, V. Gordon
1951 [1936]   *Man Makes Himself.* Mentor, New York.

Cobb, Charles R., and Adam King

2005   Re-inventing Mississippian Tradition at Etowah, Georgia. *Journal of Archaeological Method and Theory* 12(3): 167–192.

Flannery, Kent V., ed.

1976   *The Early Mesoamerican Village*. Academic Press, New York.

Ford, James A.

1969   *A Comparison of Formative Cultures in the Americas*. Smithsonian Institution Press, Washington, DC.

Fowles, Severin

2009   The Enshrined Pueblo: Villagescape and Cosmos in the Northern Rio Grande. *American Antiquity* 74(3): 448–466.

Gladwell, Malcolm

2000   *The Tipping Point: How Little Things Can Make a Big Difference*. Little, Brown, New York.

Goring-Morris, A. Nigel, and Anna Belfer-Cohen

2010   "Great Expectations"; or, the Inevitable Collapse of the Early Neolithic in the Near East. In *Becoming Villagers: Comparing Early Village Societies*, edited by Matthew S. Bandy and Jake R. Fox, 62–77. University of Arizona Press, Tucson.

Hicks, Dan

2016   The Temporality of the Landscape Revisited. *Norwegian Archaeological Review* 49(1): 5–22.

Hodder, Ian

1990   *The Domestication of Europe: Structure and Contingency in Neolithic Societies*. Blackwell, Oxford.

Ingold, Timothy

1993   The Temporality of the Landscape. *World Archaeology* 25(2): 152–174.

Johnson, Gregory A.

1982   Organizational Structures and Scalar Stress. In *Theory and Explanation in Archaeology: The Southampton Conference*, edited by Colin A. Renfrew, Michael J. Rowlands, and Barbara Abbot Seagraves, 389–421. Academic Press, New York.

Kowalewski, Stephen A., and James W. Hatch

1991   The Sixteenth-Century Expansion of Settlement in the Upper Oconee Watershed, Georgia. *Southeastern Archaeology* 10(1): 1–17.

Meskell, Lynn

1998   An Archaeology of Social Relations in an Egyptian Village. *Journal of Archaeological Method and Theory* 5(3): 209–243.

Muller, Jon

1997   *Mississippian Political Economy*. Plenum, New York.

Netting, Robert

1963   *Kofyar Agriculture: A Study in the Ecology of a West African People*. University of Chicago Press, Chicago.

Pauketat, Timothy R.

2000   Politicization and Community in the Pre-Columbian River Valley. In *The Archaeology of Communities: A New World Perspective*, edited by Marcello A. Canuto and Jason Yaeger, 16–43. Routledge, New York.

Rautman, Alison E.

2014   *Constructing Community: The Archaeology of Early Villages in Central New Mexico.* University of Arizona Press, Tucson.

Smith, Bruce D., ed.

1978   *Mississippian Settlement Patterns.* Academic Press, New York.

Thomas, Julian

2001   Archaeologies of Place and Landscape. In *Archaeological Theory Today*, edited by Ian Hodder, 165–186. Polity, London.

Tilley, Christopher

2008   Phenomenological Approaches to Landscape Archaeology. In *Handbook of Landscape Archaeology*, edited by David Bruno and Julian Thomas, 271–276. Left Coast Press, New York.

VanDerwarker, Amber M., and Gregory D. Wilson

2016   War, Food, and Structural Violence in the Mississippian Central Illinois Valley. In *The Archaeology of Food and Warfare*, edited by Amber M. VanDerwarker and Gregory D. Wilson, 75–105. Springer, New York.

Vandkilde, Helle

2016   Bronzization: The Bronze Age as Pre-Modern Globalization. *Praehistorische Zeitschrift* 91(1): 103–123.

Varien, Mark D., Scott G. Ortman, Timothy A. Kohler, Donna M. Glowacki, and C. David Johnson

2007   Historical Ecology in the Mesa Verde Region: Results from the Village Ecodynamics Project. *American Antiquity* 72(2): 273–299.

West, Geoffrey

2017   *Scale: The Universal Laws of Growth, Innovation, Sustainability, and the Pace of Life, in Organisms, Cities, Economies, and Companies.* Penguin Press, New York.

Willey, Gordon R.

1953   *Prehistoric Settlement Patterns in the Virú Valley, Peru.* Bureau of American Ethnology Bulletin No. 155. Smithsonian Institution, Washington, DC.

Willey, Gordon R., and Philip Phillips

1958   *Method and Theory in American Archaeology.* University of Chicago Press, Chicago.

Contributors

Jennifer Birch, Department of Anthropology, University of Georgia, Athens, GA.

Charles R. Cobb, Florida Museum of Natural History, University of Florida, Gainesville, FL.

Robert A. Cook, Department of Anthropology, The Ohio State University, Columbus, OH.

Martin D. Gallivan, Department of Anthropology, William and Mary, Williamsburg, VA.

Richard W. Jefferies, Department of Anthropology, University of Kentucky, Lexington, KY.

Jessica A. Jenkins, University of Florida, Gainesville, FL.

Eric E. Jones, Department of Anthropology, Wake Forest University, Winston-Salem, NC.

Kurt A. Jordan, Department of Anthropology and American Indian and Indigenous Studies Program, Cornell University, Ithaca, NY.

Martin Menz, Museum of Anthropological Archaeology, University of Michigan, MI.

Thomas J. Pluckhahn, Department of Anthropology, University of South Florida, Tampa, FL.

Christopher J. Shephard, William and Mary Center for Archaeological Research, Williamsburg, VA.

Lynne P. Sullivan, Department of Anthropology and McClung Museum, University of Tennessee, Knoxville, TN.

Victor D. Thompson, Department of Anthropology, University of Georgia, Athens, GA.

Neill Wallis, Florida Museum of Natural History, University of Florida, Gainesville, FL.

Shaun E. West, Department of Anthropology, University of South Florida, Tampa, FL.

Ronald F. Williamson, ASI Archaeological and Cultural Heritage Services and University of Toronto, Toronto, ON.

Index

Page numbers in *italics* refer to illustrations.

Van Besien site, 91
violence, 4, 36, 74, 152–53, 196, 201. *See also*
    conflict; warfare

Wall site, 75, 80
wall trenches. *See* architecture, wall trench
warfare, 7–8, 66, 83–84, 118, 99, 129, 134,
    142, 149, 154, 180, 184. *See also* conflict;
    violence
Watson Break site, xii, 140
Weeden Island, 41, 55, 58, 62, 64–65

Werowocomoco site, *161*, 163–68, *167*, 170
Weyanoke Old Town site, *161*, 166–70, *169*
Wheeler Station site, *177*, 178
White, John, 140
White Springs site, *177*, 181, 187
Willey, Gordon, 54, 193
William Klutz site, 75, 80
Wolf, Eric, 165
Wray, Charles, 176

Yanomamo, 29, 201

Ripley P. Bullen Series

FLORIDA MUSEUM OF NATURAL HISTORY

Tacachale: Essays on the Indians of Florida and Southeastern Georgia during the Historic Period, edited by Jerald T. Milanich and Samuel Proctor (1978)

Aboriginal Subsistence Technology on the Southeastern Coastal Plain during the Late Prehistoric Period, by Lewis H. Larson (1980)

Cemochechobee: Archaeology of a Mississippian Ceremonial Center on the Chattahoochee River, by Frank T. Schnell, Vernon J. Knight Jr., and Gail S. Schnell (1981)

Fort Center: An Archaeological Site in the Lake Okeechobee Basin, by William H. Sears, with contributions by Elsie O'R. Sears and Karl T. Steinen (1982)

Perspectives on Gulf Coast Prehistory, edited by Dave D. Davis (1984)

Archaeology of Aboriginal Culture Change in the Interior Southeast: Depopulation during the Early Historic Period, by Marvin T. Smith (1987)

Apalachee: The Land between the Rivers, by John H. Hann (1988)

Key Marco's Buried Treasure: Archaeology and Adventure in the Nineteenth Century, by Marion Spjut Gilliland (1989)

First Encounters: Spanish Explorations in the Caribbean and the United States, 1492–1570, edited by Jerald T. Milanich and Susan Milbrath (1989)

Missions to the Calusa, edited and translated by John H. Hann, with an introduction by William H. Marquardt (1991)

Excavations on the Franciscan Frontier: Archaeology at the Fig Springs Mission, by Brent Richards Weisman (1992)

The People Who Discovered Columbus: The Prehistory of the Bahamas, by William F. Keegan (1992)

Hernando de Soto and the Indians of Florida, by Jerald T. Milanich and Charles Hudson (1993)

Foraging and Farming in the Eastern Woodlands, edited by C. Margaret Scarry (1993)

Puerto Real: The Archaeology of a Sixteenth-Century Spanish Town in Hispaniola, edited by Kathleen Deagan (1995)

Political Structure and Change in the Prehistoric Southeastern United States, edited by John F. Scarry (1996)

Bioarchaeology of Native Americans in the Spanish Borderlands, edited by Brenda J. Baker and Lisa Kealhofer (1996)

A History of the Timucua Indians and Missions, by John H. Hann (1996)

Archaeology of the Mid-Holocene Southeast, edited by Kenneth E. Sassaman and David G. Anderson (1996)

The Indigenous People of the Caribbean, edited by Samuel M. Wilson (1997; first paperback edition, 1999)

Hernando de Soto among the Apalachee: The Archaeology of the First Winter Encampment, by Charles R. Ewen and John H. Hann (1998)

The Timucuan Chiefdoms of Spanish Florida, by John E. Worth: vol. 1, *Assimilation;* vol. 2, *Resistance and Destruction* (1998)

Ancient Earthen Enclosures of the Eastern Woodlands, edited by Robert C. Mainfort Jr. and Lynne P. Sullivan (1998)